Beaujolais in My Blood

GROWING UP GAY AND WELL-FED IN A FAMILY-RUN FRENCH RESTAURANT

ERIC NEIL PITSENBARGER

TABLE OF CONTENTS

For my parents
Gerald and Ellen Pitsenbarger

Nancy - you're my
Prom Date!
          X Eric

INTRODUCTION

This is a coming-of-age memoir, told in vignettes as a disgruntled teenager drafted at age fourteen into the restaurant business.

My two bohemian parents, Gerald and Ellen Pitsenbarger, moved our small family from Berkeley, California, in 1968 and began what has now gone on to become a legacy restaurant in the quaint Victorian village of Mendocino. Café Beaujolais was born from humble beginnings by artists with a passion for good food and wine, for embracing the rustic esthetic of the Northern California coast, for living an adventurous and full life, and for entertaining people with flair. This great adventure lasted about seven years, until it became unsustainable, with the Beaujolais then selling to chef Margaret Fox in 1976, who lifted the now-established enterprise to new heights. Currently, Café Beaujolais enjoys sustained popularity and is the preeminent experience for fine dining on the north coast. Besides the name, the cachet of what my parents originally built is still very much in evidence.

I began this project as a telling of history, to illuminate the beginnings of my family's role as progenitors of Café Beaujolais, but soon realized that much of my own experience had colored the facts. I needed to write this as a memoir, my own perspective as a kid conscripted into a new lifestyle. These collected stories are retellings of familial fables and remembered events, sometimes told through the lens of a projected, sometimes magical thinking. The life of an impressionable (and somewhat troubled) teenager produced many fantasies that overlapped what may have actually happened. I'll leave it to you, the reader, to work out which truth sticks. The truth for me is all of the above. My experience is the story I've chosen to tell. Some names have been changed to preserve anonymity.

Marked with research, interviews, the various ephemera available, and memories of being on the periphery of my parents' new enterprise, *Beaujolais in My Blood* is a poignant love letter and reckoning. I owe everything to my parents, for the many skills learned, and to the beautiful town of Mendocino itself, where I was able to discover my authentic self. This book is dedicated to Gerald and Ellen Pitsenbarger, who never really saw a true recognition of their achievements.

I hope you enjoy.

—Eric Neil Pitsenbarger

CHAPTER 1

WAITING FOR STRANGE

I was only three years old in 1958 when I got my first disturbing taste of individuation. The stark separation from Ellen's all-encompassing care and from Gerald's omniscient presence. An abrupt sense that I was different from everyone else, unique in some way, and also, I had the growing, irritating realization that I was stuck.

Wrenched from our cozy San Francisco apartment, there I was, wedged like baloney between Ellen and Gerald. Trapped in this dark, hot, loud, smoky place crowded with people all talking at once, hoisting drinks and cigarettes, and gesturing as if they couldn't get their point across without some crazy violent thrust of hands in the air. Heads glued together, beards brushing bouffants, yelling and banging, the noise so loud I couldn't hear Ellen's voice as she spoke to me. It was lucky I could read her lips.

"Have some bread, Eric." Smiling, she placed a piece of garlic toast in my small hand.

Not sitting on someone's lap, instead placed on a hard chair of my own, I felt vulnerable to the heaving bodies and noise pressing in from all sides. Apart from Ellen and Gerald, with just enough space to gape at the crowd, I felt that, quite possibly, I might be in some terrible danger.

A blue smoke trail flowed in a low current over people's heads. Flickering red candles shoved into empty Chianti bottles melted wax rivers over wicker and down onto greasy checkerboard oilcloths so old they'd become part of the small tables themselves. Tables were jammed so tightly together there was barely room to squeeze between the skinny people, who had coalesced into a shouting mob, all wearing the very same black sweater as my two parents.

Bringing the piece of garlic toast to my mouth, I observed the chaotic scene. I'd never seen adults act this way. Everyone so unruly, reckless, and loud, with no one telling them to be quiet, to shush, or to watch out! Ellen and Gerald sat oblivious, cool as cucumbers, eating pasta and bread, sipping from glasses of red wine between puffs on their own cigarettes, the twin spirals of smoke joining the river running above our heads.

I wondered why my two protectors were not in the least bit concerned. They sat unfazed by the mayhem, and it struck me that perhaps this was all quite normal. That it was OK that people were yelling and screaming at each other, belching smoke, and bumping into our checkerboard island as they jockeyed back and forth, unable to make up their minds about where they wanted to sit. Was I supposed to yell and scream too? But Ellen and Gerald remained silent statues surveying the scene (their elbows resting on our small table, cigarettes tucked in angled fingers), so I followed their example and remained mum as well, but disquieted.

Ellen and Gerald were both enthusiastic, exuberant parents who always treated me as if I were already a fully cognizant person instead of merely a thoughtless toddler. Speaking to me with their grown-up voices, they'd introduced themselves early on as Ellen and Gerald and wrinkled their noses when other people would coo and pander. I became familiar with all my toys, with books and food and the stroller, and I knew that I of course was Eric and that the two Siamese cats that shared our tiny flat were Mortiqui and Portia. This awful place, however, was unfamiliar; it was out of control, and even scary. It seemed that Ellen and Gerald, sitting still, acting as baffles on either side of me, were the only things that kept me alive.

A woman reached over me to kiss her friend who was standing on the other side of our table, and the fringe from her shawl knocked the garlic toast from my hand. I followed it with my eyes as it disappeared down into the black hole. Ellen also noticed too and leaned in with another end piece.

Completely aloof, Gerald hovered his cigarette just over the edge of our table. His snug little Basque beret was pushed backward, right hand twirled the edge of his Vandyke mustache, his discerning, angry glare from under arched brows watched something and nothing. He looked like a slightly annoyed, slightly crazy, skinny, black cat.

Ellen was his even more delicate, fine-boned, porcelain-faced double. Her razor-cut short, black hair, a skull cap, squinting eyes smiling slits of onyx. I took the second piece of bread from her long fingers and shoved it into my mouth. I was hungry, and this piece was not getting away. Ready for another, I looked again over at her, but to my alarm, she stood up from her chair, said something to Gerald, and left.

All arms and legs, she unfolded herself from the tight squeeze, stepping at impossible angles over people huddled on the floor or sitting on each other's laps. Why couldn't I sit on someone's lap?

She touched a woman's head for balance and continued picking her way across the war zone. Her stick figure finally faded away like a ghost behind the veil of smoke.

Gerald remained stoic and unmoved. Why was he ignoring me? He never responded to my sharp look of doubt, my drowned-out yelp of concern. Wasn't he the least bit upset that Ellen, his wife, my mother, might never return from wherever she'd wandered? I strained to see her sharp-edged shape returning from the haze, but there was only swirling chaos. There was a moment of panic and then, sudden rage. I'd been left on my own in this horrible place. Ellen had abandoned me.

Floating away as if leaving me were easy, Ellen had just gone. I blinked, straining to see her. This was not normal. This had never happened before, and locked in this uncomfortable chair, I was on high alert.

Afraid that I might be casually knocked by some strange elbow and tossed like a piece of toast into the abyss beneath these tables, I saw the reality of my fragile mortality revealed. I might cease to exist. This could be the end, and it seemed so ironic that just as I was waking up, it could all be over. It was absurd and unfair, and I felt tears start to rise, and then Ellen came back.

She must have seen the look of resentment on my face as she petted my curly head like a puppy's. She'd left me! Left me alone in this awful place, and all I got was a pat on the head? Gerald didn't care; he didn't even glance my way as my little arms went up, demanding a hug. I needed to connect with these two people who claimed to be my friends and parents. I needed their attention now, and a dismissive pat on the head was utterly insufficient.

"I am not a poodle!" I wanted to yell, remembering the snooty, poufy dogs that lived on our block.

It was at that moment that a harsh white light blinked onto a small stage, and a dignified, bearded man appeared, sitting alone on a tall stool. He was going to read us all a story.

The room grew suddenly quiet, and it was an eerie, woozy feeling after the bombardment of so much noise. Ellen and Gerald shifted in their seats; they stopped eating and leaned in. Everyone waited for the man (who looked a little bit like Gerald with his close beard, mustache, and dark sweater).

The entire room froze, all eyes gazing at the man on his stool. Hands floated in the air, holding either cigarettes or wineglasses; someone coughed; a whisper, a scooting chair, and then the man held up a handful of papers, cleared his throat, and began speaking.

But it wasn't a story at all. I'm not sure what I was expecting, but this was not like any story I'd heard before. There was no little bear or monkey, no red balloon, no French schoolgirl or purple crayon. It was a long list of nonsensical, rambling words all stuck together backward that went on and on. I tried to find meaning in what this man was talking about, forced to listen to this long speech about nothing, but it was useless. This was gibberish.

The man spoke in an arch, serious tone as if he were explaining something significant, something vital. He paused for effect after telling us that he was waiting for God, waiting for America, and waiting for a strange new appetizer.

Looking down at us from his high stool on the stage as if to make a point, he wanted us to understand something, but what, exactly? Severe and dramatic (as Gerald could be, telling me not to crawl too close to the front door of our third-floor apartment and to watch out for all those narrow stairs that went down, down, down), this man even seemed angry at us. I was incredulous. Why was he waiting, and why was he mad? Was he mad at all these stupid, loud people for being so obnoxious? I could agree on that point, but weren't they all paying close attention now? Why was he making such a big deal? I know I certainly hadn't done anything wrong.

The longer he read, the more impatient I grew, still waiting for any of this to make any sense. Even more frustrating, people around me were smiling, nodding, and exclaiming, "Yes!" as if this were the very best thing they'd ever heard.

This was terrible. There wasn't one picture. It was random words bunched together as if the man had cut up a real story and pasted it all back together while hopping around blindfolded.

Amazed at this ridiculous display, I once again looked to my two parents for reassurance. They couldn't think that this stuff's any good. It was garbage. But to my dismay, they loved it. They were smiling just like all the other weirdos in this hot, smoky room.

I couldn't believe it. Ellen and Gerald, my parents, the two most influential people in my young life, were eating this stuff up. I slunk down in my hard chair and stared at a red splotch on the greasy checkerboard. It looked like a scowling face, just about ready to scream.

But still, I didn't make a sound. Something in me had changed.

Struck dumb, I didn't know the words to describe this ugly, dark feeling. A creeping dread filling my heart with something bitter, something like fear. Frustration, disappointment, a sense that even as I sat here locked in this chair, I was completely and utterly lost. Even in a room full of people, I was all alone. Still only a child but judging the artistic choices of my parents, I worried that somehow, by not comprehending, I was indeed in some very deep trouble.

This ridiculous reading was something I didn't understand, something I didn't want to understand but felt that I was supposed to understand. But it was impossible. I didn't have a clue. My irritation became a gap, falling into a valley, spiraling down a ravine. I was squashed toast.

And then suddenly the "story" was over. The man finished, gathered up his papers, and left the stool and stage with people clapping, whistling, and also, oddly, snapping their fingers. I guess he'd finished waiting, and thankfully, he didn't come back to read anymore. I saw him in a corner smiling, shaking hands with someone, other hands patting him on the back.

There was one last piece of garlic toast on the table, and I snatched it before anyone noticed. Bread was my favorite food, and it seemed a just reward, the very least compensation for having to endure this torture. But the last piece of cold, hard, buttery toast couldn't satisfy the dark hole appearing deep within me. Even then, I knew that no amount of toast could fill the existential dilemma I faced. I had freedom, was very much my own person, but there was a tricky price to pay. I was also on my own.

CHAPTER 2

THE BLUE TABLE

In 1962, we moved to Berkeley, into our own little house on Bonita Avenue. Still the little princeling, I was eight years old with my own bedroom. Ellen and Gerald continued to treat me with deference even though there was now a new member of our family. Little sister Greta was only five and was still fed mush from a highchair, wore snap-up onesies, and was often referred to by Ellen, Gerald, and me as the Creature. A tendency to scream a lot, Greta was jealous for attention, and there were a few times when I fantasized about smothering her in her sleep.

One day, we were gifted with a large, solid-oak door, and I thought, there must be some sort of major redecorating happening. A wall was probably going to come down or a new room built for this extra-wide, imposing door to have a purpose. I cringed, anticipating all the noise, the mess, and the mayhem.

Watching my thin, long-legged daddy huff and puff as he and his friend hauled this beast of a door inside was an event all by itself. Even though he was just a twig and always wore only spotless black (looking like an extension of the piano bench with all his sharp angles), Gerald was stronger than he looked. There was a lot of grunting and groaning, much back and forth, angling and shifting of weight, testing, tilting, figuring out just how to get the monster door into the house without taking out a window, damaging the wall, or mashing a hand.

And once the great slab was inside, Gerald and his friend flipped the heavy door over onto two wide sawhorses, and voilà! They'd instantly repurposed this great door into our new dining room table. The door would now be painted and glazed to complete the transformation.

Ellen and Gerald had collected and then taped pictures of ornate Chinese lacquered cabinets, medieval stained-glass windowpanes, and Egyptian sarcophagi to the wall for reference. You could spin in place and traverse the globe, fly back and forth in time, all in a glance.

Ellen and Gerald were so capable and smart, but oddly they couldn't decide which color to choose for this door. Red or blue? Oxblood or lapis lazuli? The blue won out as Ellen said she couldn't see herself sitting down every night for dinner at a table that looked like there'd just been some sort of pagan sacrifice.

The process I learned was much more involved than just slapping down paint. There were detailed preparations to be done before the actual painting itself, and they had to be just right. The correct brushes would be purchased, two sets made of horsehair, imported all the way from England. None of the mangled brushes Greta and I offered from our homemade easels would suffice, and there needed to be just the right amount of glaze and a solvent to clean off the brushes once they were all done. Gerald told us that this solvent would dissolve skin from bone, so unless I wanted a hook for a hand, don't touch! I thought, those English horses must be pretty tough.

A week's newspapers were collected in a pile by the front door and a king's ransom spent on the few items used for this one big project. The extravagance seemed excessive, but only the very best would do for my parents (and for us kids, by extension). There was an anticipation of great things about to happen. Our life would be larger and better once the new table was complete.

The dining room became an impromptu studio with newspaper laid out, tools arranged just so, and small cans of translucent electric-blue glaze set upon the table and opened with great solemnity.

When Gerald pried open the cans, oohs and ahhs greeted the twin pools of liquid night. The glaze seemed like gateways into another dimension. You could see deep within the two paint cans, the swirling clouds of space and time, and I wondered what lingered beyond all that celestial matter and what would happen when it was applied to wood?

We were reminded not to touch, to stay away! The glaze looked eerily radioactive, and with my parents' constant warnings to keep back, I guessed it must be quite poisonous. Why they had it in the house in the first place and were now using this volatile substance to paint onto a table we'd eat on seemed weird. What if some of this gunk ate a hole right through the table, burning like acid through the floorboards, and then melted all the way down to China? This mighty effort Ellen and Gerald were making must be worth all the trouble, and I hoped they knew what they were doing, risking life and limb and possible planetary destruction.

Both Ellen and Gerald spent many painstaking hours applying the deep-blue glaze in a careful, choreographed fashion. They asked for quiet, and we kids stared in awe as they practiced as if for a performance. A slow, deliberate dance, they took a pose, then with delicate precision, dipped a new brush into the can of infinite deep blue, gathering up just enough paint; their arms gracefully bowed and then slowly lowered to touch the table edge. They extended each long stroke from one end of the table to the other in a descending and then ascending pattern without breaking momentum. Slowly, deliberately, after about a million strokes, the glassy surface was revealed in the ever-deepening glaze. They began the dance repeatedly, touching the spot marked by the last stroke and then off, down to the other side and back in endless repetition. There were many deep sighs of relief upon reaching the end and much shaking of cramped arms.

It was a game of nerves. Would they make it? Would there be enough glaze? Would their concentration hold or falter? Would I poke bothersome Greta to make her yelp so that Ellen would jerk her brush and have to start all over?

Observing from a chair nearby, after briefly putting down my copy of Magnus, Robot Fighter, I remember being eventually won over by the seriousness with which my parents tackled this mundane project, the painting of a door. It had at first seemed so dull and not worth any of the ridiculous sweaty effort, and yet, they were willing to endure obvious discomfort.

The outcome was essential, and our life was put on hold until the door was finished. Dinner waited. This was not just another painted door (our house had many colorfully painted doors); this door would be a work of art. That they had conceived of turning a door into a table was awesome DIY moxie. Ellen and Gerald were a couple of geniuses, but I was still confused.

With the painting finished, we still had to wait for two days before we could even think of putting anything on the table. Once again, it was: Do not touch that table! They erected a barrier of string tied around the backs of several chairs, all marching around, stationed, protecting the table. Honestly, I loved my sweet, eccentric parents, but they were so naive. Did they actually think that this would keep anyone's reaching hands from scraping the edge and leaving tiny, cryptic sgraffito of winking aliens?

Our dining room became a gallery display space for the blue table. The string looked so thin and white against the deep blue, a flimsy pretend fence or a vapor trail ribboned around a frozen lake.

For two whole days, we watched paint dry, admiring the perfect lacquer finish as it deepened; finally, Gerald proclaimed that, now, we could all collaborate and perform the final finishing touches. And this involved dancing.

He dropped the needle on Missa Luba (an African choral mass that had the magical effect of making feet move), and he told us to go ahead and take our shoes off (but leave socks on) because we were now going to be dancing on the table.

As we kids kicked off sneakers and our parents nimbly lifted the table from its sawhorse perch and onto the floor, I wondered if they might have been sniffing too many paint fumes? Somehow, the table had gone from a danger zone to a dance floor.

"OK, kids, let's do the twist!" Gerald exclaimed. We all hopped onto the heretofore untouchable tabletop and scooted around in our sock feet. With the jubilant chorus of African song propelling us, we bounded about, swinging each other around and around, sliding back and forth, busy little legs shuffling and buffing. At one point, I held little Greta by a finger as she pirouetted around and around like a balletic baby swan. Screams of laughter as we slid right off the table, crashing into parked chairs, must have alarmed our neighbors. What were those crazy people doing?

After we were all too tired to dance any longer, Ellen and Gerald once again put the table back up on its sawhorse legs. Then, leaning in, getting right up close, they began petting the table as if it were a new baby, buffing and caressing it with mitts made of sheepskin. Of course, we all wanted to be petted, so those mitts wore many hands and buffed many faces.

Polished and protected from the raging elements of our wild household, the blue table dried to a hard, permanent sheen that not even scraping plates, Tonka trucks, or wrestling Barbies could scuff. The finishing touch was a tangled string of Christmas lights hung around the dull lamp overhead. Transformed into a nebula of stars, the lights reflected within the deep space of the table underneath.

The two wizards masquerading as my parents had created a magical pensieve, an enigmatic surface that could look upon the universe and reflect your innermost thoughts, allowing me to gaze upon the endless expanse of space, all from the comforts of home.

The sudden luxury and civility of elbow room and now being able to face my ever-widening arc of work while seated at the table (just like an adult instead of childishly sprawling on the floor, like Greta) was an epiphany. My hands were now free to pick and choose which drawing to master and which star in the endless constellation, now beautifully trapped within the table, to explore. Which crayon would I use in drawing the residents of heaven, the exploits of ancient Greek deities, or the menacing robot invaders?

Mercury, with his stylish winged feet and streamlined helmet, zoomed across the sky, bearing urgent messages. I drew his sharp wings farther bent to the wind, for without his successful delivery, without crayon poised and my cunning hand hovering just above the table, the fabric of the cosmos might unravel.

The blue table was a force of nature, and by some mysterious coincidence, it had manifested in our house. Enabled by my two parents' prescience, the blue table held the potential for deep magic, and I joined with it.

I took my new responsibility as an arbiter of divine intervention quite seriously. As the son of demigods, I looked upon our new universe with awe and appreciation, the tingle of ultimate power flowing from the sparking fingers of my right hand into a sharpened crayon. From here, hovering above the universe, I would create a perfect world. This would be fun.

CHAPTER 3

THE RED ROOSTER

It began at home in our little kitchen, evolving later into a full-fledged business, but we always considered it playtime even when it became crushingly hard work. We could never really take it seriously.

Born from the desire to make dinnertime "more interesting" and engage the family in a shared activity, we created the Red Rooster, our very own exclusive, pretend restaurant. We used as our logo an image found on mass-produced kitchenware of the 1950s, the clichéd silhouette of a red rooster crowing happily against the rising sun or a pointy barn, evoking a welcoming, simple, country environment.

In 1965, I was eleven years old and took the comforting theme to heart. Living in an uncomplicated, nostalgic world, slipping between time, these roosters represented a faded utopia now made even more appealing with the patina of age. This simple, wistful atmosphere remains one of my favorite chosen refuges, with the kitchen as its epicenter. Plus, the kitchenware had been used by people from an unknowable past, people who'd died, people who'd maybe turned into ghosts.

We had the tools and food we needed to make a feast at any time of day or night: Our kitchen was a magnificent room stuffed with shelves stacked high with a survivalist's supply of Campbell's chicken noodle soup, Chef Boyardee sauce, Armor Star corned beef, and Vienna sausages. Boxes of Kraft macaroni and cheese, Sun-Maid raisins, Kellogg's Corn Flakes and Rice Krispies, giant cans of V8 tomato juice next to the jar of Heinz sweet pickles, the tin cabin of maple syrup, see-through honey bear, and ubiquitous Bisquick pancake mix. We would never starve as long as there was a box of Bisquick.

The refrigerator worked overtime to keep milk, juice, butter, eggs, and Jell-O from turning. The Velveeta slices and prepackaged Swiss or cheddar never lasted long enough to mold. A ziggurat of Tupperware was filled with tuna, baloney, and stew; each box was labeled with a date; most had my name scribbled on the side. I dreamed about tuna fish sandwiches. Ellen put pickles in them.

We had a porcelain sink as big as a small tub to clean up in, to wash each lettuce leaf, bunches of bright little radishes, and dumped green beans, or to fill up a flower vase. And the stove with its glowing-hot electric grills, scary oven, and buzzing timer was the big bang in our shiny, condensed universe. Copper pots crowding overhead were gleaming, clanking stars.

An organized laboratory, appointed with objects either purchased new or collected from a box at the flea market. Everything functional and designed for use; even the blue glass bottles lined up with Ellen's delicate hand-lettered labels: anise seed, cardamom, garlic, and ginger. The grizzled toy kitchen witch hovering overhead helped to keep Ellen from spilling gravy or burning the toast.

Our crowing red idol's likeness first appeared on the face of a battered kitchen clock that hummed at night in the dark. Guiding me tiptoeing to the bathroom at 3:00 a.m. for a groggy pee, I'd squint at the stoic, proud rooster standing guard. That clock marked the moments of anticipation between epic events like school, *The Addams Family*, dinner, and bedtime.

Eventually, there were glasses, plates, a matching pitcher, cloth napkins and their best friends, the napkin rings. Coasters, swizzle sticks, salt and pepper shakers, dish towels, and a well-used cutting board.

Displayed as the raiment of the holy sacrament, our roosters gathered together on the shelves or in open cupboards, each one crowing about the thrift store we'd liberated them from. When they were taken down and arranged about the kitchen or on the big, shiny-blue table, it signaled that a special meal would be prepared, served with flair, and enjoyed with the knowledge that we'd made this together. Roosters gave our little clan a sense of belonging. We were a family.

And we spent most of our time in the kitchen. Making meals and talking about what the world looked like outside. We told each other stories, explained profound mysteries, and counseled each other on the dos and don'ts of life.

"If you want something, Eric, you've got to ask nicely," advised Ellen. "Otherwise, if you just demand and not ask, it may not go your way."

I was skeptical but couldn't help acknowledging that she did have a point. There'd been plenty of times when I'd been ignored as I yelled my bitter disappointment that ice cream remained an unfortunately rare food staple.

"The word *please* really is a magic word," she continued. "It's amazing how the world opens up just by you using that one word, and a courteous thank-you seals the deal." She carefully spread peanut butter on my favorite, doughy Wonder Bread.

"People will remember you and your manners. They'll remember what a nice boy you are." Ellen was a wise woman. Her calm description of behavioral nuance gave me confidence. So, I pondered. If I repeated *please* over and over, might I have a better chance of getting chocolate chips for breakfast?

When I finally grow up, I thought, *my dream kitchen will have a big stuffed sofa to lounge on so we can encourage the cooks, raising a glass of Kool-Aid from the comfort of our velvet slouch.* Why, I asked myself, was there a separate room in the house for living when most of the living we did was in the kitchen?

Over time, dinner themes expanded to include exotic Asian food as we attempted to re-create the lively, fresh, spicy, vegetable-heavy dishes we'd eat at Sichuan restaurants around town. It was like taking a trip to another world, with the fragrant aromas of sesame or red pepper lifting the mood. Ellen always used a great technique of slivering and then sautéing almonds in butter first so that they would be extra crunchy, splashing some teriyaki over steamed vegetables, and then add a very odd new ingredient, tofu. I was surprised at how much I liked eating tiny cubes of crispy, salty sponge. Ellen made anything taste good.

I became adept at cooking rice (timing is everything) and separating big bunches of cauliflower with Ellen's little abalone-handled paring knife. I gave the sugar snap peas a tip and toe and grated lemon peel just enough (so I didn't also grate my knuckles). But what I truly excelled at was setting the long, blue table.

There was no question, the spectacle of a sit-down family dinner with fancy food and dessert, anticipated and celebrated as an event, must be decorated accordingly. And in attempting to re-create the dynamics of the actual restaurants we frequented, we put on quite a show for ourselves, with a flock of red roosters as star performers.

The deep gleam of the blue table was complemented with Ellen's blue silk sari or vivid Mexican serapes draped over it. My collection of sparkly mica-infused rocks found at the beach weighted down intricately folded rooster napkins, while a fountain bouquet of peacock feathers and blood-red amaranths dripped.

Saturday nights, family dinners required menus and invitations and costumes, and I took it upon myself to direct the proceedings as if they were a grand fete. Nobody stopped me.

My imagination spurred me to open Ellen's library of cookbooks and look at them, asking her, what did mincing garlic look like, or how did you bake Alaska? I needed information if there was going to be progress. The evening needed to be perfect.

"Ellen, all these recipes ask for vegetable shortening." I had been puzzling over her new book about East Indian food, which seemed like a potential treasure trove of endless feasts. In the bookstore, I'd whooped. "Look, Ellen! It's your sari!" The book's photographer had wrapped a sky-blue sari around lamb kebobs for the cover. That book was an easy sell.

"Think about it, Eric." Ellen turned to look at me with my nose in the curry section. "It's not butter, by the way." She'd given me a hint, waiting while I worked it out.

"Is it, uh, Crisco?" I queried, remembering the colorful can of slippery goop Ellen always dipped into when she was making pie crust.

"Very good. Now tell me about curry." She was testing me.

All I could think of then was: "It's old, as old as the caveman." This was almost correct, but besides it being ancient, I knew that curry was an essential spice in the large blue jar since it didn't last very long.

Soon, Indian food became my reigning favorite. The sweet-and-sour flavors, the colors, the textures, and the decorating possibilities were endless. I would concoct elaborate menus pairing lamb korma, assorted condiments of lentil dal, creamy yogurt, chewy dates, mango chutney, and steamed spinach, with coconut rice pudding for dessert. All delicious. I studied that book of Ellen's and was in a constant state of craving, asking, please, please, please (very nicely, I might add) if I could have a potato samosa with the meatloaf she'd made. Leftovers dipped in gravy carried me over until the next royal repast.

Imagining that the only other house where you could get our kind of banquet was at the Taj Mahal, I spun scenarios from Scheherazade's *One Thousand and One Nights*. I spent afternoons constructing cardboard menus, sometimes with gold leaf or pop-up features, and plotting just how the food should come out of the kitchen and then forced my patient, obedient parents to lend a hand. I cast Ellen as chef while Gerald became my personal assistant. He once helped me haul a whole tree limb, fallen from the blossoming plum out back, to hang overhead, then swept up all the fallen petals after dinner. Little sister Greta of course wanted to be involved somehow, but she was of no use to me as a trustworthy workhorse, so she usually helped Ellen shell peas or stir cake batter. I begrudgingly accepted that it was only fair that she then got to lick the big wooden spoon.

I scattered roses, lit incense, and lay tiny mirrors across the table to catch the sparkling candlelight. The beaded bamboo curtains hung between kitchen and dining room were constantly swinging. Ravi Shankar hypnotized the air with his sitar accompaniment. I wore a towel for a turban, Ellen her silk sari (if not already on the table), Gerald stuck a glass jewel on his forehead, and Greta tied a long scarf around herself. She looked more like a small mummy than an Indian princess, but she would not be left out of the proceedings.

I served up mulligatawny soup in the deep-red rooster bowls, then prowled around the table slurping madly. I always finished first and paced impatiently around the dining room while everyone else ate. When they'd taken their last sip, I reached quickly in on the right (just like I remember a haughty waiter doing), collecting the empty bowls from atop the larger rooster plates underneath.

Next, out came the large, teak salad bowl, presented to Gerald first, who, with great panache, took the two long wooden rooster-head serving spoons and maneuvered a bunch of greens to his plate, never dropping a leaf.

I stepped around the table, even waiting for little Greta as she struggled with the oversize spoons (more like shovels in her tiny hands) until we all had a nice bunch of lettuce. I of course served myself last but again, always finished first while skirting the edges of the room. I was way too busy to sit while the show was in motion.

The large, red rooster dinner plates were all stacked in the warm oven, and once salad was finished and plates removed, I put on a red rooster mitt and took each larger plate out, organized perfect spoonfuls of rice next to a cut of lamb or pot roast, a glop of stew, or steaming stir-fry. A sprig of green parsley to finish, and then I balanced two plates between the fingers of my right hand and a third in the left, serving my family like they were hungry, paying customers. Ellen and Gerald waited while I arranged my plate, but Greta didn't care about manners.

Dessert was, if not rice pudding, a duo of carefully considered ice creams. A perfect round scoop of rocky road and mocha chip brought home from Mr. Botts was usually the unanimous choice. Sticking one Pepperidge Farm ladyfinger in at a jaunty angle, a spoon on the other side, I whisked the rooster cups out, and we shuffled away from the formality of the blue dinner table to gather around the warming hearth of our black-and-white TV.

Those theatrical dinners were so much fun, but after a while, it just wore us out, and we reached saturation point. Work was work, and it was becoming too serious. We were at home, after all, and wanted to relax.

My commitment to all the prep and then cleanup faltered, so we took a break. The immortal hamburger, cheesy pasta, or spicy meatloaf, still served on red rooster plates, made a welcome resurgence. Easy to make, these always pleased us kids, and by not spending all night devising elaborate meals, we could slump on the couch, turn on the TV, and sit cuddled up with plates of spaghetti, surviving the Wild West of *Gunsmoke* or navigating a hostile universe with the space family Robinson.

Lost in Space had become my favorite show, and it was a bonus that everybody else seemed to also get a kick out of the sci-fi soap opera. Ellen laughed at the goofy monsters popping out from behind glittery papier-mâché rocks. Juicy, mustard-covered hot dogs were the perfect food to shove in your mouth while spaceships spun across the screen.

In fact, hot dogs on a bun, with relish and mustard, briefly became my exclusive TV-time dinner. Delivered automatically (hand to mouth), barely tasted, eyes glued to the action, I pondered one of life's great mysteries: am I in love with a robot?

Those swinging, efficient pincer arms that became ray guns when needed. A deep, authoritative voice and seemingly godlike best friend status broadcast confidence and a warm sense of security. The Robot could detect and protect; he could figure things out super quick. He was full of computer chips, electricity, and heart. This was the person I wanted to be! Powerful yet gentle, infinitely smart, self-sacrificing, and universally loved. His stylish metallic suit invulnerable to the ravages of cosmic mayhem, he personified my ideal of a gentle warrior.

Watching the predictable travails of this perfect suburban family guided by a hunk of dapper, masculine metal gave me some confidence that I, too, could be master of my small world. Plus, they also ate hot dogs in space.

It was during one of these evenings, with a simple all-American construction of dog-on-bun perched in my lap, with the lights off and the eerie glow of the TV turning our faces ghostly pale, that Gerald quite suddenly got up from the couch, and right in the middle of Dr. Smith's whining excuse as to why he'd lured young Will into that cave, changed the channel.

"It's time to start watching something intelligent for a change!" he proclaimed. "We're turning into zombies. Our minds are mush."

Gerald hadn't asked or even suggested — he'd just acted — and I knew that once he had pronounced his edict, it was all over for Will Robinson. I sat in shock on the arm of the couch. Gerald, my dad and faithful assistant, had declared mutiny.

He flipped around and around until he found what he was looking for: a cooking show. A giant woman in an apron, talking as if she still had a mouthful of half-chewed food, slapped a lineup of different-size chickens on her table. She picked one up and started squeezing it tenderly as if it were her baby and then explained how she was now going to roast it.

I suppose I should have been more interested in what she was saying, given my general investment in dinner, but as she danced the chicken around like a dead puppet, sawed its neck off, stuffed its butt with herbs, and then proceeded to sew its legs together, I felt my mood shift. This beast of a woman (and my dad) had ruined everything.

I watched in dismay as Ellen and Gerald leaned in, transfixed. They ate their asparagus tips one by one like zombies mesmerized by the light. I recall protesting that my show had been preempted, but Gerald shushed me, putting a hand up as if to block me from view, not taking his eyes from the TV.

I chewed my rubbery hot dog in silent desolation as this large, loud lady skewered the poor chicken with a spear, tied it all up, and as promised, shoved it in the oven. I knew what roasted chicken tasted like and the captivating, inviting smell of it. Once the televised bird had been cut up, the dripping fat glistening along the edges of the big TV cook's serving board, the cold, dead pig parts fell abandoned on my plate, what I'd swallowed thudding hard in my stomach, a tasteless brick. I wanted chicken. We all did. Ellen and Gerald were licking their lips, not finishing their food either. We sat there on the couch, staring.

I don't remember what else we watched that night, but from that moment on, the benign and powerful inspiration of Julia Child informed what happened in our kitchen. Red roosters were brought down and arranged as before, but instead of curry, stir-fry, meatloaf, and hot dogs, there was an entirely new fare: the cuisine de France enveloped our world. My parents were obsessed, and I couldn't help but understand why. The food was amazing. So delicious, so elaborate and elegant, yet just as accessible as any hot dog.

Our approach to food was irrevocably altered. We started paying much more attention to what was in the grocery store and what we brought home. How everything was prepared, how the foods interacted and then tasted, all the way down to presentation, and then finally (most satisfyingly), a discerning critique of a meal became the main topic of conversation at dinner. The fluffiness of the eggs, the crispness of vegetables, herby potatoes, silky blended soup with a subtle hint of saffron, the earthy tang of truffle.

"I like how the black tea comes through in the custard." Ellen licked the spoon. It wasn't even dessert. She'd made a tea-infused custard to go with the broccolini sprinkled with sea salt.

Enthusiasm for fancy dinners returned with a vengeance, and I tempered my space-faring adventures with the enraptured study of Madame Child's cheerful instruction. Greta squirmed as Ellen, Gerald, and I sat staring, shushing her without glancing her way, our hastily prepared family picnic of chicken liver pâté, Anjou pears, Stilton cheese, and baguette sampled during commercials. Nothing was ever the same again.

CHAPTER 4

DANGER, WILL ROBINSON!

One early October morning in 1967, Gerald and I took a long, four-hour drive north along generic suburban highways that then detoured off into a never-land of country farms and roadside apple stands. It was the kind of trip kids in the backseat whine about.

"Are we there yet?"

We turned off the gradually thinning thoroughfare of Highway 101, and almost suddenly, I got this palpable feeling that we were crossing over into someplace…different. I questioned Gerald's every move when we made that turn at Cloverdale.

"Why are we going this way?" I demanded.

This was an event—a father-son road trip in the beat-up Rambler. Ellen and my two younger sisters, Greta and smaller Kristin, were still asleep when we'd left. It was just me and Gerald.

Down the slope past a fallow vineyard, winding up and around and down those hairpin curves and dips into sheep land; past little farms and viney old trees hanging off the eroding edges of the road, beckoning and warning.

"This will be fun," Gerald announced, adjusting the ever-present beret to the back of his head, declaring the beginning of a project. He had a small bag of granola in his lap, a thermos of coffee balanced in the groove between seats, and a large Texaco road map regularly opened and refolded, referred to, and then shoved aside again. Where were we going, Canada? Gerald and Ellen talked about that all the time.

The Vietnam War was raging, people were rioting in the streets, and at thirteen, I was inexorably getting closer to an age when the army might call me up for the draft. I didn't want to join the army, go to war, or die! Canada seemed the obvious alternative. But Vancouver, I knew, was still many hundreds of miles to the north. Where was Gerald headed?

Gerald had only said that it was a surprise. A surprise? The only times I drove around with Gerald were to or from school or those brief Saturday jaunts to an opera or the museum. Mounting suspicion told me that he had some sort of plan, and the surprise could be either good or bad.

There was a strange look in his eye, and I didn't like this road; it was different and curvy. He was very mysterious, and when Gerald doled out cryptic, dramatic bits of information, that usually meant there was something substantial at the end of the mystery. Like a birthday blowout, ice skating at the rink in Oakland, or going to the doctor for a painful tetanus shot in the butt. Gerald would make broad proclamations resulting in either a magnificent or horrifying revelation. The new sweater, the altered beret, and most importantly, the pointed lack of info. Yes, the signs were all there: the surprise was probably bad.

"Look at the map, Eric." Gerald indicated to the dashboard where the confusing, rumpled map had ended up. "This road leads to the coast. We've never been this way."

I was aware that I'd been discussed by both parents and teachers recently. Beside the impending, threatened army conscription, they were concerned about my education. I was spending all my time at school conducting an ongoing role-playing drama in the lean-to shack in the field, away from the main buildings. The alternative "free school" out in the loose farmlands of Martinez was where I spun fantasies and experimented with social interaction, where I entertained the notion that I might be an enfant terrible, an idiot savant, or just a terrible idiot.

Almost immediately after getting off the bus at school, a small group of us would find ourselves…lost in space. My obsession with directing the proceedings as the all-powerful Robot had the grown-ups scratching their heads. I never did a lick of bona fide studies, playing my game all day, and as the game became serious business, such mundane things like math and English were ignored, even avoided. There was a disconnect somewhere. Anticipating the crackdown, I figured this road trip was probably the beginning of the inevitable.

Gerald's solution was that now he was taking me to some run-down, wretched boy's school for the dim-witted. Where blackboards covered in indecipherable calculus squiggles lined the cold, gray hallways, where brutish matrons marched you into freezing offices to inspect your teeth or, worse, your wiener. Or some wide space in the road where he'd just stop and say: "Son, that time we've talked about, the one where it's time for you to grow up? This is that time. We've arrived. Here it is. You're on your own now. I love you, but will you please get out of the car?"

Quickly perusing the map and all the red lines wandering over the state of California, I found Cloverdale toward the top, barely visible. A teensy dot connected by a short road to another spot along the coast. It looked rough and was probably dirt; there would be plenty of places for an anonymous car to pull over.

"We're on 128!" I exclaimed, letting Gerald know that I knew exactly where we were. I checked to see if I'd fastened my seat belt. I wouldn't be shoved out of a moving car without a fight.

"That's right," he said. "And 128 leads us to the coast route. We'll see some surprises along the way, I'm sure." As he kept both hands on the wheel, his eyes slid sideways to glance my way. There was that word again: *surprise*. A chill went up my spine.

I always got carsick, even seated up front. Any road trip for me was like Columbus on the high seas. The passenger window rolled down enough for me to stick my hand outside. Cold air rushing over fingers, somehow alleviating thick nausea bubbling up. I put the map down and concentrated on not vomiting.

Riding the ocean-rolling movement around curves carved into hills on roads meant more for buggies than cars (and driven with a hint more impatience than Gerald would admit), I found 128 a nightmare. With the open map still on my lap, ready to catch barf, my hand caressed the cold metal roof of the Rambler, familiarizing myself with all the dings and dents.

This torture was only the beginning, though, because, at the end of this road trip, there'd be a disciplinary hearing and punishment for wasting valuable (and expensive) study time, and I would, of course, have no defense. It had to end this way.

But as we zipped around a tight curve and began snaking down the slope of a twisty hill, I encountered something new. A lush, musty smell of roadside weeds, trees, cows, sheep, and the scent of bacon signaled a change. We were in the country! The bleak future of my extended stay in a garbage-bag folding facility didn't smell like this. I was expecting urban decay, smoke, burning rubber, screeching metal, and old warehouses with rusty tractors and dark pits of sulphuric sewage. Instead, I heard birds, the air was sweet, and those were poppies popping up.

Swerving past a weathered farmhouse plopped down via a Frank L. Baum cyclone, I imagined Mrs. Butterworth behind her kitchen stove frying up the bacon. I asked her if I could stay, please! My dad's taking me to a boot camp. The pancakes are piled high, with hot syrup dripping, and she wipes her big hands on that stained apron.

"Oh, you poor dear! Of course you can stay with me. We'll make your dad shovel cow poop while I squeeze you some more orange juice." And then with another rush of green, her little house flew past, and we climbed up and around another curve.

The closer we got to the coast, the closer to the road the trees grew, gathering almost as if they'd anticipated our presence and were less than happy about it. Didn't Gerald see that No Trespassing sign back there?

We drove from the city where sidewalks, store windows, cars, and constant movement reflected my image of the world. Where larger, tougher, more masculine boys threatened my very existence. Forbidding stands of rough, red-barked trees remained still as we passed. Very strange things. Taller and broader than any building, these big bully trees were closing in; they were going to beat the shit out of us. Farmland faded away, and we were lost in the Dark Realm: the Redwood Kingdom.

"Isn't this amazing?" Gerald craned his neck, looking up at the towering, encroaching trees. "These trees are hundreds of years old, maybe even thousands. These trees were big when America was new."

It made sense. Nothing else survived as long. They were squashed by these ancient, lumbering, malevolent trees.

"No one but us can stay here, and you're not one of us," the trees seemed to be communicating, crowding so close. We were swallowed up, surrounded, huddling underneath. The whoosh of our Rambler echoed off the narrow road, with an occasional loud crack of a branch falling, just missing us.

"It's like being in church or a cathedral," said Gerald. He was in awe. He was impressed. He would know about church; he used to sing in a choir.

On the rare occasions when I'd been taken to the Unitarian church in Berkeley either to hear Gerald sing or to have the Sunday school experience, I'd come away with the impression that it was all some elaborately disguised, gussied-up death cult. The very serious grown-ups worshiped this beautiful, skinny man who'd been nailed to a wooden cross. He kept bleeding and was stabbed by mean Romans. It was horrible and sad, but people wore their best suits and ties and Easter bonnets, and when I wondered aloud if I was going to be stabbed or nailed to a cross, we started going to flea markets on Sundays.

But the analogies were real, and I was forced to experience reverence and wonder and a bit of dread. Don't make a sound. Don't laugh or shout, and for goodness' sake, don't fart! Don't slump or put your feet up on the pews or eat all those holy crackers in the holy bowl on stage. And for god's sake, don't wake these trees up. You don't want to know what they're saying: the deep rumbling and sighing that is tree talk.

I looked up through the window, trying to see the tops of these monster trees: a flickering light-and-deep green. There was a flash of water somewhere beyond. A terrified bird, or was it an evil were-elf? There was the sensation of movement and also of standing still. A waking dream and the distinct impression that as I gawked, I was as well being observed. These ancient, immortal trees assessing, not at all pleased that these two clumsy humans had insinuated themselves, defiling the sanctity of this sacred place. We were intruding, and it was best we kept driving because if we stopped, we might never be allowed to leave.

But by some miracle, we were released through a sudden, widening gate of trees. A sparkle of water glimpsed was revealed to be a river sliding along with us, curving with the road. The trees marched away, 128 evened out, and the Pacific Ocean was visible between lumps of small hills. There was a small island sprouting from the widening river, an idyll of mossy decorative rock where an egret posed in elegant angles. Breathing a sigh of relief, I smelled salt.

Past an old verdigris metal bridge that took the road up left into another group of trees, we instead forked right onto Highway One, up and up and up into a bobbing cumulous cloud of a climbing hill with a broken picket fence clinging, wildflowers scattered like confetti. The road ribboned around for a bit then finally arranged itself in a soft line as the land dropped away into a vast mirror.

"Behold! The sea!" Gerald gestured as if sharing a private treasure. A panoramic, endless expanse of water. The largest body of water I'd ever seen. Glassy gray-green with flecks of white. Outcroppings of the cliff had broken off from the mainland and floated like ships, while the sky rushed away into space to meet water on a far horizon. My road sick was replaced by wide-eyed wonderment. It was silent in the car as we marveled, and it felt like flying.

But we were still driving. Highway One continued its curvaceous nature around hillocks of wild grass and wind-bent fences. Strategic, cliff-dwelling trees leaned and pointed their drunken, twisty arms. Drive this way, right off the cliff!

We passed small roads that led up and off into other territories away from the ocean. I saw locked gates and lonely mailboxes. The character of this community began to emerge. A rusted green road sign declared that this was a town. Albion: population minuscule.

A few homes appeared, again, as if they'd arrived via the hand of God, placed intact if imperfectly on a cliff's edge or nestled between the folds of a hill. Little pointy homes with weathered, peeling paint and cute decorative detailing, and all with more than a bit of sad, solitary melancholy. Enduring, once-pretty faces looking at an empty sea. We crossed another high bridge made of rusted tinker toys, and far below, I saw a gray river's slow pour into the ocean. A jumble of sad-looking boats hunkered close together, as if in collective misery against the cold. I smelled damp, old wood, and fish. Everything was ghostly and forlorn, abandoned. I bet the zombie fishermen only came out at night.

"Keep driving, Gerald."

Thankfully, he did, and the road took us down a gentle slope through another tiny cluster of banged-up gingerbread houses, the tiny township of Little River. The river was so little I couldn't even see it, but there was a grand, scarred, white mansion that could be Wuthering Heights. We didn't pull over, so I guessed this wasn't my new penitentiary, but as we passed, I was sure that was Heathcliff roaming the creaking halls, looking at us right then through a window, waving madly, trying to warn us. "Don't go that way! It's a trap! Look at me. I got suckered into a road trip and ended up here."

Downhill, a small beach appeared, all gray and littered with drift-wood. A few stick people wandered about all bundled up, with the wind blowing their hair in impossible directions. They stood like statues or bent down to pick up things from the sand—lost souls in limbo.

"Do you want to stop and look for shells?" Gerald asked.

"No," I almost yelled.

I was crushed into the warm bucket seat, wishing that I could be back home with a comic book, pursuing more exciting adventures with the likes of Spider-Man or Dr. Strange. More accessible than this desolate place.

I would also pick up a math book and read it like it was the latest issue of the Fantastic Four. If I cleared my head, started all over, I could make it work. I could understand what everybody was studying so diligently. I wasn't broken, only misunderstood. So I hated math and football. I would make any necessary adjustments in attitude, and I'd learn to love them, if only we'd turn back now.

But then, as we made another slow climb up yet another bouncy, mossy hill, Gerald exclaimed at the rustic grandeur of a tilted mansion resting like a royal forgotten on its throne. It was surrounded by an ink-black field of dirt blooming a thousand orange pumpkins. I saw a farmer loading a pickup truck full.

Whereas the beach back there was so empty and grim, this bucolic, elegant homestead had the warmth of a feather bed. I wanted to snuggle up and never leave. I could study in this place. Adjust the fluffy pillow, hunker down with a plate full of cookies and my fascinating new math book (with lots of pictures drawn by Jack Kirby). It would be perfect.

"That movie *Johnny Belinda* was filmed here," Gerald explained.

I of course had no idea what he was talking about. If it didn't have a robot, a superhero, or some tragic heroine, like Carmen or Mimi from *La Bohème*, I was bored. Perhaps, I said to myself, *Johnny Belinda* was the next movie I should see. Victorian robots from space threaten an innocent farm girl who happens to be a superpowered mutant. She kicks their ass.

"I wanna see that movie, Gerald."

He smiled and nodded, impressed that I was taking an interest in something he thought was cool.

We came to the edge of the hill and paused, like a cart on a roller-coaster track getting ready for a tummy-caving descent. The impression of weightlessness, and then, hovering over a twinkling bay, there was a birthday cake.

"There it is. We're almost there." Gerald pointed at the obvious target. A long line of white, oddly shaped buildings and grassy cliffs lay out over the sea. Embraced by dancing trees, ocean, and blue sky, the town floated, framed like a frothy, frosted cameo. I saw the tiny, pointy steeple of a church, tiny streets, and tiny cars. There must also be tiny people and a tiny civilization. It was like the lost city of Kandor. This was the surprise? At least it looked pretty from here. I stared and tried to discern what exactly it was I was looking at. From this distance, it looked like a long, sugar-coated pastry, but it was probably just another strip mall, and we'd driven this entire way for the same old frosty cone or plastic motel chain. If we were lucky, there would be a pool and a TV.

"Is it...Disneyland?" I asked hopefully, my impression of Gerald suddenly lifting. Was he on my side after all? Instead of chucking me off a cliff, was he going to indulge in some serious playtime?

"Oh no, no, not Disneyland. That's way in the other direction." He was chuckling. "This is Mendocino. We're going to have a look around and see what we shall see."

CHAPTER 5

PETRIFIED WOOD

Almost like a welcoming gesture, a fork guided us left off the highway and down into this old town. Seagulls wobbled around the half-moon smile of a beach, floating then lurching, flapping madly or diving. My eye followed a zigzag path down the cliff cutting through leaning trees, weeds, and wildflowers. I saw a kid in a windbreaker tempting fate by jumping off a huge log. His arms aloft, he flew up into the air, then landed down onto the plane of sand. That kid seemed strangely familiar, and as we swooped down through wisps of fog, I asked myself, could I do that? Scramble down that cliff, slog through all that sand, and jump off a big, wet log? I was not quite sure, but even from my seat in the car, I could feel the grit collecting in my shoes.

Past a tiny cemetery, a solitary stone-gray horse stood grazing. It was early afternoon, but there was a thick morning drowsiness as if we were still asleep and this was a dream. A haze of fog hung low over the town, filtering the sun, colors bleached to a daguerreotype pale.

My head felt like a lead balloon lolling this way and that, my right hand a block of ice (having been glued to the car roof for hours), but it was worth it, since I was not throwing up. Creeping into town, I was relieved, knowing that this road trip torture was almost over, that we were going to have to stop soon, or we'd go right off the edge.

The town rested on an outcropping of land with the ocean all around. I would gladly step onto the sand and grab hold of a gritty, wet log as long as I didn't have to get back into that car for a while.

All along the sides of the street, I noticed cars parked at odd angles, like scrabbled dominos or tossed litter. The drivers had pulled over and stopped dead in the dirt. Are people crazy in this town?

On either side of the street, there were sad-looking old homes with slumped picket fences, unhinged gates, and scrappy gardens. In a window, old-lady lace curtains hung tired around the outline of a cat who watched us as we drove by. A witch's familiar or a taxidermy warning?

A family of abalone shells, each sprouting alien, leggy succulents, marched down porch steps and into the yard where a rake was left teeth up, waiting for someone to step on and get a face full of stick. I watched *The Three Stooges*; I knew how it worked.

Even the streets were cracked and full of unexpected lumps, bumps, dips, ruts, and rough patch jobs. Dry grass exploded from breaks in the road, and the wiggly pavement was edged with plain dirt and forests of Queen Anne's lace. The relatively new highway we left behind continued merrily onward while Gerald and I shuddered and rumbled through a town built on chewed-up bubble gum.

This whole place was a spooky, dilapidated antique. Every house either an abandoned barn, haunted mansion, or fisherman's shanty. Everything old and tired, made of bent, moldy, rough wood. Everything in desperate need of some repair, a paint job, a facelift, a strip mall.

A grand, knobby old tree grew defiantly right in the middle of the street, demanding that we make a right-hand turn. So, Gerald obediently swerved right, up the hill farther into town, passing a greasy garage and the beginnings of what looked like a cartoon sidewalk, also made of wood. He craned his neck around like a bobblehead doll, eyes twinkling, mouth half-open as if he was about to exclaim in wonder. He was glad to be here! He liked this horrible, bedraggled, sad place. It was as if he had discovered a magnificent secret treasure. What happened to my highbrow, elegant, sophisticated father? Who was this strange person who drove like a maniac and reveled in dead things? I did a quick internal measure of whether there was something about rotten fish, lopsided Victoriana, and dried weeds that eluded me? Was there something I was missing? Did all that sea air freeze Gerald's brain? Had a ghost possessed my dad as we entered past that graveyard and into this surreal Victorian village?

That was it. Tired from all the mad swerving around endless cliffside hairpin curves and the deep concentration it took to pretend he was on the Indy 500, his mind weak from the effort, from avoiding cows and slow RVs, Gerald must have collided with an errant spirit floating about in this foggy soup. I blinked tired eyes in a mix of chagrin and dread. My dad was gone, replaced with the lost soul of an undertaker or fisherman—someone who used to live in this awful place, someone who'd never driven a car.

With a conspiratorial little smile on his face, he finally pulled over willy-nilly, like all the other cars. Parking like a circus clown (or possessed person), he was right at home. Now what? Was I supposed to get out of the car? Should I run for my life?

"C'mon, Eric, let's explore" he said. "Bring your coat."

After all that worrying about being shuttled away to boot camp, the hours of driving, and the car sickness, it was nice to have stopped, but I asked myself, explore what exactly, and with whom? I could see it all right there from my car seat, thank you. Everything was old, run-down, and so boring. All of it one color: cold-porridge gray. No movie theaters, no stores, no parks, no nothing. What was this new dad so intrigued with? Was he going to take me back to that graveyard I saw and show me his headstone?

A clump of tourists shuffled by wearing ugly, chunky sweaters and wide-brimmed hats, the kind that kept the sun off faces while on safari or bird-watching. But here there was no sun, and only seagulls were looping in and out of fog trails. The bird-watchers huddled together, scuttling along that wooden sidewalk, pointing cameras in every direction. What was so fascinating? It all looked the same.

A goofy Tinkertoy sidewalk that rolled up and down the street, the droopy, gray dollhouses, frozen-frosting scrollwork around door frames, all along the tops of roofs, and at the sad edges of things, everything, all of it, made of wood. The tiniest details blunted. Ornate flourishes all molded together by the fog.

A lanky, lopsided dog loped by, breaking my trance. On its own and knowing exactly where it was going. Patchy in places, ears flopping, it galumphed up the wooden sidewalk. Though it looked harmless enough, I was still suspicious. The only dogs I'd ever seen off-leash were the wild hyenas at the zoo or in Disney wildlife documentaries. Wild dingoes chasing down and ripping apart bunnies or small deer. Maybe this one was out hunting with the rest of its pack waiting around the corner in ambush. Or maybe it was rabid. I looked for telltale foam as the dog ambled away. No, it couldn't care less about me; the dog was going home for a snack. I wished I could go home.

As I stood there by the Rambler, its motor off, myself not moving and feeling the blessed ground under my feet, everything stopped. It was so quiet. Those scary redwoods were far behind us on the lost highway, and with no dog bites to bandage, I was relieved.

Gerald stepped up onto the wooden sidewalk and put his hand on my shoulder. He was still looking wide-eyed and excited like he wanted to join in on all the fun; his little Polaroid camera swung by the strap.

"OK, Eric," he said, "which way should we go? Are you hungry?"

Which way should we go? *Any direction would be just as boring as the other, but let's avoid the graveyard, shall we? I am a bit hungry.*

The sensation of g-forces subsiding, I got my bearings and looked up to follow the gaze of the bird-watchers. On the steeple of a wooden church painted mushroom white was the statue of an old man balancing a scythe in the crook of his arm while braiding the hair of a maiden standing in front.

"It's Father Time," explained Gerald, snapping a picture.

Then it hit me. This whole place was Disneyland, sort of. This was a little Victorian village theme park where at any moment, a craggy old lady wearing mourning black would ride past in a horse-drawn buggy. Or a man in a tweed suit and handlebar mustache would step out onto the wooden sidewalk, adjust his brown derby, hook a thumb in his vest pocket, and check the engraved watch to see what time it was. The watch had stopped because time had frozen.

A pillow of deafening stillness pressed in on me; there was no traffic, no bustling crowd, no buses, sirens, no neon, not even a real sidewalk. I was standing on a wood plank path plunked down and nailed right into the dirt a very long time ago. It rolled over the ground like a petrified carpet.

The curiosity of a barren field appeared behind the church, wild weeds pushing up against the gray sky. The air was fresh and sweet with a salty sea tang. The radioactive dust that had collected in my poor head was suddenly vacuumed up.

Standing still, breathing this new air, I realized that everything felt surprisingly...better. The heaviness evaporated, wooziness settled, and I could see straight once again. Suddenly, everything was crisp and bright, it was as if I'd grown new eyes, and I had to ask myself, *Could I ever live in a place like this? Oh no, of course not! I'm a city kid. This is a ghost town.*

A hand-painted sign points toward The Sea Gull Restaurant; it was right down the block and looked like a big, gray barn. I was hungry. I wanted pancakes and bacon.

CHAPTER 6

IRONIC SEASCAPE

The wooden pergola entrance of The Sea Gull bristled with thumbtacked flyers and notices, bent business cards and handwritten requests for rentals or part-time jobs. Every time the front door opened, the entire community of papers flapped and rustled. One card tore loose, flying away.

Inside the entryway, a massive carved wooden sculpture of seagulls flying up was meant to be the inspirational mascot for this place. Still, the hard brown seagulls looming seemed as much a threat as an invitation. I'd be crushed flat if that thing fell over. The blackboard menu overhead announced: "Chowder is our specialty."

Pale, dusty, overgrown plants hung everywhere from rough wood rafters. Gerald and I stooped underneath drooping tendrils of carnivorous, malnourished plants as they dragged our hair, hungry and reaching, hoping for a human snack. Assorted glass balls, bloated spiny fish, wooden oars, fishing nets, life preservers, and boards painted with names of boats floated about as if washed in by the tide. If we made it past this aquarium, we could eat, but not chowder.

A lady with magenta hair leaned out from a dark wooden booth, like the animated fortune teller from the Playland amusement park. Smoke from her cigarette flowed out in a bitter fog. She looked me up and down, deciding whether I could enter.

Grabbing two huge menus, she marched us to a long slab of lacquered wood. This was like our table at home but with people's names and goofy drawings carved all over, exactly like the school desk of a juvenile delinquent. How did she know? Was this some sort of test? Then I noticed that all the other tables were also slabs, all carved up. All the malcontents in town must have eaten at The Sea Gull.

The big windows next to our table were hung with dingy macramé curtains, an outbreak of bulging wooden beads woven throughout. I touched one, but the curtains were heavy and solid, molded with years of smoke and grease, and they barely moved. They shuddered.

The lady dropped our menus on the table as if they'd suddenly bitten her.

"Enjoy your breakfast."

There was something about the way she said it. It was a command and a warning. It sounded as if she was also saying: "Or else." This might be my last meal.

Looking through dusty holes in the macramé, I saw a large wooden figure of an Indian standing across the street. His stiff right arm was reaching out, offering cigars. Even the wooden Indians here smoked.

Sweet Mrs. Butterworth smiled kindly from her squeeze bottle at the corner of our table. She looked right at home here, stuck with the wooden salt and pepper shakers and the plastic basket of rocks our waitress called muffins. When she finally returned to take our order, it seemed like it was the last thing she wanted to do, and that instead of pancakes, we'd asked her to recite from memory the building blocks of the periodic table.

After our food arrived and we'd eaten a couple bites, Gerald poked at something the waitress had had to write lots of notes about to get right.

"They don't know how to do a proper Hollandaise."

He stirred the yellow goo puddling around his eggs.

My pancakes were falling off the plate—a leaning tower of pancakes.

Bacon floated in a moat of syrup, and I'd dripped some down my shirt.

"Be careful what you wish for," said Mrs. Butterworth. I wish I'd asked for another napkin; the waitress had forgotten all about us. She was leaning up against the giant seagull sculpture, smoking.

Our late breakfast finished, Gerald and I struck out on our tour of this strange, silent stage-set of a town. A veil of fog drifted down the street, and I heard a faraway raven cry out.

The wooden Indian seen from behind dirty macramé had been standing out there on the street for so long that his moccasin feet were now patterned stumps. His once-elegant carved headdress had melted into a blunted bonnet. A solid lump of wood whittled by an artist's knife, rendered into the vintage likeness of a proud chief had been reduced to schmaltz. One moccasin stump inched forward from the storefront, stepping from this world and into the next. An icon of endurance, he now seemed to be waiting to become, once again, just a log.

I could see the remnants of bright paint scratched, peeling off and visible under a frosting of decorative bird poop. Reaching out with a sticky finger to touch one of the wooden cigars gripped in his fist, I sensed the ancient spirit trapped within. His woodgrain eyes stared back at me with a dull ache. A sudden gust of chill wind echoed his silent entreaty:

"Blow the birds off their course. Keep them from my face so that I may see the world."

Glancing up, I glared at the gang of seagulls as they maneuvered the wind, waiting for a chance to mock the chief with further indignities.

The small store he stood guard over featured several shelves of large glass jars, each filled with an assortment of colorful candy placed annoyingly out of reach. There was no way I could sneak around and grab a handful without being seen, or was there? Gerald was distracted; he was chatting to a lady with big teeth. If only she could keep him busy for just a little while longer. There might be a short window to snag some toffees. No such luck—they both turned and looked right at me as if sensing my criminal intent. Why did adults always suspect the worst from me? Candy stayed in the jar, itchy hands in pockets. *Nothing to see here!* Another candy crime averted.

There was a corkboard gallery of paintings arranged like mismatched tiles, each picture a different version of the very same ocean: crashing waves spitting foam over sharp rocks, spilling into glassy tide pools. Gray, green and blue, they all hung as if the tide had been pushing them askew. Framed with rough planks of wood, the sign read: "Real Redwood." All these paintings would make you seasick and give you splinters.

A huge net slung like a lumpy hammock between two corroded metal buoys bulged with a school of fake fish. Caught and staring at nothing for years, their lidless eyes peered down at me from the holes in the dusty net. A ragged bouquet of fishing poles was poking underneath in a galvanized garbage can. The sign said: "Please see owner for lures."

I was not lured in any way to see the owner. I was even a bit leery. He looked like an ogre who could quite possibly have a taste for children. He was slumped in a ragged armchair smoking a cigar, clutching a newspaper with big-knuckled, hairy, sausage fingers, the splotchy red stain on his plaid shirt all that was left of his last meal. I was not going to be the stupid but innocent kid lured behind the counter by all those candy jars and that tricky sign.

Not a comic book rack in sight, and the last thing I wanted to do was to inquire about fishing. That would be like me begging the gym teacher to please, show me how to grip a football correctly behind some other boy's butt. Football: an exercise in humiliation and torture. The ridiculous rules of all male competition, really, made me want to run in the opposite direction. I heard the sniggering from mean kids bouncing off the school hallways: "I know what your real name is: Eric Picks-his-boogers!"

I'd rather be at home drawing robots or melting GI Joes and Barbies into cojoined mutants dressed up in each other's clothes, zapping Godzilla or bullies with glitter and flame.

Come to think of it, it felt strangely comforting to be lost in this backwoods tourist trap run by cannibal ogre fishermen. I was invisible there in that museum of generic, tacky crap. As unnoticed as all those dust balls hanging from fake fish. It was the weekend, and school was over, the bullies far away. There was no homework. It was just me and Gerald sneaking around this weird old town, pretending that we lived there, pretending that it was cool and that we fit in. Those hick artists slopping paint on redwood burls out back seemed like they knew what they were doing, painting the same crashing wave every time, hoping they'd be noticed at the back of the store. I had to hand it to their single-mindedness. They were determined to keep going, even if their work sucked and nobody bought their stupid paintings.

Back outside, escaping the sad little store and leaving the Indian chief alone to his fate, Gerald and I walked a bit farther down Main Street, looking in other windows, all displaying "Fine Art" and "Real Redwood." It was like going into a grocery store and all the shelves had the same bright box of Rice-a-Roni, and because it was "the San Francisco treat," everybody had to have it. Tourists would buy anything.

Here was a gallery proudly displaying several mottled-brown, lumpy ceramic vases with shells and broken glass stuck all over, sitting on a fake beach of sand and dead crabs. This flotsam looked like horse poop made into pottery. Already a culture snob at thirteen, I recalled the posters Gerald had plastered all over the house: Picasso, Degas, Renoir, Chagall, Magritte, Cassatt, O'Keefe. I'd been to many museums and galleries with both parents. I'd puzzled over abstract, spattered paintings, classical portraits, and grand landscapes; wandered around monumental sculptures and then examined tiny, detailed objects; admired plenty of Japanese raku and Greek Corinthian pottery with naked men jumping bulls; and handled many potted plants. Still, I'd never seen poop repurposed into fine art.

I was curious and found myself caught between two worlds. This forgotten Victorian theme park and our fine-art bungalow in Berkeley. How did poop become art and then make it into the windows of these galleries? It seemed lazy to me, but then again, someone put thought and effort into this stuff. To me, it looked like crap, but was it? Was I wrong? These galleries all had such big, clean display windows and yet were all directing my attention to things that felt fake and wrong. It was confusing and a little depressing. Art was so subjective.

When (if) we finally made it back home, I'd create a seascape as my special surprise for Gerald, a souvenir of this memorable road trip. Or I could scoop up a handful of dried dog shit, stick some of my collected marbles in it, and present it at dinner one night. I love you, Dad.

Main Street was a long, sloping, wooden boardwalk that ended quite abruptly, falling off into the slate-colored Pacific Ocean pudding. Held together by a splint of bent trees, wormy fences, and overgrown berry bushes, the powder-dry cliffs somehow pushed back against the relentless waves. It could all go at any second.

The wall of fog was moving toward us, overtaking even the ocean, enveloping the sky. There was a bite to the air and a sprinkle of wet. Gerald's black sweater had little beads of moisture all over it. He looked like a stylish Christmas ornament. Seagulls loitered seasick overhead.

An Addams family mansion sits above the street, jaundiced and forlorn. Its sagging columned porch leaned into an overgrown garden of bent, dead flowers, mashed-down bushes I swore were dented into the shapes of screaming faces. Shutters hung like a sad old lady's tattered fake eyelashes. The front screen door with a big hole in it was her crinkled old mouth. Lipstick long worn off, she was wailing, "Nooooooooooo!" as she sank into the garden, sliding back down inexorably into the ocean. Gerald and I made it there just in time to witness this slow-motion disintegration.

About halfway down Main Street was a fenced-in brackish pond. A couple of big geese, brown ducks, and a lone seagull floated about, avoiding each other. Kids were tossing bits of their sandwiches in, right over the hand-painted sign that said: "Please Do Not Feed the Ducks."

It was a mad dash for the ham and cheese! The geese had first dibs, muscling past the smaller ducks while the single seagull observed the mayhem, floating quietly alone in the middle of the pond, slumming it;

after all, it had the whole ocean only a short distance away.

A few steps farther, and there was The Hotel. It was a grand old building that seemed to have a central place of importance on Main Street. I asked myself, couldn't they have come up with anything else more original to call this place besides The Hotel? Something other than the glaringly obvious? The clodhoppers round there needed things spelled out simple, I reckoned. The fancy, thick-cut glass door had an elegant, fat, brass knob right in the middle, bigger than my hand. Did it work like a hobbit hole? Victorians made odd choices.

Through the distorted bevel of glass, I saw people sitting by a fireplace reading newspapers and sipping amber-colored drinks. People pretending to be guests in an old hotel on the edge of the world at the turn of the century. Or were they ghosts masquerading as guests, moving through smoky glass, appearing and disappearing? They died a long time ago but never left. Having conversations with unsuspecting tourists, buying them drinks, discussing current events, fooling everyone.

On the wooden curb outside sat Rip Van Winkle waking up from a hundred-year nap, The Hotel built around him as he dozed through a century. His matted hair hung stiff like dried kelp, a wild, frizzy beard poking in all directions. He was wearing a necklace of bones and a long, wilted black feather hung twisting around a knob of hard hair. Sleepy, red-rimmed eyes squinted at something across the street, and I followed his gaze. He was being watched by a big raven sitting on the fence. They were having a staring match. That bird wanted its feather back.

"Damn hippies!" Gerald glared disapprovingly down at Rip Van Winkle. "Human garbage."

Gerald was right—poor Rip had a rising stench. Sickly sweet, clinging to my clothes and tongue. I'd smelled it before, at the university where Ellen worked. Old leather, wet dog, dried sweat, urine, and something else. Tables on Telegraph Avenue sold it in little brown bottles with psychedelic labels: "Patchouli and Sandalwood. Imported from India." The distilled essence of rotten fruit. Rip Van Winkle must have spilled the bottle.

"Hippie grease!" Gerald reared as if from a rotting corpse, sneering in disdain. Gerald at least had the good sense to smell like ripe citrus and to clip his beard. I'd never seen him wear a feather or anything other than black. He looked somewhat like a ballpoint pen with arms and legs. The small Basque beret on his head came off only when he went to bed.

Next to The Hotel was a little bar called Dick's Place. I envisioned the pervy patrons inside all getting drunk and exposing themselves. Drunken old men with their dicks flopped up on the bar, comparing sizes. There was one leering at me right now through the window.

"Hey, kid, look at this! I've got a kielbasa!"

Bumpkin artists, zombie hippies, and geezer perverts, Mendocino was a vacation paradise.

A giant pocket watch hanging outside broadcasts a Victorian's penchant for stating the obvious: what a surprise—this repurposed house was a museum of clocks. A big room smelling of old wood and oil with every kind of timepiece, big and small, displayed like rare objects. Walking through a maze path created by long glass display cabinets, I examined ornately monogrammed gold pocket watches, big, fat bankers watches next to petite ladies watches barely hanging on to filament thin gold chain. A flock of cuckoo clocks sang madly from assembled gingerbread condos. A somber column of grandfather clocks leaned like coffins against the far wall, their muted, clunking tones droning impending doom.

On the next block, a small, dark room in the back of a whitewashed building had all kinds of old books, more lumpy pottery, an assortment of tools, and tons of smoking equipment. A deep, woodsy smoke hung above the bookshelves and rolled over counters. Arranged all around were pipes of every shape, size, and color. Carved stone pipes, Ma Kettle's corncob pipe, even a tortoiseshell pipe like the one Beaver's dad smoked.

"You want to keep your pipes in working order," the bearded gnome behind the counter told me. "You need to keep them clean, so it draws."

He showed me a variety of tiny screens and buffing cloths. There were bouquets of different-colored pipe cleaners stuffed in a clay jar. The gnome puffed on his stubby little purple glass pipe and shuffled a pack of oversize, gold-edged cards. As he turned one over and placed it face up on his counter, I saw a medieval skeleton wearing a black cowl with scythe raised.

Gerald came into the store from where he'd been outside making notes and taking pictures of old houses advertised in a real estate office. He looked pissed off. But I hadn't done anything! "Let's go, Eric." He gave me a small shove out the door while speaking loudly to the thick, blue air. "Smoking is bad for you. It can even kill you."

The stupid people who lived in this lump of a town had nothing better to do. Maybe they'd rather be dead, or perhaps, it was because they were already dead and just didn't care. Maybe Gerald and I were also dead and didn't realize it yet. Run down by a marauding logging truck on that corkscrew highway. Both Ellen and Gerald smoked when I was a baby, but then they stopped. Did something change, and I didn't notice?

At the end of Main Street was a big, wild field of high, dry grass. Little houses were bumping together against the cold. There was nothing else, just ocean beyond and the wall of hovering fog. I smelled wet seaweed and salty, damp wood. The wind rushed up, pushed us through the field, and cried.

"Be quiet. Listen to the sea. It's coming. It's here. It's all around you."

I was so sleepy, so drained. The urge to lie down in the tall grass and let everything go was overwhelming, so tempting. I could hear the Wicked Witch of the West cackle.

"Poppies will make them sleep! Pooopppiiieeessss!"

Gerald shivered and said his famous line: "It's as cold as a witch's tit in a brass bra on the shady side of an iceberg! Let's go find our hotel, shall we?"

Wait, what!? We're staying the night? I was incredulous.

"I want to have a look at a couple places before we go home tomorrow" he said. Gerald always had a surprise or two up his sleeve.

CHAPTER 7

THE END

My experience of Berkeley in 1968 was of an endlessly fascinating, adventurous, and fun place to grow up. Nothing like that horrible hole-in-the-wall ghost town Gerald had dragged me to the year before.

Colorful and quirky, Berkeley hummed with energy; it was made up of an architectural potpourri and curlicue hill-jumping streets, roundabouts full of wildflowers cutting off the flow of traffic. There was every type of store, and the scents of restaurants or a grocery's bounty of produce around every corner mixed with the fragrant surprise of magnolia or jasmine, coffee brewing, cedarwood burning, croissants baking, incense wafting. The city's famous university generated a magnetic flow of activity that radiated outward, connecting everything. Cosmopolitan yet familiar, with the fabled California sun spreading its relaxed vibe, Berkeley was a happy terrarium for curious, restless explorers.

The Sunday farmers' market burst with jungle bouquets of wildflowers, fistfuls of fresh herbs, and cookies as big as my little sister's head, and lucky me, every other neighborhood boasted a fancy sit-down soda fountain offering one million and one flavors of ice cream. I could almost reach out and grab a slice of pizza, bag of cashews, or salami sandwich from the deli down the block. It was a special night out when our family would pull into an A & W drive-in and crowd around the driver's seat, yelling our orders at the roller-skating waitress. Burgers tasted so much better when they were delivered on roller skates, accompanied by a frosted glass mug of root beer.

Sometimes Gerald would drive us all around with no real goal in mind other than to observe our fascinating city. Nurturing a comforting mouthful of raspberry Razzles in the back seat of the Rambler, I'd slump down and peer over the window's edge as we slowly cruised past darkened film-noir-looking industrial neighborhoods. Desolate, cast in shadow, the cracked glass-brick windows watched us suspiciously as we sneaked by—a dark taste of foreboding stirring together with the tang of raspberry gum.

There was a Daliesque landscape of driftwood sculpture along an isolated beachfront; elsewhere, a long, lonely avenue of uncertain neon hotel signs all proclaimed space-age-travel or rooms with pools and a TV. Even the river of brake lights lining up to cross the swooping Christmas twinkle of the Bay Bridge was a kinetic, hypnotic performance.

Great oak, dark redwood, and aromatic, whispering eucalyptus trees hugged colorful succulent-centric gardens in quiet neighborhoods of arts and crafts bungalows, matronly Victoriana, reimagined turreted Tudor mini-mansions and arched Greco-Roman temples. Gray brutalist cement government buildings and boxy, midcentury modernist puzzle pieces jutted out of hillsides, posing on stilts, or hovered over creeks— every architectural style within one block and banging up next to one another. The city looked like a well-lit, lived-in Hollywood set.

We'd moved to a typical one-story stucco bungalow plunked down on top of sloped Carlotta Avenue. With a colossal agave plant out front, prolific plum tree and shingled playhouse in the backyard, and the wilds of Martin Luther King Jr. High School's playground just beyond the linked back fence, our little patch of paradise lay in the middle of everything.

Our neighbors were teachers, doctors, architects, secretaries, or artists who drove slightly dented Citrons, dusty BMWs, or VW Bugs. Their kids, my friends, and I regularly hung out building futuristic forts, marathon TV watching *Three Stooges*, or playing spin the bottle in the nearby church basement.

Still, I spent most of my time on my own, exploring the endless maze of parks and paths that wiggled between people's houses. Wearing my standard Star Trek blue velour turtleneck, cuffed jeans, and P. F. Flyers, I was an alert and comfortable civic colonist, ready to tackle any terrain, familiar or obscure.

I maneuvered past museums and banks and downtown to the library, pausing at movie theaters to examine blaring posters and wonder if Clint Eastwood was good, bad, or ugly with a six-shooter hidden under his poncho. Or (if I stared long enough) would Raquel Welch pop out of that fur bikini?

I'd dip into antique stores to examine rusty kitchen tools all lumped together in melancholy disuse, the families of lonely scroll-back chairs sitting around with no one to entertain, or a majestic, tilted grandfather clock tick-tocking alone in a corner. I could relate. Being alone was tricky. I wanted to engage the world, but it had to be on my own terms.

I'd make a pit stop at my favorite corner drug store to peruse the latest issue of Mighty Thor or X-Men, contemplate a Ken doll in his plaid shorts, and then grab a handful of sustaining bubble gum.

After hiking up steep hills past houses, up, up, up to Indian Rock and then down into the shaggy forest of Tilden Park, I'd collapse exhausted in grassy fields, listening to birds or watching silent, careful deer tiptoe out of the woods, look over to consider me for a moment, and then disappear back into the trees.

I'd walk for miles all the way into Oakland to marvel again and again as Elizabeth Taylor made her ostentatious entrance as Cleopatra at the Grand Lake Theater. Or (if I was feeling particularly restless) I'd hike to Children's Fairyland and scrutinize colorful cement renderings of classic fairy tales. I'd crawl through Alice's rabbit hole, sit down to tea with the Mad Hatter, or lean over upside down to watch just how puppeteers nuanced life into blocks of wood in the front row of the little marionette theater. Walking back home, I'd scheme a repurposed Wagnerian opera with puppets, staged for my lucky parents.

There was the ritual refueling at Caffe Med on Telegraph Avenue for a grown-up espresso. Sipping slowly while establishing my cool credentials, I'd observe the cavalcade of interesting people, from students of the university to just everyday oddballs, and I imagined that I was pleasantly lost in some European country or had somehow been transported to a strange yet sophisticated alien planet.

Then I was back on safari, surveying the ever-extensive grounds of my endless estate. Italianate hillside homes buttressed with a rash of violet bougainvillea or protected by huddled pine and cedar. The shapely sidewalks shaded with dense, hanging arbors of Cecile Brunner roses. Stately palm trees befriended mutant fuchsia, a corner cornfield was caged behind a cartoon picket fence, dancing bare-breasted metal-and-sea-glass folk-art mermaids erupted from behind a wave of ivy.

Occasionally, I'd escort my two younger sisters up the hills to the elegant Rose Garden or the cement slide in Codornices Park—four-year-old Kristin, in her yellow Twiggy dress, surfer-girl hair cut flat over her big eyes, hustled forward by older Greta, as she swished along in her homemade denim bell-bottoms.

They'd both often leave the house barefoot, without a care in the world. No shoes or coat, gregarious and free, nimbly missing any broken glass or dog poop, hopping curbs, and running across crosswalks like feral ponies skipping through clover.

In Greta's fierce determination to do everything better than me, she'd sometimes launch ahead then call back impatient as if she were the parent and we the dawdling children. Greta would act as a tour guide, reminding little Kristin what was coming up and what was around the next corner, of how much fun that slide was going to be. Her mane of chestnut curls shimmered orange fire (in the right light), matching her temperament perfectly. Bossy and demanding, she could think she was in control as we walked along, but I knew the way to go.

And they loved that cement slide. I'd cheer them on as they slid down on flattened cardboard boxes, landing breathless in a tangle. I rode down occasionally myself. This first meant ascending the narrow, steep steps. The gauntlet included a large tree limb bending low over the trail, just waiting for me. Crouching down, contorting my tall body underneath, despite every effort, I'd always bang my head. At fourteen, I was forced to remember how much older I was. This was a slide for children.

We'd romp in the streams that ran through the sprawling, Romanesque campus or ride up the campanile tower elevator for a quick peek of the dusty, stuffed gorilla housed in a tiny room near the top. A dedicated pilgrimage to Mr. Botts for a double scoop of carob and bubblegum ice cream and, our perennial favorite activity: storming the gates of the outdoor Greek Theatre to enact an elaborate, shouting melodrama. Our performance for an audience of stoic, oblivious pigeons perched on poop-spattered cement seats always culminated with a furious sword fight and the gruesome death of all players. We'd parry and thrust and die again and again until we were all just too tired to die anymore.

We ruled this city, and besides the occasional loud antiwar protests, smelly hippie encampments, or swarm of riot police quarreling in the distance, Berkeley was an oasis of middle-class tranquility.

When our parents were available, our typical family outing was to walk up a few streets and buy coffee beans from a guy named Peet. Then Ellen would, of course, have to get some of that stinky English cheese she loved so much from the tiny store next door, appropriately named The Cheese Board. Like a small chunk of blue marble chipped from a cliff, this new cheese was certainly not cheddar, Swiss, or Velveeta but was strangely delicious in small amounts and particularly good when eaten with Bosc pears.

We'd then mosey down eclectic Telegraph Avenue to our place of worship: the bookstore Cody's. Among stacks of shiny new books, I had time to reflect in a silent epiphany that I was a fortunate kid who lived in an extraordinary place.

Sitting cross-legged in a comfortable corner, I'd lay out a treasure trove of large art books. Staring wide-eyed at Picasso's grotesque, flat-nosed cyclops women, Monet's multihued gardens, or Magritte's floating derbies, I reconnected to my very first memory. As a baby, I'd look up from the Persian carpet at every wall and ceiling surface in the living room plastered with prints of these great artists. My eyes rolling around, getting lost in Van Gogh's swirly *Starry Night* or riding Chagall's *Circus Horse*, I thought that my beloved parents had collected all these pictures and given me this wonderful place to explore. Here on the floor of Cody's with a ready collection on display, I felt right at home.

Gerald would disappear into the music section while the girls morphed into one person, staring dreamily at picture books about horses. Ellen stood glued by her shoulder to a tall shelf stiff with cookbooks. Her left hand supported a massive bible of recipes as her lips moved, right pointer finger tracing.

An hour would go by before we'd reconvene and continue our walkabout, inevitably stopping again to press our noses against the large display windows of Frasier's. A fancy furniture store more like a museum, it had picture windows that revealed a diorama of sleek, modern living rooms. A lean, square couch upholstered in olive fabric and dotted with round orange pillows; the arching metal lamp turned on for some stylish ghost to read the *LOOK* magazine conveniently open there on the kidney-shaped glass table.

Ellen and Gerald went into a kind of meditation, pointing and murmuring, clutching us kids a little bit tighter. They'd ask each other if that sofa would fit in our living room or how much that chrome lamp might cost. We never did get anything from that store, but the window shopping was almost better, the fantasy intact.

Berkeley was a glorious, bountiful, cinematic feast for the senses, providing the ground upon which I built my sense of self. Life was good, and I was content in this civilized, picturesque utopia. Everything seemed so settled and accessible, so calm yet plugged in, with a crackle of energy flowing down every street and up every hill. Everything was in its place and perfect in its placement. I was confident on these streets, excited about what I might discover on my many sojourns, mapping out my life to and fro. I knew every block and alley, the secret ways to get around. I knew store clerk's names and had my well-used library card and a collection of movie ticket stubs. This was my world, and I could only see myself growing up to become a bon vivant, culture-savvy artist, shadowing my parents' dapper example. Then we moved.

CHAPTER 8

THE BIG BANG

We lived in the back of behind-nowhere, on the edge of a cliff at the end of the earth. We were all alone, if you didn't count all the hard-faced hairy hill folk who lived down long dirt roads in weird tree houses, hung out on street corners, or drove beat-up, mud-spattered trucks filled with chopped wood or manure. Berkeley was now just a rosy, idyllic memory along with my childhood. It was a place I'd never see again.

Our new home was a lonely, forgotten place. Removed from everything, from normal life, from civilization. Lost down a maze of vomit-inducing, zigzagging, roller-coastering two-lane highways and within an impenetrable layer of all-concealing, intoxicating fog, we were trapped. The oppressive army of giant, malevolent redwood trees that grew everywhere made sure we'd never leave. Those trees grew so close even birds had a hard time flying. I knew I'd never see the sun again or visit Ellen in the architectural department on campus. The ice cream parlors were closed, my library card revoked. I'd never walk those sleek Berkeley sidewalks or visit Sam at the deli. My private rotating art collection at Cody's lay abandoned. All my friends, favorite park benches, and my secret hole-in-the-wall store, The Body Shop (where I'd spend my allowance on patchouli oil), were left behind. I didn't know any-one in my new home and didn't want to know anyone.

Solitary scrawny horses were grazing in soggy, desolate fields. Dirty, drunken seagulls circled overhead, laughing to each other as they shit on everything. There were goats. It rained all the time, and there was nothing to do except work. My new job: dishwasher. My bedroom win-dow looked out onto a cemetery. I'd be there soon enough since my life was over.

For a fourteen-year-old city kid, it was like suddenly being relocated to the moon. What was I supposed to do here? How could I become the person I'd felt was my destiny in this godforsaken place? What the hell had happened?

Our new home seemed by comparison to Berkeley beyond the reach of natural evolution. Everything had just stopped. Preserved by an unex-plained time shift, locked somewhere between the Age of Aquarius and the late 1800s, this little village was like an up-ended Victorian snow globe, abandoned and cracked, with all the glitter poured out. Every moldy, bent house was a monument to hardscrabble, against-the-odds subsistence. Only the hardiest, or stupidest, of people lived here. I must belong to the stupid family.

When my parents announced that we were moving to Mendocino and would open a restaurant, I had a rather epic meltdown. A foot-stomping, door-slamming yelling match during which I thought I could convince them that it was a terrible, ridiculous mistake.

I recalled with a sinking dread the backwoods wide space in the road Gerald and I had visited last year. It had been a neat thing that he'd taken me on a father/son road trip and not dumped me off on the side of the road or handed me over to drill sergeants. But to consider now actually moving there was a nightmare. Were they serious? Just when things seemed to be working out so well for me here in the real world.

I'd never been more resolved in my complaint as I was then. Standing tall, facing my parents in direct opposition that was the first time I'd ever attempted to argue with them, and there was something cathartic and strengthening in that. I felt closer to what an adult must be—surprised at my new backbone, the force of my opinion, all the words coming out of my mouth. Underneath the tirade, I was also thinking, *I like this new me. Even if I lose (and it looks like I'm going to lose), I kind of also won something.*

Marshaling every convincing argument I could think of, all the logical reasons why it wouldn't work, I presented my case, but they remained unfazed. Acknowledging my distress, they said they'd already considered every angle and swept aside my doubting resistance. They'd bought a house.

As sudden as their decision seemed to be, it just as suddenly seemed I had something to lose by leaving. I'd just kissed a girl, and that was a quantum leap. I was also secretly messing around with Charlie in the playhouse out back (and in the basement, up in the attic, and out in the garage). And they were taking it all away from me. Didn't they know that I learned best by repetition? Now I'd never get to kiss Carol again; I could never touch Charlie. I'd have to start all over. Would Elly May Clampett or Bigfoot be my next love interest?

Whereas I used to be able to go get gum, a sandwich, or pizza from the store right down the block, now I'd have to go out in the rain to the icky, muddy garden and pull a hundred carrots out of the dirt, wash each one, and chop them all up (along with the potatoes, celery, beets, beans, and onions), peel and squish the garlic, pluck the basil, and shave the parmesan every day if I wanted to eat. Besides being thrown into a junior high school class full of strangers, I have to work!

I used to be able to watch cool television shows, scribble comics with my pal Tristin, and dress up as Mr. Spock (reading minds with my fingers). Now I washed a million dishes; my hands withered into slimy fish paws. I had a life once; now, I was a kitchen drudge with no future, other than becoming what my dad merrily referred to as a restaurateur. From the looks of it, it was the last thing I wanted to be. All my parents did was work, and when they were not, they were exhausted and worried about everything, and if they were worried now, I certainly had nothing good to look forward to. Mendocino was a dead end.

Today, it's common for locals to call their town Mendo-Scene-O or Mendo-World. Commercialized and branded, a charming Disneyfied Victoriana. It's all in the label on a jam jar or bottle of wine. Potato chips taste better if they're from Mendocino. Salsa, coffee, pickles, and cheese from Mendocino are synonymous with refined gourmet sensibilities, with the American Good Life. The caché of vintage homespun funk married to highfalutin taste buds. You go there to get away from it all and to experience a foodie's satori in an environmentalist's idyl.

But it didn't used to be that way. Mendocino was once a little artist community kept secret because of the inhibiting gauntlet of travel time and potential for getting lost. Before it was "discovered" and became the destination it is today, it was just a peculiar little spot where travelers filled up on gas for the rest of the trip, and before that, it was a run-down former logging town. No one ever stayed in a place like that. And before it was renamed in memory of a Spanish explorer, and its Pomo people brutally displaced, it was called Big River, in honor of the big river running nearby.

This was a cataclysmic, heartbreaking disaster. Being yanked out of my hard-won security and deposited into this hillbilly slave camp, I contemplated the idea that I'd have to unlearn certain things and then learn others. I'd have to get along with less and to perhaps grow a pelt of fur just to stay warm.

Compounding my dismay was the fact that suddenly I didn't know my parents as well as I'd thought. They'd made this life-changing decision all by themselves, without any family meeting or debate. They'd yanked the carpet out from underneath and consigned our fate. They wanted to become hillbillies.

The schism was almost too much for me to comprehend. Moving from the convenience and sophistication of Berkeley to the backwoods mud hole of Mendocino exposed my once-elegant parents as the pretenders they were. They'd succumbed to their old white trash roots.

They'd given up and dragged us underage appendages with them.

Gerald had told us a few horror stories of his miserable childhood growing up on a farm in Iowa where he was forced to milk cows at four in the morning and walk in the blinding snow uphill (both ways) to and from a one-room schoolhouse. Ellen shrank whenever she spoke of the flat, dusty nothing of her home state of Texas. And now, with sickening finality, it seemed like we had come full circle, had moved back to a place where cows were revered as family members and wearing shit-stained overalls worked as your Sunday best.

On that last day in Berkeley, as I stood there on the sidewalk regarding the comfortable house we'd lived in, a great war of feelings collided. Rearing up, flaring hot, then canceling each other out, I ended feeling hollow and numb. Nothing made any sense.

Berkeley had been more than our home, more than just a place. It had defined who I was. Now, Eric was gone yet I still stood there, an empty husk. I empathized even further with my robot mentor from *Lost in Space*. Circuits fried, brain wiped, about to be reprogrammed. Put on an assembly line with everything I'd been and done flushed away as if never having existed.

As everyone (except Gerald, who had a job and got to stay in Berkeley for now, commuting on the weekends) waited for me inside the new VW bus, I continued to stand frozen on the curb. Without asking, I knew Gerald wouldn't let me stay with him; instinct told me I needed to get into that car and go with Ellen and my sisters.

Finally, sitting up front with the window rolled down (to let in as much life-giving air as possible), I watched our house, and our block, and our old city, and our former lives disappear into the maze of freeways. Gerald had waved goodbye from the sidewalk. With Ellen at the wheel and us kids tucked in, with our lives shoved into every corner of the bus, I stared in a daze as Berkeley receded into memory.

Joining the flow of traffic, Ellen drove carefully in the slow lane with frustrated drivers zooming all around us. It was as if Berkeley held on, trying to drag us back. Ellen kept on driving, though, and I soon begin to recognize the twisting country roads that lead away from the world. I knew this route and didn't need a map. Just keep driving, right off the cliff.

CHAPTER 9

THE HAUNTING

My parents were brave, crazy, or both. They begged, borrowed, and scraped together $30,000 (more money than they'd ever seen)—all that money came into their hands and then flew right out again. All of it spent on a small Victorian house with an adjoining one and a half acres.

In 1968, purchasing property was a big deal for them; they'd always been renters. Suddenly, they owned a house; they were the landlords of themselves. They had a mortgage and were both excited and somewhat terrified.

Plus, it was way more than just a house. It was a whole new beginning. There was the responsibility of making a family-run restaurant work. A new business, something only imagined but never tested. I could see the thrill of realization flash across their faces, shifting from amazement to panic, then back again to excitement. They were going to build a dream.

While my parents were crafting a plan of sorts fueled by passion, faith in their newfound abilities, and the bonds of our family support to make this work, I just had what I could see. All that money spent on an old house perched at the abrupt end of quiet Ukiah Street where it turned into a short dirt path leading through a gate and then into a small, sloping cemetery. It was like the set of a gothic horror film.

Anticipating moving into a potentially haunted house was both a macabre thrill and an uncomfortable wake-up call. Along with everything else, could I deal with this? The thought of possibly becoming the next generation of ghostly inhabitants would be cool, I suppose (if I wasn't already so attached to being alive). I still wasn't over my displeasure at being forcibly removed from my last reality.

I'd make a nasty poltergeist, taking out my frustrations on any unsuspecting tenants who followed. They'd have to condemn the little house and board up the place, this part of town becoming off-limits.

"No one goes near that place, not since the Pitsenbargers moved in." Locals would shudder and shake their heads. "There should be a warning sign about the evil that lurks at the end of Ukiah Street."

Buying this house was such a huge commitment, especially in the face of a potentially hideous disappointment. However, it was out of my control, and there was nothing to do but hang on. Things were changing, and we were all in for the ride of our lives.

Out on the street among unloaded boxes from the VW bus, I looked at the leaning picket fence barely holding back the forest of neglected roses scrambling up and over the garage. I thought of Sleeping Beauty's thorny protection from handsome admirers or the mysterious Secret Garden where dreams fluttered in shadows like tiny moths.

Tilting wooden shutters and lace curtains looked back at me from a long set of variated discolored window teeth, a disarming benign smile that said: "Come in! Come in...and then die!"

The enclosed front porch had a fist-size brass doorknob sprouting from heavy paneling, a wolf's head door knocker at shoulder height. If not the Munsters' place, then this must have been the local undertaker's house, and now that he'd mysteriously passed over himself, the place was most likely haunted. Silently, patiently waiting for us to move in and to let our guard down.

Room for a restaurant on the first floor, our little family living right upstairs, the house was two blocks from the store, down the street from the school, and up a path from the beach. The post office was three blocks thataway, a volunteer fire station was 'round the corner, and we could practically just roll into a plot in the cemetery next door.

As I took it all in, I suspected that this odd little place, the tiny town, and now our poor, innocent family had been caught up somehow in a weird vortex. Pulled into its magnetic swirl, we were now (for better or worse) a part of it. I wondered if we might already be dead and just not known it. Our new "lives" would be spent as wraiths playing restaurant in a haunted house.

Something was said about me now being "the man of the house," with Gerald left behind in Berkeley. Even though I felt entirely out of the loop, leery of added responsibility (not feeling manly in any way), I was drafted as second-in-command while Ellen was in charge.

We were told that Gerald would come to visit us on weekends and work the rest of the time as an apprentice at a fancy restaurant, Norman's, back in Berkeley, learning how to become a chef really fast. He'd spend days at the library, cook in the evenings, and then after work sleep in the back of the old Rambler.

I pictured him at the end of a long shift, parked along some quiet, tree-lined street, laid out in the back of the car, tucked in a sleeping bag reading by flashlight. He'd wake up super early (before everyone else) and zoom away before being discovered. Gerald had become a gypsy secret agent chef.

Breaking up and shifting the roles of our tight little family unit, moving away from everything familiar to this moldy Victorian question mark, and leaving poor Gerald all on his own was all scary. And I missed him.

Thinking back, I realize the drive up from Berkeley was like passing through a portal, and a rift slammed shut after we passed a certain point.

I couldn't drive yet, but I could manipulate the lozenge-shaped side-view mirror. One slight toggle of a knob and I could see up close or far away. There went my city, receding into the past, and here came the roller-coaster roads with weeds growing like the Amazon.

Sitting upfront in the VW, I pretended to be Ellen's copilot, but it was mostly pointless, as just taking my eyes off the road for a second undermined any self-control. I might barf at any moment.

I tried to be valiant, but even when I wasn't carsick, I felt sick. Unfolding the recently excavated Texaco map (usually kept mashed in the glove compartment of the old Rambler), I recognized these horrible little roads and the names of towns I'd tried to forget. I was astonished to find myself once again on that dotted red line, now actually moving to that tiny, circled blip on the coast. Knowing what I did about Mendocino, this was a bona fide horror story.

My other task was to watch over all the boxes piled on top of each other and make sure nothing came toppling over to bury my two sisters, although if a bump in the road knocked one small box off to hit Greta on the head, it was strictly coincidence. The bus was loaded with boxed valuables. Ellen had packed everything. All the stuff wrapped meticulously in newspaper, tied up, boxed, and labeled with her unmistakable calligraphic handwriting: "Dishes: Red Rooster. S+P, plates, cups & saucers, clock." All the stuff we'd need right away once we landed on the moon.

To witness Ellen in control was a lesson in grace under pressure. Her slim frame held taught, both hands on the wheel of the new sky-blue VW bus, her sharp eyes darting from the rearview mirror to those on either side of the car. Hawklike and alert, elegant with her short, black hair and fine-boned face, she drove differently than Gerald. Not like a race car driver with a fondness for speed and then sudden braking but at precisely fifty-five miles per hour and with more anticipation of what lay ahead. She drove like I would have. Ellen took her blessed time around the curves and up the hills, frustrating truckers and retirees in their block-long RVs, all impatient to get around us, in such a big hurry to get to the end of nowhere faster.

"You know this route, don't you, Eric?" she said coolly, glancing my way.

It was like revisiting a nightmare. These corkscrew curves were my nemesis. Even with Ellen's careful driving, the molasses swooping around and around evoked nausea. And with that piled on top of the hopeless, sickening reality of my kidnapped predicament, it was a testament of how much I loved her that I didn't fling myself out of the car.

"Everything's going to be fine, just you see. We're going to have a great new life, and the future is bright." She was smiling, but she was also gritting her teeth.

Why didn't I believe her? Although she seemingly had control over the car and all our lives, she was also acting a bit nervous. Her slim fingers gripped the steering wheel as if it might try and get away from her. I knew that grip; it was no-nonsense and usually preceded stern words. But she was trying to be extra cheerful, curving her words into a forced smile.

"I know it's hard moving, but you haven't lost anything. Think about it," she encouraged. "You're gaining everything."

Who was she trying to convince? Even as we pitched forward with everything and everyone packed up, a spot chosen on the map, it was still a mystery as to where exactly we'd end up. Who knew what would happen. My trust in what I saw and felt was in contradiction to the story Ellen told us. She was hiding something.

The girls in the back were all chirpy and excited about a cool road trip to the next adventure! They didn't realize that everything they knew was being stripped away and replaced with a set of chores that made taking out the garbage seem like an Easter egg hunt. All our friends, the beautiful neighborhoods, our amazing school, the parks, stores, museums, and energy of the city were all being replaced with Paul Bunyan–themed rest stops and tacky galleries featuring lumps of carved driftwood. At the end of this sickening corkscrew road was a cultural sinkhole where we would be forced to cozy up with our new best friends, the Beaverbottoms.

Even at this meandering pace around curves, my stomach heaved. When we pulled over to let a honking parade of traffic go by, I got out to stand in the dirt, feeling the solid ground not move. While my head spun, I prayed that I could just die right here.

"Just leave me," I wanted to say. "I'm going to lie down here and disappear into the scrub. Good luck with the restaurant and all. It was fun being Eric, though now I think I'd rather be a tree instead."

After a few moments, though, I got back in, Ellen patting the seat. "C'mon, Eric. It won't be long."

Oddly, though, still furious with my parents for changing the rules of the game, I had to admit being also begrudgingly impressed at the great efforts they were making to comfort us. The lengths they went to in arranging everything, the sacrifices made, and the big chances they took. I felt a bit guilty for putting up such resistance and was even proud of Ellen as she drove us so carefully around and around and up and down, away from our former lives in Berkeley, right through the fabric of reality.

There had been a moment years ago when I realized what a responsible, loving, and clever woman Ellen was. On one of those late afternoons, we three kids had walked from our little bungalow to pick Ellen up at her university office. Taking a route home through People's Park, she'd suddenly grasped each of the girl's hands and calmly said, "OK, kids, it's time to run."

At first, I was confused. Then I glanced over my shoulder to see a wave of scrambling hippies being flushed out by cops pumping tear gas into the trees. The yellow gas roiled close to our heels as we bounded through the park and then across the street.

My little sisters were none the wiser, but I realized that day that our mother was a hero.

Even though Ellen's hands were on the wheel, the car did almost seem to have a mind of its own and to drive itself. The fancy new blue VW shuttle craft locked on a one-way track toward the inevitable end of the line. Ellen could have slept the whole way (I know she could have used it, as she and Gerald had been packing for days). She and the car took those turns like we were on the edge of a large, flat butter knife.

Careful and smooth.

Ironic that my parents had invested in such a fancy new space pod since the place we were moving to preferred beat-up, rusty trucks with tailpipes dragging and hay bales piled. We would stick out like Day-Glo clowns barging in on a witch's coven. I wondered how long it would take for this fancy new car to get stolen, to become just another junker?

Ellen and Gerald must have called the VW factory directly, requesting the long, pregnant roller skate with squishy padded walls, secret compartments, and a special picnic shelf right up front. Like Flash Gordon's fort house on wheels.

"We want it to look like the observation car on an Amtrak train, and it has to be blue—that's Ellen's favorite color."

As this was a special picnic, Ellen had collected everybody's favorite snack foods. Apples, carrots, juice, crackers, and nuts. The prerequisite PB&J sandwiches made with the rough stuff Ellen churned out of a huge upside-down crock at the co-op. There were baggies with sunflower seeds, cheddar cheese fish, and sesame crackers, all with our names on them. We each had our stash. No one got more than the other, or there would be anarchy.

There were specialty items: a box of animal crackers just for Kristin, Japanese rice candies (sealed in edible rice paper) for Greta, a chunk of halvah and a plastic cup of mandarin oranges for me, and a crisp little bunch of green grapes just for Ellen.

Stuffing our faces, this familiar comfort went a long way toward putting us at ease. Who knew what people ate in Mendocino? This could be our last meal.

As she drove laboriously around the curves of Highway One, Ellen placed the grapes right in her lap and popped them into her mouth one by one, tossing the stems out the window. Concerned that we'd be pulled over by the police for littering, I gave her questioning looks. We were always being told not to throw stuff out the window.

"It's OK," Ellen explained. "It's organic. It's going back to the ground."

I didn't know what organic meant, but I surmised that candy wrappers didn't rot, sink into the ground, and grow into Milky Way trees.

When we finally reached Mendocino, the girls had to be woken up, and suddenly, it was party time! Their crushed crackers and spilled nuts flew off them like confetti. Our new house! They wanted to see, to explore, and to claim their rooms.

Ellen had the keys ready, and as we all crowded around the front door, I could see her hand shaking; she was nervous. What was on the other side of that door? All the preparation and anxiety had come down to this moment, like a gasp just before leaping off the high dive.

The key fit, she turned the lock, the door creaked open, and the girls burst in, ignoring Ellen's plea to be careful. Touching everything, disappearing through the foyer into the back rooms, the kitchen, into closets. I heard them opening doors and stomping upstairs, their faraway voices squealing and yelling and then becoming strangely quiet.

They were taken...just like that. They'd rushed right into the empty house, dashing headfirst right into the waiting mouth of this death trap. The evil, lonely house hungry for tender, innocent souls sweetened up with animal crackers and rice candy. Would I ever see my two sisters again?

I took Ellen's cold hand, and we walked together in silence up the front steps and into the house. Her eyes just as wide as the two girls, she was excited to be here too, or was it terror? Gliding wordlessly in, Ellen already seemed rather ghostly. She, too, so quickly claimed by this creepy, silent old house. I expected at any moment to feel the life force drain from my own body.

Stepping into the short foyer, I felt the peculiar sensation of being transported back in time. Everything was just as the old lady who'd lived here before us had left it. There were a few sewing articles placed on an old chair. Pieces of quilted material with delicate pink stitching, the needle still hanging loose. A messy, well-used wicker basket spilling sewing notions. Was she still here, waiting for us, just gone to the attic for the pink thread? Ellen knitted her eyebrows and picked up the sewing project.

"I was told that when it came time to move, the woman who lived here didn't want to go. She'd changed her mind. They had to remove her. This was her favorite room."

The place smelled old. The kind of smell that seemed to linger around old ladies. Dust, lavender, dead skin, and herbal sachets. Gerald called it *poopery*, a riff on *potpourri*.

On the wall was a faded picture of handsome young Jesus looking down at two wide-eyed children, his bloody hands touching their shoulders. A little white crucifix hung from a hook under his image; another lay forgotten at the foot of the chair, perhaps fallen off the old lady's lap as they dragged her away to the retirement home.

I looked for the garlic hung over the door to ward off vampires, for a rabbit's foot, an upside-down horseshoe. I worried that I hadn't paid enough attention to that black cat darting across the street.

There was a distinct vacuum of displaced energy—a hush, like when someone left the room after saying something important. "The mystery of place," Ellen called it. I always felt it in silent rooms or buildings I was exploring, a delicious tingle of magic.

The old lady was still here. Sitting right in front of us. We just couldn't see her. Maybe we couldn't see *them*. There was, after all, a graveyard right next door. This foyer was the perfect junction for ghostly old ladies sitting and resting for a moment before entering the great beyond.

As the cold, blue sun beamed through the long windows, illuminating floating dust particles, I almost expected one of the sewing needles to start levitating and hover in the air for a moment, then pick up where it had left off.

"Oh, we're going to have to fix this," Ellen said as she played with the rattling green kitchen door hanging cattywampus on its hinges.

Inside the kitchen, more evidence of the old lady. Her little stove was covered with pots, a mixing spoon forgotten next to a burner. Had she been making soup? A small duck vase with a chipped bill was stuck mid-waddle to the stove's upper shelf by grease. Nope, there hadn't been any cooking on this stove for a very long time.

There were cupboards everywhere. One whole wall was a puzzle of different-size wooden doors, each with a differently colored knob or handle. One right at waist level pulled out, revealing a long, wooden cutting board; another, lower, deep, metal-lined trough folded out on hinges.

"That was where the flour was stored," Ellen said.

So much flour! I imagined this old kitchen turned into a bustling pizza parlor, Ellen throwing disks of dough above her head.

Another door (built at an angle in the corner) opened into a small cave and a large circle of spinning wood, the scent of sweet apples wafting out. What oddball, outmoded thing was this? Ellen said it was a cooler, where bulk items were kept fresh longer and that this wooden circle was a lazy Susan.

"Remember, Eric, when this house was built, there was probably no electricity, no refrigerator."

The cabinet was just big enough for me to get in and spin around a couple of times. I felt like an overgrown Alice in Wonderland, hunched over, grown into her giant self. Dried lumps of what I hoped were apples lingered as I turned around slowly in the darkness, my head bonking the top of this perfect hiding place. I thought about poor, lazy Susan, kept in the dark cupboard when she didn't do her chores.

"The old lady's late husband built all these great cupboards for her." From my hideaway, I heard Ellen's voice echo through deep wood shelving. She was excited again; this was like Christmas for her. An entire kitchen of hidden compartments, ready to be filled up with whatever she wanted.

My two sisters came running back down the stairs, breathless.

"There are three bedrooms up there, and one of them has a secret door!"

Well, I had to see that. This would be a dream come true, a room with a secret door. Where did it go, and were there skeletons? A gateway to another world? I imagined a bookcase folding inward to reveal the old lady's secret laboratory, or a torture chamber.

The steps creaked and cracked under our machine-gun running up the narrow stairwell, built for tiny old ladies, dwarves, and children. Worm-eaten whitewashed boards lined the walls, and I saw the bones of an old fish. This was what Jonah must have felt like being swallowed up by a whale.

The first room on the left was the largest, and of course, loud-mouth Greta announced that this was her room, setting the stage for a sibling quarrel. I'd wait to inspect the entire premises more fully before passing final judgment, then perhaps invoke my eldest prerogative. She could sleep in the hallway for all I cared.

I was almost disappointed when the secret door turned out to be just a connecting entry from the larger into a smaller room—tacky, scenic wallpaper slapped onto a piece of chipboard swinging from hinges. There was a stage-set, temporary feel about it, and I kind of liked that. Here was hidden potential for drama.

What lay on the other side would always be a mystery, and mystery meant that I could make it anything I wanted it to be. Still, I wasn't sure; there was no grinding masonry or dark tunnel, no special effects of any kind. I could always paint a trompe l'oeil bookcase right here on the board, one book slightly off to indicate "the secret." Quite suddenly, my opportunity to trump Greta lost any clout. I wanted that smaller room. Wrestling with the laying down of arms, without arguing, I marked this moment as a possible steppingstone toward peace.

The attraction of occupying a secret room outweighed any desire to struggle with Greta.

After all, I did have a secret, didn't I? I was an alien (so far going unrecognized by the others).

This small room could be my refuge. I could expose my inner, more vulnerable self at night, gathering strength for the days when I walked among the ignorant, dangerous humans. Here, I could shed the skin of a fourteen-year-old geek and examine suction cups that doubled for hands. Flex my extra-sensitive antennae, indulging the kinetic storm of space noise, receiving instructions and encouragement from others of my kind who were out there, somewhere.

I could practice my alert powers of deduction, connect the dots of a confusing and dangerous day-in-the-life, and I could think about my attraction to boys and how cute they always looked in tight shorts.

"This can be your room, Eric," Greta proclaimed. As if it were her generous gift to me, her freak of an older brother. *Yes, I will take this small room with the secret door, and I will also strangle Greta with my newly freed tentacle while she sleeps.*

From upstairs, I heard someone knocking on the downstairs door, and like an avalanche (girls first), we all charged back down to see who could be visiting us already.

At the side kitchen door, two little heads peeped in over glass panes. Two little girls very politely, almost too sweetly, introduced themselves. Ginger and her sister Maddy were daughters of the people who ran The Sea Gull restaurant just down the block, and they'd come to welcome us to the neighborhood—and to check us out. They were spies!

Stubby little secret agents, so close to the bottom edges of tables and chairs, easily bugging the place with mini microphones wedged in bubble gum. Their mascot wiener dog was frantic to make our acquaintance, all happy tail wagging, face licking, and on command, standing up on his hind legs, pawing the air, and singing a whiny, yippy dog song.

"Sing, Skipper, sing!" the two girls both commanded, encouraging with their upraised arms for their little dog to hypnotize my sisters. I felt like I was turning the pages of a cautionary Dick and Jane preschool novel.

"See Skipper sing. Sing, Skipper, sing! See Ginger chew wads of gum. Chew, Ginger, chew! See her plant a miniature homing device in-between the doorframe and the creaky screen. Chew, Ginger, chew! See Ginger's parents tune in to their spy screen and snicker at sweet little Skipper brainwashing my sisters. Sing, Skipper, sing!"

"Why don't you kids go outside and explore the back yard?" Ellen suggested, indicating the back door. She'd posed a question, but her sharp, expressive hand and tired eyes said something else. Remembering that I was her second-in-command, I shooed everyone out, now a counterspy in the sudden restaurant wars. I needed to keep an eye on these two in-nocent little girls who'd so suspiciously appeared out of nowhere. My poor sisters so easily duped by the cute dog, they were a lost cause.

Greta and Ginger, now instant best friends, bolted for the back porch. Who would be first to discover the exciting treasures that lay hidden out back under all the overgrown rosebushes and collapsed sheds? Kristin and Maddy sheepishly followed while I, the awkward older brother (put on earth to chaperone little girls away from trouble), skulked behind, looking for traps.

The back porch was like the wooden prow of a boat hanging precar-iously over rough seas. This acre backyard had been too much for the poor old lady to keep up on her own, so she'd just let it go. With the jungle steadily growing outside, she spent her remaining days sewing in the front of the house.

Now, the backyard was a turbulent green ocean of shifting grass-es and mutated primordial wilderness. Erupting splashes of color burst through the drowning green, the whole acre quivering with reaching, undulating, uncurling energy.

I could smell the wet, wild scent of flowers and grass reaching up, pulling me toward the edge of the porch. I could dive right in and swim out to those gnarled apple, cherry, plum, and apricot trees all leaning topsy-turvy and seasick with fruit, limbs sprouting makeshift splints, caged in fragile halos of string and wire. A red currant bush exploded against an old fence, leaning dangerously inward, its slow-motion fire-works being sucked into the whirlpool of hungry grass.

Fountains of roses cascaded up listing old trellises, then spilled back down to the ground, their tiny pale-pink buds littering the path. Nasturtiums were everywhere, at war with the grass. They held up the back stairs, the foundation of the house. Growing up and over the porch, their march could be traced from way back in the yard. I could see them creeping over the back fence, flowing into the street. It was an invasion.

Next to the protective porch, a mammoth fuchsia bush trumpeted purple in every direction, claiming its share of sun. An army of bees, dragonflies, sparrows, and hummingbirds zoomed back and forth, desperately trying to keep up with the jungle. A delicate tendril of nasturtium poked through the wooden deck. Soon, it would consume the entire house.

A butterfly separated itself from the air traffic and landed on my sneaker, taking a moment. The grass shifted and seemed to grow another half inch.

The girls had explored an old chicken shed and already run the entire length of the yard. They came stomping back up the narrow back steps squealing and laughing, scaring the butterfly away.

"There's a creek with strawberries growing!"

"A chicken shed with old eggs in it!"

"I saw a salamander!"

"A whole patch of four-leaf clovers!"

"Horseshoes are hanging under the garage! We can have a horse!"

"I found a frog!"

Kristin opened her tiny hand to reveal the pebble-size body of a lime-green frog. It calmly sat there in her palm, trusting. It knew that sweet little Kristin was only too careful with small creatures (being so small herself), and she would never harm it. I felt a swell of pride that she'd made an effort to be so gentle and to share her tiny treasure with me even as the other loud girls were clamoring. I turned them off and squatted to admire Kristin and her frog.

Kristin was my treasure; she was like a fairy child, so different than Greta or I, or anyone else. She was quiet and strange. We wondered aloud that maybe she was one of those foundlings who got left under the cabbage for us to find, her birth parents, the king and queen of the fairy kingdom, abandoning her to our care. I had become her protector.

Kristin had the look of a Renaissance waif or Twiggy on a bad hair day. She adamantly refused to brush her long, blond hay bale hair, and we just left her alone after a few screaming fits with the brush.

"Give her time," Ellen would say.

Her big eyes were wide and wary, wise beyond her five years, a Keane portrait come to life. Kristin barely spoke. But when she did, it showed that she had been listening and paying perfect attention. So smart for such a tiny little thing; we looked at her with a certain awe. Who was she? What was she? An unassuming fey presence, she'd stand there observing you, saying nothing while I rattled on about how that episode of *Lost in Space* was the best thing I'd ever seen and that I wish I had a life-size computer that could control the world. She would quietly, pointedly look down at my drawing of an animated robot waving metal arms, shooting electric rays, vanquishing scaly aliens, and calmly say: "Kablam."

I'd been thinking of the exploding word balloon above the robot's blinking head and what it might say: "Kablam." Kristin read minds as well.

Greta and I were always quarreling about who was first and the inequality of portions when candy or ice cream was handed out. "She got more than I did!" or, "You like him better!" was our gripe to the parents at any party, every Christmas. Five-year-old Kristin accepted graciously, quietly, any treats and all attentions as if they were holy grail, with no demands or repercussions. Serenely occupying her corner of space, stoically contemplating the ever-expanding and contracting universe while her unruly elder siblings squabbled in chaos. The calming, seductive weight of her eyes taking everything in was almost scary. I looked for the signs. I knew from experience that aliens walked among us. There were always more questions than answers with Kristin. It was FYI on a strictly need-to-know basis. We learned to respect her boundaries and didn't harp on why it was that she had chosen us as her human family.

The tiny frog was quite at home here on Kristin's palm, warmed by skin, in the aura of safety. Tiny webbed feet clinging, large, glistening green eyes looking up at her.

Hello, you. I know you, child of wild places.

Kristin acknowledged the smiling eyes of the frog and then looked at me. I looked at her; she looked at the frog; the frog closed its big eyes and rested, content to wait for whatever came next.

"Look at this! It's a merry-go-round!" Greta proclaimed. She was referring to the old wooden laundry carousel built on the edge of the porch, a grayed wooden staff sprouting six hinged arms connected with rope and an army of wooden clothespins. I explained what it was, picturing the old lady slowly, slowly pinning her faded old-lady clothes to these splintery arms and turning the carousel out and off the porch over the green sea to drip dry.

Greta reached up and spun it around. *Clickity-clack, clickity-clack.* It wasn't just an old laundry carousel; it was a tilt-a-whirl in our own private amusement park!

"We can ride on this! Me first!"

A vapor of caution wafted quickly in front of my eyes. It was plausible, even possible. These girls were small enough; the rope looked sturdy enough, the rotation short enough. A cheap thrill on this back porch mechanism adapted for use, our amazing funhouse ride. We were so clever!

I hoisted Greta up onto one of the rope swings, and she held on to the bar above, laughing with pure joy as I turned her slowly, creaking, out off the porch and over the yawning garden.

Turning upside down for a moment, daring the jungle below to grab her—this was so much better than those tame swings in the schoolyard. She came wheeling back onto the porch and jumped down triumphant.

"My turn! My turn!" Ginger and Maddy were our guests, so they each went next. Kristin was assured that she'd get her turn. Just be patient; it was the natural order of things. Ginger was heavier than Greta as I lifted her, but this carousel held her just fine. It groaned a bit, but it was old. Ginger wasn't quite as brave as Greta the daredevil but so happy to be initiated into our exclusive back yard adventure. We all laughed and cheered.

"Yeah! You survived! Safe from the lava pits below!"

Maddy was a bit shy about getting on, but we all assured her that it was fine, the other girls had ridden around, and it was OK.

"C'mon!"

She climbed aboard and held on tight. I swung her out, and she held her breath while we cheered. Now, it was Kristin's turn. I was particularly careful helping her on to her seat.

"Here, hold on here, OK, you got it? Don't let go. Hold on tight—you ready? Whoohoo!"

Off the porch she went, slowly, wood creaking, girls cheering. Kristin's eyes were two plates of white light. She looked at me the whole time. She wasn't enjoying this but was such a trooper, wanting so much to be a part of the group. I felt a tinge of guilt for encouraging her, wanting to bend the rules for little Kristin. I wanted her to find some freedom in the pretense of flight and the joy of conquering her fears.

She was on her way back in, the girls reaching for her, laughing, when suddenly the arm of the wooden carousel snapped and broke in half (finally pushed beyond its limit), and Kristin went falling away from our frantic grabbing hands and onto the stone path below.

Kablam.

She just lay there. Greta and I rushed to her. She was in a flattened heap of roses on the stone path, so still.

The broken piece of carousel lay on top of her, and I threw it aside, screaming her name. We turned her on her back, pulling bits of wood and rope and shattered roses away, her tangled hair from her face. She looked at me, but it was different; her eyes were straining, her mouth gaping, gasping for air!

"Oh god, look!" Greta stepped away in shock. Kristin's right hand was screwed up weirdly; her arm was stiff, sticking out funny. Oh Jesus! Little squeaks were coming out of her mouth, and she started to look scared.

Omigod Omigod! What have I done!?

Instantly, the call went out:

"MOM!"

I gathered Kristin up from the terrible stone path. Her twisted hand fell onto the smudged Twiggy dress, her tight fingers loosened, and the little frog hopped out onto the ground, back into the green. I also noticed that our new friends Ginger and Maddy had disappeared, run back home to tell their parents what horrible people we were.

Ellen was in the front of the house, directing two large men in dirty sweatshirts as they heaved the banging upright piano in from the street. The just-arrived Bekins moving van took up the whole block; all our furniture lay half-unpacked, chairs and tables, bed frames, and lamps shoved into corners; towers of boxes. There was just enough room to carry in a broken little girl.

Greta was screaming, clearing the way with a wedge of noise, alerting the gods of terrible trouble here on earth. She threw open the back door, rushing to Ellen, the one who would save precious Kristin. I was right behind with my damaged little sister held gently. I banged past stove and tables, cupboards and stepped over willy-nilly boxes. I was a long-distance runner forging past the gauntlet of fire. I had to get to Ellen.

We lay Kristin down on the floor between the piano and a dropped box of toys. Greta breathlessly explained our disastrous ride on the laundry tilt-a-whirl. I was crying, apologizing, trying to smooth Kristin's hair. Ellen told us to be quiet and asked Kristin something, and when Kristin looked up at Ellen, suddenly to our horror, we saw that her skin was turning a pale shade of blue! She wasn't breathing!

Ellen told me gently but firmly to calm down and call 9-1-1. I was still Ellen's copilot. This was the call that would save Kristin's life, so I'd better do it right. I'd never called 9-1-1 before, but I put my finger in the little hole, and the dial of the rotary phone went around, and around, and then around again. So slowly! It gave me time to screw up my courage to talk with an operator, a stranger who had the power of life and death. With the phone pressed to my ear, I looked at Ellen bent down over Kristin. They had become one person.

The phone rang and rang and rang. No one was answering! Greta was crying. Then a lady's voice on the other end, sounding so far away like she was in some underground bunker.

"My little sister fell off the porch, and she can't breathe and is turning blue, and it's all my fault, oh god, I'm so sorry!"

The operator asked me something about where we lived, but all I knew was that we were in the haunted house next to the cemetery that we'd just moved in to, and I'd killed my little sister. She told me to calm down and that help was on the way. So, I hung up.

"Where do you want this, lady?" The two moving men held the large, lacquered-blue door we'd used as a dining room table. Suddenly it was junk and in the way. Ellen must have given them a look because they just propped the blue door up against the wall and went back outside.

Surrounded by a village of abandoned furniture, Ellen looked scared. Kristin had stopped squirming and was just lying there, a little blue girl in a dirty yellow dress. Greta was sobbing, wailing like a siren in the schoolyard that demands you to line up for a fire drill. Her mouth was a round speaker box of hurt.

"Go outside and look for the ambulance," Ellen directed me.

What I wanted to do was turn back time. Reel Kristin back into my arms and hug her, cheer, and proclaim that she was safe and that she mattered and would never be alone on this earth, that I loved her and would look after her. What I'd done instead was encourage a stupid risk when I knew better. I'd put her in harm's way and failed miserably as her protector. I'd failed as Ellen's copilot, failed our absent father, who depended on me. By my negligence, I'd caused this accident. I was a big brother in name only, pretending to be anything other than a blob with arms and legs stumbling around avoiding disaster, until now. I found myself contemplating life without Kristin, and it was inconceivable. But this was happening.

The side kitchen door opening was real, the splintered white picket fence I touched was real, the air on my hot face and my feet on the stone path that led out to the front gate left ajar, me standing alone out in the street—that was all real. The faraway, wailing air raid siren also seemed to be real. It was rising and falling, crying sorrowfully around corners, up and over the little houses and through the fog. Dogs were howling.

The blob of an older brother spun around and around, past the moving van and to one corner of the street, down the block around another corner, into the cemetery, bounding over headstones to the highway just beyond, looking for a racing ambulance, for the cavalry.

There was nothing. Empty streets, silent wooden houses, bent old fences, only the wailing siren and a rumpled old raven looking down at me from its high-wire perch, laughing.

"Idiot! Moron! Asshole! You're cursed! Forever! Forevermore!"

Then something stirred at the other end of Ukiah Street; something shifted in the distance. I looked hard, willing it to be an ambulance, but it was a crowd of people running full tilt down the street toward me, toward our little house. The wave grew like a sudden flash flood as more people joined and rushed forward, filling up the street, and leading the charge were Ginger, Maddy, and happy, barking Skipper singing high with the siren. Ginger spotted me in the street and pointed, calling to the cresting wave of people behind her.

"This way! This way! The new people are in trouble!" She pumped her arm like a traffic cop.

The blob in the street gestured madly toward the house, and the tide of people poured in past me, filling up the path, clogging the doorways. Suddenly an old fire truck came screeching up, its siren separating from that of the firehouse, and stopped in the middle of the street. Men in suspenders and big boots were leaping off and pushing their way in. The sight of them and the great commotion they made by tromping in with authority, shoving everyone out of the way, told me that these are the guys who would save my sister. I pushed my way in after them and stood behind Ellen as she frantically described the incident to one of the men, a big, stocky guy with a beard and massive arms.

It was Paul Bunyan himself; raising his voice and a thick arm, he asked people to step away and clear the area. But nobody moved. Everyone leaned in closer to see what he would do. Collecting his large body, he knelt and started giving Kristin CPR, his big, grizzled-bearded lips blowing big gulps of air into little Kristin's blue mouth. Ellen silently stroked her hair, tears flowing down her face.

We all held our breath, and then suddenly, Kristin gasped as if coming up from the deep end of the pool. Everyone cheered, and many hands patted Ellen and Paul Bunyan on the shoulders. I was jostled back against the wall by the shifting crowd, people murmuring and chatting, starting to squeeze out of the house.

I felt a cold hand touch my back and looked up to see an old lady with tight, curly, blueish hair and horn-rimmed glasses. She looked like an owl blinking at me.

"It's going to be all right, dear," she said. "Your sister will be just fine. It looks like she might have broken her wrist, but that will heal."

I looked at little Kristin, now crying openly, now able to cry. As the color came back to Kristin's face, Paul Bunyan gently placing the injured arm on her belly. One big hand went on her forehead while his other arm was around Ellen's shoulders. He was talking to them; Ellen was nodding, saying something.

When I turned around to acknowledge my relief, the old lady had gone; there was only space where she'd been, and suddenly I was floating. The room began to move in a slow, woozy spin, and there was a sharp ringing in my ears. Everything began to swirl slowly, the colors of the wallpaper and everyone's clothes, the wood floor, the light beaming in through windows all meshed into a muddy puddle. As I instinctively reached out to grab something, there she was again, the old lady standing right behind me.

Kristin was now suddenly being lifted overhead on many hands and carried carefully outside, passed from person to person, like a rock star, out the kitchen door down the path to the ambulance that had finally arrived. Ellen followed in her wake, Greta and I joined her, and at the last second, as little Kristin was being tucked into the back of the ambulance, she raised her good hand.

"Mommy."

The tableau of Ellen amid a crowd of strangers having to make a split decision was like something I'd seen on an opera stage. The tragic heroine torn between a fateful choice contemplated the moment when destiny changed everything, and as if right on cue, the old lady appeared once again, offering to take care of Greta and me for the night. She lived right next door.

Ellen promised she'd call us, to be good kids, don't get into trouble, and she gave me the house keys. I was still her second-in-command. She got into the ambulance, and off they went, sirens blaring.

Greta and I were left standing there with a receding tide of people, the old house becoming quiet once again. I noticed that the big moving van had gone, everything unloaded. Ginger, Maddy, and Skipper had returned to their restaurant, and the fire truck drove away with Paul Bunyan hanging off the back.

The old lady had told Ellen that she lived right next door but hadn't said in which direction. Was it that little house tucked behind the water tower or that new mound in the cemetery?

CHAPTER 10

JESÚS, WRITE MY JOURNAL

Wednesday morning: I had this crazy dream last night where I'm trying to get away from these dogs. I'm trying to fly up, but it's not working! Pumping my arms up and down, slowly pushing off the ground with these foaming, snarling dogs biting my feet. Why isn't it working? I've had these great flying dreams where I can just lift off effortlessly. I swoop and hover, but not this time. I see the sad little house we've moved into and the weird water tower over there, the uneven, cracked street just below my feet, but I can't seem to get any higher. The dogs pull at my shoelaces with their yellow teeth. They're having fun taunting me! I woke up angry. *Fuck you, you fucking horrible, mangy dogs!*

I couldn't believe it. This was our house. This was where we lived. Did I wake up, or was I still in a nightmare? This old, dusty, wooden building was scrunched up at the end of the street.

Built with long redwood floorboards running the entire length of one room without a break. Tall, ancient trees turned into boards before Gerald was born. Before his dad. Birds probably used to live in the foyer. Old, old, old. So old, older than dirt. As old as the hills. As old as the Crypt Keeper.

Later: The branches from that giant tree were made into shelves that wrapped around the entire kitchen. Brown medicine bottles, old seed packets, and broken utensils were stuck to the paint, and if I touched something, it had dust or grease or something worse on it, something dead. I'd never washed my hands so much in my entire life. We lived in a mausoleum.

Dark, musty cupboards deep enough to store a winter's supply of grain. You could park a bicycle or easily win (and get bored) at hide-and-seek. Why did I bother hiding in here? Did the girls even try to find me?

Narrow stairs marched up to the second-floor rooms. Each step creaked and groaned, even after we'd finished walking up or down. I'd be standing at the top landing, and they'd keep snap-crackle-popping as if ghosts were following. Shadows flickered in my peripheral vision; a chill passed by even though there was no open window. Proof positive that this place was haunted.

Heavy doors on wobbly hinges had different-colored, rough-cut diamond doorknobs jiggling in their sockets. They would fall off in my hands, and it was such a pain in the ass to get them back in.

Push-button locks in recessed panels squirted dust when pressed. The last time this door was locked was probably a hundred years ago. Tall windows slid up on ropes and locked with corroded green latches; dust flew off everything. I was sneezing, coughing, and losing brain cells, it was so dusty.

There was a different-patterned wallpaper in each of the front rooms: Country scenes of horse-drawn buggies, farmers tilling, and children turning hoops along cobblestones peeled back in the foyer. Mismatched red stripes paraded around the main room. Woven cornucopia spit fruit, flowers, and medieval musical instruments all over the smaller side room. Everything was yellowed, warped, and torn. It probably used to be kind of cheery when the old lady lived here. Now, it was just creepy.

Spidery chandeliers hung lightless, and their exposed wires clawed the air, bulbs burnt black and broken. Crown molding was painted over with layers of green and pink, dripping solid fingers over buggies and bouquets. The walls looked wounded. Built-in glass cupboards were the final resting places for dead spiders and mice, their final scrabbling paths etched in the dust.   Were there mummies hidden somewhere?

Layers of chipped art deco–patterned floor linoleum hopscotched over each other in competing angles. Whoever laid this tile didn't care about getting it even at all, and I got kind of dizzy just looking at it. The whole place made me feel like I'd fallen down a tunnel, been drugged, or was still asleep.

I wanted to know: Was there a god, and if so, why did he decide to cast us into this purgatory where the world had stopped at the turn of the century? I'd also wondered for a long time, what was the meaning of life? And…who was I?

The weathervane permanently pointed west, and cracked slate stepping-stones walked around the front of the house into a jungle out back. I could get lost and never be found.

Thursday morning: I couldn't remember my dream, but it didn't matter because I was not sure if I'd woken up yet. Fog covered the sky. Thick, gray fog clamping down, pushing down the street. There was not a sound in this gray muck, no birds, no cars, nothing. I was underwater. I was drowning.

At the very end of quiet Ukiah Street, surrounded by a leaning picket fence, this old house looked like a squat, wrinkled, and forgotten old lady, practically invisible behind the soupy fog. Our nearest neighbors were a couple of dingy double-wide trailers shoved together behind chained link. I never saw anyone go in or out. A tiny aquarium-green cottage down the block. The creepy wooden water tower was just like an antique H. G. Wells Martian invader stopped dead, mid-invasion. There was a grand gingerbread mansion and the lumpy cemetery next door. The people who settled this town way back in the 1800s all buried right over there. This whole town was a graveyard. That made me the living dead, right?

Later: One and a half acres of overgrown climbing vines, leggy flowers, thorny berry bushes, propped-up fruit trees, elbowed roots grasping for water, rotten-apple landmines in the grass. Bugs were everywhere. Earwigs, potato bugs, Sal bugs, dragonflies, and mutant vampire mosquitos. A big ladybug landed on my arm, and remembering that they bring good luck, I didn't swat her off right away even though she tickled, since I needed all the luck I could get.

A falling-down chicken coop in the far corner of the yard stank of rotten eggs encrusted under dried shit and abandoned nests. A large shed next to the back porch had a sink and short, rickety ladder climbing up to a small loft. Rough, exposed beams were homes for spiders, bats, and slivers seeking reaching fingers.

That shed leaned into a small creek that seeped in from underneath, filling a small well. Tiny green frogs, orange-bellied salamanders, and a little brown turtle lived under leaves and in puddles. Everything was held together by a giant, swooping wave of nasturtiums climbing up, then pouring down over the roof. The garden was swallowing the shed.

Migrating birds were right at home in our wild backyard. Insane chirruping reverberated from the trees and deep grass, an orchestra of discordant prettiness, like a savage, long-lost Eden. Every flower and bush was fighting for light. You had to hunt for the water spigot and hidden hose snaking in a petrified mass. There was a large, rusted wagon wheel propped against the house, just another frame for climbing vines.

A vacant three-car garage was littered with boxes of old tools and rusted farm equipment. There was the long, sharp shadow of a wood-handled scythe, held precariously in a cobwebbed corner—the shrouded figure of death hiding right there in plain sight.

We discovered antique brown ceramic beer bottles and jugs half-buried and used them for vases, window jams, and paperweights. A large chunk of shiny black obsidian was perfect for holding open the screen door.

The laundry carousel on the back porch was regarded as sculpture after Kristin's fall. No one touched it. We barely hung socks up. I'd push it around occasionally just to hear it creak as a sort of prayer wheel, acknowledging a karmic debt. I almost killed my little sister. I was a terrible big brother. I also reminded myself that Kristin was OK. She lived.

Saturday morning: Gerald drove up from Berkeley on the weekend just like he promised, calling us early in the morning from the Owl Diner in Cloverdale.

He was almost home! I was waiting for him on the front porch as he slowly pulled up in the Rambler. He'd driven all night (leaving Berkeley right after his shift at work), and he was exhausted, and for some reason, he was only wearing underwear.

"It's an old trucker's trick," he explained. "You take off a piece of clothing to jog your tired mind." I helped him gather up pants and shoes as he tiptoed barefoot into the house.

Ellen made him put his clothes back on before eating breakfast. We made him a bunch of rooster-shaped pancakes, but he barely finished and fell asleep where he sat in the rocking chair. Covering him with a blanket, letting him rest, we unpacked the many boxes of paint thinner, rags, dirty gloves, a huge tarp, old buckets, paintbrushes, and all sorts of scary-looking scraping tools. Ellen said that we were going to remodel the house.

"It's going to be a big project, and I'm going to need your help, Eric," she said. "You are still my second-in-command, remember?"

How could I forget? I was already tired just thinking about it. Being responsible was exhausting.

To start, we'd rip all the wallpaper down and the linoleum up, scrape the paint off moldings, windowsills, and door frames, and then sand, stain, and polish the floorboards. I was worried that we'd have to do it all while Gerald was still sleeping. Wouldn't we disturb him? Maybe not, because he'd slipped into a coma. Slumped over in the chair, he was not moving, barely breathing.

But Ellen said the remodeling would take weeks and weeks, maybe as long as three months. Wait a minute. The whole summer? That was just fucking great! That was exactly what I wanted to do with my summer: scrape paint off molding.

Later: Gerald finally woke up, and Kristin showed him her new cast, and they spent a long time sitting together. He drank more coffee, reading to her and brushing her hair. Brushing hair wasn't a big deal any longer, as Kristin had experienced much worse. She told him the whole story of meeting our new neighbors, of riding the laundry carousel and falling off the back porch and breaking her wrist, of not being able to breathe, of being kissed by a smelly giant, and then of spending the night in the hospital.

The rest of the day was kind of fun. Ripping all the ugly wallpaper down. Screaming and yelling behind our tied-up pirate bandanas, tearing away at the thick sheets of flower baskets and dried fruit. Unfortunately, there was more of the gross lime-green and faded-pink paint underneath. It was like the walls all had a disease.

A fine powder settled over everything as we mangled the vintage scenes of idyllic countryside. Once it was all torn to shreds and stuffed into garbage bags, Gerald dragged them outside while I swept the floor. Greta followed with a mop. Don't forget the corners. She always pretended like she was doing a good job, and when Ellen or Gerald pointed out that it didn't get done, she said she didn't know. She was such a liar and got away with murder.

Ellen and Kristin wiped up as much powder from other surfaces as possible. Our life was dusting, washing, cleaning, always cleaning. Well, Ellen, Gerald, little Kristin, and I cleaned; Greta just pushed the dirt around. Why was she so lazy?

When all the tools got put away, and our hands were washed for the five hundredth time, Ellen lay out a picnic on the floor. I could see all the spots Greta missed, and it was totally obvious. Why didn't Ellen say anything?

The old checkerboard tablecloth we used in Tilden Park was set with unpacked Red Rooster plates and glasses. Cheese, apples and crackers, peanut butter cookies, and chocolate milk. Gerald and Ellen sipped glasses of red wine, their new favorite: Beaujolais.

"A fun, fruity red wine!" Gerald licked his lips.

Sitting there in the middle of the floor with the naked walls echoing, we raised a toast to our strange new home. Yeah! We lived in a dilapidated, filthy haunted house.

Sunday night: Gerald went back down to the Bay Area, and we were left alone in this sad, dirty place. Now, what did we do? The wallpaper was all torn down, the linoleum tile was gone and thrown away, and the rooms were now even uglier with the old, glazed, green and pink paint. We'd have to do something about the walls if we didn't want to throw up every time we went in there.

Monday morning: We looked around all the rooms with laser vision, removing every stray bit of clinging, glued-on meadows, buggies, stripes, apples, and corn. Digging in corners, lifting up, and then scraping away, we removed every last piece of the room's former life. It seemed weird that scenes illustrating the same stereotypical simplicity Ellen and Gerald loved had now been ripped up and thrown away. They wanted a different version.

Ellen said we'd put new wallpaper up over the vomitous pink and green (so we could just leave that for now). Still, all the molding would need a thorough going over. Couldn't we just paint the whole house pink and call it a circus?

Later: More sweeping, more dusting, some snacking, and then a nap. Ellen and I wrapped our faces back up, lay down the massive tarp, put on gloves, and started applying paint remover to the baked-on green and pink crown molding. Even with all the windows and doors opened, it still felt like we were poisoning ourselves, the toxic fumes most likely causing irreversible brain damage.

The girls were told to stay far away, and I wondered if that meant I somehow was more expendable. Instead of Ellen's second-in-command, was I only just a convenient pair of long arms and legs put to good use? I wondered, if my brain melted, would anybody notice or care? Would they even remember me? Greta might be young, but she was power hungry, and she'd be the one to take over.

The rest of the day was spent straightening upstairs while the downstairs paint slowly bubbled up, turning all the molding into oozing blisters of key lime pie and Pepto-Bismol.

Tuesday morning: my scraper brought down long, mushy strips of lime- and pink-colored puss. Peeling back puke-colored buttercream frosting, I felt like I was carving into a melted clown castle.

Later: This was the messiest mess I'd ever made! It all came down in taffy sheets or sticky, drifting confetti, covering everything with a layer of candied ash and sticking to my hands and hair, gunking up the scraper, every fold of the tarp. Even the pen I wrote with. Half the job was cleaning up the cleanup. This was taking for fucking ever!

Wednesday morning: It looks like someone left the cake out in the rain! The smell was sickening. Slushing through party-colored, saccharine-scented puke. Something died in here. A bird flew in the open window, and I had to shoo it back out with the old broom, bristles covered in dead cotton candy paint fuzz.

The actual wood grain on the molding was beginning to reveal itself, and it was beautiful. All the curvy lines swirling, the natural warm shades of hardwood were comforting and elegant, even in raw form. Suddenly, we lived in a treehouse.

Thursday morning: We'd cleared all the wallpaper, all the dead paint and muck away, and now we were ready to get to work. Ellen said that after breakfast, we were going to wash every inch of the house. *Are you kidding me?* With what, a fireman's hose? We needed to flush the whole place out.

Ellen had made a solution of vinegar and soap. We scrubbed under and over and in-between every millimeter of every board, inch by inch. The girls in the lower cupboards, me up on a ladder with a rag tied around the broom, Ellen smoothing out all the shelf surfaces and light fixtures. Every cobweb, every dust bunny, every bit of dirt and dried-up bug. Now the rooms all smelled like Easter.

Friday morning: While we were sitting around the shiny, blue table eating Ellen's perfect omelets, wondering what project we'd do next (and exactly how to do it), someone knocked on the side kitchen door. A long-haired, bearded man passing through town was looking for work, and the only payment he wanted was food and lodging. His name was Jesús (like the son of God) but the way he said his name, the *J* sounded like an *H*.

My mouth was full of cheese and egg, and I was thinking about old fairy tales and some obscure passage in the Bible. I seemed to remember something about mercy for the weary traveler. We all looked him up and down, at each other, and then way too quickly, Ellen said, yes. Was she crazy? *Don't let him in, Ellen! He could be a psycho killer!*

"You couldn't have timed your visit any better." She welcomed him right into our warm kitchen. "We've just moved in and have more than a few big projects, and we could certainly use the help."

I could see that she was relieved, and I was sorry she was so tired. I wished I were better at helping, that I could do more. Now this strange guy was going to take over, and I'd missed my chance. I just pretended to know what I was doing anyway. Second-in-command was an empty title. Maybe I should be glad Jesús was here to do the job. Ellen whipped him up a large omelet and toast.

Later: Jesús was dressed in a plaid shirt and tight jeans cinched with a leather belt and wide metal buckle in the shape of an Egyptian ankh. His leather hiking boots looked like they'd been walking for a while. His army surplus jacket was stitched on the back with a big purple peace sign, and he smelled a little bit like sweet hay. He looked like all the other hippies I grew up with in Berkeley, but he was not drunk or stoned, he didn't stink, and I imagined what he'd look like with short hair, his beard shaved off, wearing a suit and tie. He'd look just like any normal person. I guessed I liked his long hair much better.

He looked you right in the eye when he spoke and smiled a lot; he was very polite and careful not to let the screen door bang as he dragged his big backpack and rolled-up sleeping bag into the front room. Our house, his new crash pad.

Later: He didn't seem like a psycho killer, but I was still dubious and watched Jesús closely, ready to call 9-1-1. I knew how to do it now and would call at the first sign of trouble.

Quickly making friends with him, the girls showed Jesús all around, touring the house and yard. He was taking notes on a little pad, occasionally reaching down to grab a tool found along the way or a daisy, broken off a bush. He tucked the flower behind an ear, flipping his long hair back.

From an upstairs window, I watched them walking around, and when they disappeared into the shed for a long time, I practiced a few karate chops on my pillow in case I needed to take him out.

Later: Ellen went over his list, nodding in approval.

"Yard cleared, prune trees, drywall, floors stripped & finished, windows resealed & washed, gutters cleaned, doors leveled." It was a short but deceptive list. I knew that each item all by itself would take forever.

"Eric will be your assistant." Ellen cheerfully volunteered me. Everything she said after that, all the gobbledygook about learning something new and following direction, blah, blah, blah, went in one ear and then out the other. I hated my mother. I had no life.

He was starting in right away, hacking at the overgrowth that blocked the stone path and the back gate with a wicked-looking machete he found in the garage. He took his shirt off and attacked the backyard Amazon, leaving a trail of thrashed rose vines, nasturtiums, and weeds. Right behind him, I scrabbled everything into piles, picking over the ground, collecting rocks, sticks, and other bits of junk. The muscles in his shoulders were flexing a lot. His chest was like a superhero's.

Would I become strong like him if I kept pulling weeds and swinging a machete? A strand of hair was stuck to his sweaty back. His butt looked good in those tight jeans. *Don't look at his butt!* He was a whirling, chopping hurricane, leaving a path of destruction for me to gather up. I kept my shirt on, though.

Later: Jesús had chopped the entire jungle down and put aside the machete, he now started using the old scythe. He reminded me of those figures on the wall I ripped down last week or a younger version of that statue on top of the bank. After raising the rusty scythe high, he swung it out over the grass and took a whole chunk out. Now, he was mowing what was left with an old, clackity-clacking lawnmower. Back and forth and back and forth. His arms flexing and pushing, rounded shoulders tensing, now glistening. Occasionally, he stopped to throw stones, pieces of wood, or clay beer bottles into a pile, then leaned on the lawnmower to rest, closing his eyes and taking in long breaths. He went somewhere else in his mind, and I watched his breathing slow down, his body relax.

Dipping his big hands into the well and splashing cold water on his face and then down over his sweaty body, he took several long drinks, and now he was all wet. I could see all the little hairs on his chest smoothed in one direction. I hope he didn't accidentally swallow one of those frogs.

The yard was beginning to look like a different place, like it had a bad case of mumps. A practically vacant lot dotted with decorative mounds of debris. I had so many blisters on my hands. Well water cooled them off.

Later: Ellen had made us all tuna fish sandwiches. I loved her so much. Always thinking about our well-being, feeding us, making sure we're OK. After lunch, Jesús encouraged the girls (who wanted to help) to gather up all those little piles and load them all into the wobbly wheelbarrow, then dump them into one big pile in the middle of the yard. We were going to have a bonfire later. I was full of tuna but already thinking about hot dogs. While the girls worked, he called me over.

"Let's begin a garden over there." Pointing to the yard farther out.

"We'll build some raised beds and use some of this chopped-up grass for mulch." I didn't know what "mulch" was, but I knew he was talking about a whole bunch of new stuff that wasn't on his original list. I was tired, dirty, cranky, and hot, my hands hurt, and I kind of wished that this guy hadn't shown up in the first place. Hadn't we done more than enough for one day, Jesus Christ?

Later: Jesús found a couple of shovels, a pickax, a hammer, a bunch of old boards, and a bag of nails that he said we could repurpose into some raised-bed gardens. Wasn't that fantastic, wasn't he just so smart. He directed me to start digging along the edge of the yard (and then pile up the dirt). We'd then sift everything through a bit of thin wire fence, cleaning the dirt even more. I thought this guy might be nuts. We were going to sift dirt.

"You've got some lovely rich soil here." He was grabbing hand-fuls of wet, black dirt and letting it fall between his fingers back to the ground. "Just look at all these earthworms." He was excited about worms. "Earthworms mean that the soil is fertile and aerated." He didn't explain any more, but I couldn't stop thinking about the ground full of squirming, slimy earthworms. I was probably going to have to squish a few.

Jesús built two long, rectangle frames and then lined the pits with chicken wire "to keep the gophers out." I massaged big clumps of dirt (and a few worms). So gross! We shoveled all the dirt back into the new boxes and leveled it off with leftover boards. Perfect, flat boxes full of dirt. I wondered what Ellen would want to plant out there. Carrots? Tomatoes? String beans or peppers? Maybe I could experiment with some of those old seed packages we found?

"We could make another small one for an herb garden," Jesús sug-gested. "Or maybe you could build that later, yourself?"

Oh yeah, sure, I'll get right on it.

Jesús had dirt smudged all over his arms, torso, face, and hands and looked like a handsome caveman. If he had a club or jawbone, he could get a part in that opening sequence from *2001: A Space Odyssey.*

Friday evening: Gerald was there! And he was wearing his clothes this time. Probably because Ellen told him that Jesús was staying with us. I could imagine her saying: "We have company, please keep your clothes on." Was my dad a pervert?

Gerald said he almost doesn't recognize the place.

"What happened to the jungle? The yard got a haircut!"

Even in the dark, it looked different and a whole lot neater. Jesús lit the bonfire and had collected a bunch of long, thin metal fence ties from the garage to use as hot dog skewers.

Gerald reminded the girls that they couldn't cross the long gutter surrounding the fire.

"Don't burn your hair off."

Ellen wanted to make sure the hose was turned on. Hot dogs tasted better with mustard and pickle relish on a paper plate. Jesús ate four; he worked hard today.

Saturday morning: Gerald and Jesús walked around the front rooms with a tape measure, taking notes, scribbling small maps, and talking in low, serious voices. Ellen made more omelets, and I helped. Swishing the butter in her new pan until it bubbled, then quick, pour the eggs in. The sound of sizzling meant that it was the perfect temperature. Sprinkle in cheddar cheese and diced chives. Fold over with the wooden spatula and then a pinch of sea salt. Jesús loved omelets.

Gerald had brought up all these new and slightly used aluminum and steel pots and pans of every size imaginable. Deep soup pots, little saucepans, and wide sauté pans with long handles.

Ellen loved her new omelet pan. She had to "cure" it first with butter, then wiped it out before even dropping an egg in.

Soup ladles and scary-looking knives of all sizes, each wrapped in paper and packaged in their box. More little boxes of heavy, fancy silverware and a couple of weird glass vases pinched in the middle. A wooden cinch tied around with a leather thong. Gerald called them Chemex. They looked like large laboratory beakers or transparent, voluptuous Gibson girls.

"We'll make filtered coffee for guests. Café filtre." He said the French with a twist of his hand. "Freed, Teller & Freed will be sending us bags of roasted beans, and you can grind them up in the evenings." *Oh boy! We're not even open yet, and he's already finding things for me to do.*

Later: I was being dragged along, up to depressing Fort Bragg and a noisy lumber yard where we wandered stacks of wood, past busy, gruff-looking men stomping around in dirty jeans and plaid shirts. Gerald and Jesús were talking with Paul Bunyan's younger brother about asbestos, acoustic plaster compound, stilts, studs, screws, and delivery of standard sheetrock with a level five finish versus tape and joint compound. I made notes and drew a picture of Jesús swinging a scythe.

Sunday morning: Gerald had decided that today, we were not going to do anything.

"Today is the Lord's day," he said, raising his hands like a priest giving his blessing. "And today, we're going to the beach."

It was a perfect day. The sun was already warm, with no sign of fog. We would have a picnic next to one of those large logs that had washed up. Maybe I would build a fort.

Later: We got in the water. It was cold but also kind of refreshing. Jesús was the first to jump in. When he came out of the waves, his skin was covered in tiny goosebumps, and there was seaweed clinging to his long hair and the tight cutoffs he wore. He looked like a merman without his tail.

Monday morning: A truck arrived loaded with huge panels of sheetrock, and two lumberjacks unloaded everything into the front room. Gerald told me the night before (before he left) that these boards were going up over the remnants of melted-ice-cream puke on the walls, flattening and smoothing, making everything the same.

"Jesús is going to need lots of help putting up all these boards." He stated the obvious. "It'll make a man out of you, to measure and lift. Do what he tells you to do, and I'll see you when it's all done."

My stomach caved in, and I was super nervous about messing it all up. I'd never cut a piece of sheetrock before! I was going to fail, fail at becoming "a man" if I couldn't lift these ten-ton boards. What would happen when I messed it up or broke my back? I'd be a cripple who couldn't leave my upstairs room, fed oatmeal from a spoon. I thought Gerald was glad he didn't have to do anything, that he got to escape. I hated my fucking parents.

Jesús put his warm hand on my shoulder, and he could tell I was scared. "It's a little heavy, but we can do it!" He smiled, and I believed him.

Getting right to work, Jesús set up two sawhorses, and I helped him lift and then lay a big board down. It was even heavier than I thought. I was using all my strength and could feel my back straining. It could snap at any moment.

"Use your legs," Jesús grunted. I watched and copied him, lifting from the middle of the board with one hand, the other bracing the edge. I couldn't believe that I was doing this. It felt like it was made of cement. I kept thinking: *The more I lift, the more manly I'll become. Use your legs.*

Jesús had measured with the pencil (the one that lived behind his ear) and then cut the top off one board. We lifted the first piece to the spot on a wall, and I could hear him sigh with relief behind his white, alien, athletic-cup-looking mask. The piece fit perfectly. That was only the first board, though. There were a hundred more to go.

Friday night, a week later: The front rooms looked like a big empty gallery. All the walls were flat and white. Jesús and I worked all week, and now it was finished. He did most of it, all the hard stuff. I just helped lift and pretended like I knew what I was doing when he asked me to go ahead and measure one board. He'd always double-check and then nod his head, so it must've been OK. I got to cut a couple of boards with the knife, crack them down the seam, and then put them up on the wall on my own. Jesús said it was perfect, but I could see that it was a little crooked. He was just being nice. He cut a long triangular sliver to fit into the small gap I'd left at the bottom. Then it was perfect.

Jesús had taped a big plastic sheet over the arched entry and moved his sleeping bag into the foyer, so he didn't have to breathe dust. White plaster dust was everywhere, covering everything. Like it snowed inside. Occasionally, the girls would come in and wipe something up or draw pictures of horses with their fingers.

I could tell that Jesús was relieved and proud of himself. He stood there with his dusty white hands on slim hips looking around the rooms like it was the prettiest thing he'd ever seen. I was a walking bruise. There wasn't a muscle or bone in my body that wasn't sore. I'd been lying down a lot. It hurt even to lift my arms. Jesús and I had each been taking lots of hot baths.

Ellen had been making us many fancy dinners. One night she made us a whole roasted chicken stuffed with lemon and garlic and an entire chocolate cake! They were the best things I'd ever eaten.

When Gerald arrived, he told me: "Next week, I want you to take the Greyhound bus down to the city and help me go hunting for furniture."

What? A solo journey on the bus? I'd never done that! Down to busy San Francisco? What if I got lost or mugged or took the wrong bus and ended up in Nebraska? What if the bus broke down on the freeway, and they had to evacuate us all to a shelter in Sacramento, and I got drafted into a biker gang? What if I got car sick? Who was going to watch Jesús?

"I've discovered some wonderful antique furniture warehouses." Gerald's eyes got big. "We'll choose the tables and chairs for the dining rooms, and maybe if there's enough money left over, we can get a grandfather clock." He wanted that clock, I could tell. If I made it down there in one piece, I'd help him choose.

But before I traveled down to the city, Jesús wanted to sand and then stain the floorboards. Back in Fort Bragg, he rented a huge machine that looked like something between an old lawnmower and a Tonka truck. Big, flat strips of rough sandpaper got clamped on. After we'd cleared everything out, Jesús plugged the monster in, strapped back on his face mask, and started to drive the roaring thing slowly along the edge of the room.

Saturday: Imagine what it sounds like having a jet plane rev up in your living room. The old wooden floor didn't like having its skin shaved off. The top layer turned into sawdust, flying everywhere. Jesús slowly pushed the beast along the floor, leaning into it, struggling to keep it in a straight line.

He yelled something at me from behind his mask, but all I could hear was the jet engine screaming. I had to get right up next to his face to hear anything. His brown eyes had flecks of gold in them.

"Watch how I hold the handlebars, here." He took my hands and put them on the two vibrating rubber bars, putting his bigger hands firmly over mine. "Hold on tight. Use your shoulders. Don't let it get away."

It was what I imagined riding an angry steer in a rodeo might be like. The machine wanted to gallop off in any random direction, but I was gripping the thing with all my strength, leaning in like Jesús, pressing and pushing, guiding it slowly forward, sore bones rattling, rubber band muscles flopping around.

Jesús was also still holding on, standing right up against me. His body pressed tight, I could feel his big ankh belt buckle mashing into my back, his hands covering mine. We were like one body connected to this crazy, howling machine, holding on for dear life, trying to control where this thing wanted to go. My hands got numb from the pressure, and I started to panic a little bit. What if I couldn't hold on? It was going to pull away any second and rip my arm off!

Jesús could tell when I lost confidence and pressed in tighter, steering the bucking sanding machine and me, grinding over the old floor.

Monday morning: I was on the bus watching Mendocino disappear behind the uni-cloud. The fog was back, swallowing everything. Up the hills, down and around the cliffs, over the bridge, past the fields and barns and squiggly roads climbing ridges.

I sat in the middle by a window so I could see the world go by and hopefully not get sick. So far so good. The big bus was like a solid, cushioned living room sliding over the road. It was cool in there, and if I kept my eyes on the landscape and concentrated as the familiar scenes whooshed by I'd be fine. *Don't barf, don't barf, don't barf.*

I'd walked the few blocks to the pickup spot on Main Street in front of The Hotel and waited on the same curb where Gerald had sneered at a hippie once. When the bus pulled up, I was relieved. I didn't miss my ride. But now I was nervous because now I had to get on. The driver took the money Ellen gave me and wrote a ticket on mimeographed paper, ripping off my pink copy.

Don't lose it. I needed it to get back on the bus at the transfer point in Santa Rosa.

I peed a lot before I left, but I was still worried. What if I drank too much coffee? What if it wasn't enough? What if I fell asleep on the bus and miss the transfer point? Would I make the connection in time and the other bus? How would I know where to get on? I was willingly trusting the say-so of strangers. Did they know where to get off, how to get to San Francisco? What if they lied to me? What if they saw how nervous I was and purposely guided me in the exact wrong direction, toward the skeezy part of town where all the bums lived? Would Gerald be there waiting for me? Would he be late? The bus driver might be drunk and drive us off the road, not paying attention as he turned the big steering wheel, swooping around that curve before the road dropped off a cliff. This could be my first and last solo bus ride.

When I came creeping down the stairs this morning, Ellen had made me breakfast and packed a bag lunch (like she used to do for school). Everybody else was still asleep. The sanding machine was still sitting there, parked in the corner where Jesús had turned it off for the last time. The wood floor was stark naked, glowing white. I guessed now he'd have to stain and finish the floor by himself. What would it look like when I got back? Would I recognize the place?

Later: I walked around the block when we stopped in Santa Rosa and then found my same seat again. I'd screwed up my courage and asked the driver what to do, how to make the transfer, and whadda ya know, it was the same bus, with a half-hour layover. Just present your ticket and get right back on. I had time for a sandwich and a stroll. There was a tacky beauty salon in the lobby with ratty wigs on chipped mannequin heads, sun-faded pictures of suburban housewives with fancy up-dos. A drug store on the corner where some guy asked me for a cigarette. I bought a pack of Juicy Fruit gum.

The Golden Gate Bridge wasn't gold; it was orange. The closer we got to the city, the more traffic there was. I felt like one tiny blood corpuscle rushing together into the current, pulsing faster toward the heart of the city. Everybody was in such a big hurry. Horns honking, tires screeching, people, people, people, streetlights and storefronts, and tall buildings crowding. We somehow didn't crash. Then we went underground, into a series of tunnels, the bus motor growling, echoing, lights reflecting off tiles. When the bus finally pulled hissing up to the curb, and the driver opened the door, it was the end of the line, and I knew that I was going to have to get off. I had to walk out there by myself.

Standing on the ramp, still gripping my bus ticket, I searched faces, looking for Gerald. Where was he? Then I saw him walking toward me, his black beret slid backward.

"Let's go get some furniture, shall we?" he exclaimed. I'd arrived. I made it.

Monday night: Driving back up to Mendocino in the dark, I thought all the roads and fields looked the same. What changed was the smell. When I rolled the window down, it was the weeds and damp and then the ocean. When the curves started, down came the window, and the country poured in.

Late: I must have slept through the redwoods because when Gerald tapped my shoulder, he said, "Look, Eric, we're almost home." There was the twinkle of Mendocino floating in the darkness just beyond the bridge. I was dreaming of watching all the new vegetables in the garden grow into elegant, scrolling vines that reached up and up. I remember thinking in the dream: I want to climb these vines into the sky, like Jack on his beanstalk, and I heard Jesús say: "Use your legs."

Much later: Everyone was in bed, asleep and quiet, tucked away under blankets, doors closed, lights off. If I listened hard enough, I could still hear the roar of the sanding machine, feel chalk dust slide between my fingers, see a shirtless Jesús with a rusty scythe raised high above his head.

When Gerald and I unlocked the side kitchen door and creeped in, I looked for him in the front rooms. Was that his sleeping bag bunched up in a corner, the sanding machine still sitting there? No, they were chairs pushed together, the tarp folded up. Jesús was gone.

"He left right after he finished the floor" Gerald whispered. "He did a pretty great job on our little house, yes?"

I turned on the light and marveled at the smoothed and shiny floor, now stained a vague coffee color, the walls a uniform blank canvas. There was a tang of turpentine and a cold emptiness, the stacked chairs and tarp looked lonely. Jesús was gone.

"I never got to say goodbye," I said. "Will we ever see him again?"

"Who knows where he'll go next," Gerald replied, looking apprecia- tively around the rooms. "We never did learn where he came from. Off to his next adventure, I imagine."

I wanted to walk around and see for myself, but the floor was still curing, still sticky, the chairs holding back any traffic. I remembered the blue door and of how long it had taken for the varnish to fuse solid.

"I think another twelve hours, and we can all walk in there." Gerald turned the light off. "Maybe by morning, we can have another picnic."

A family picnic on the shiny new dining room floor, and once again, it would be only the five of us. Jesús was gone.

CHAPTER 11

CAFÉ BEAUJOLAIS

Ellen received a hand-typed letter from the town postmaster, Don Burleson. They must've had a conversation over the counter as she bought stamps or set up the new box where we'd receive our mail. He was requesting an interview, wanting to write a short introductory story about our family's arrival and the new restaurant.

Besides postmarking packages, Don was a reporter for the local newspaper, where he discussed events or announced any noteworthy development. A new restaurant in town was certainly big news. He already had an opening line.

"Save the gas and stay in town for a night out."

Located in the center of town, the post office was where everyone would meet and share tidbits of their lives, while also taking the current temperature of a community. People talked. News or gossip moved faster than any letter could travel, and Don propitiously placed as postmaster knew absolutely everyone (and conceivably everything) about this small village.

And as a columnist for the *Mendocino Beacon*, Don had an audience beyond the unincorporated town's limits. Stretching up and down the coast, inland into wine country, circulation covered the entire length of Northern California. The *Beacon* was regarded as the voice of the Mendocino coast, while Don (ensconced behind the main counter of the post office) was the town's well-informed, kindly face. His own return post office box was number one.

It was a bit of a cultural earthquake that something as exciting (and controversial) as a second restaurant opening was happening in town. It was already the topic of discussion as people waited in line for special delivery.

There'd only been The Sea Gull, where (like the post office) everyone in town would gather. People were concerned, and it struck many as insensitive, even invasive, that a fancy French restaurant would be just down the block from the town's well-established watering hole. Two restaurants within walking distance of each other? People were skeptical and protective of the status quo.

We'd already made quite the grand entrance with Kristin's accident, our house filling up with locals responding to the volunteer firemen's siren. I imagined the very same townsfolk who'd stormed down the street to save my little sister now gathering up pitchforks and torches to run us out of town.

A story in the *Beacon* (Don emphasized) could go a long way to help settle people's nerves and prepare for change, even legitimizing our new business. A story would do more than simply introduce the Pitsenbarger family and the concept of something different. It could set us up for success.

"He was so...enthusiastic." Ellen recalled her encounter. "He frantically took notes for questions that he said needed answering. It was more like an interrogation."

A newspaper story. Free publicity. The brewing resentment. Only five minutes in town and Ellen was already a media sensation.

And now this letter offered up Don's personal diagnosis of the small town's prevailing taste, laying out his suggested approach to attracting tourists and locals alike, balancing between those who weren't necessarily looking for something new and the more adventurous. *Welcome to the neighborhood—now here's what the town* (aka Don) *needs and doesn't need. Make it easy, but also different. A fancy night out, but not too fancy; make it affordable, but not cheap. Make it the perfect restaurant for Goldilocks living right around the corner and for her relatives visiting from the Bay Area.*

Halfway through the letter, Gerald was rolling his eyes. "Oh, my goodness, but he is such an awfully big fish in a teensy-weensy puddle!"

The presumptuousness of these strangers dictating unsolicited advice, telling us what we should and shouldn't do, listing obvious ideas (ideas Ellen and Gerald had already thought of and built into their plan).

Don went on to confess that he and his wife had at one time studied the possibilities of just such an enterprise (a restaurant), wishing themselves for a place with nice food and wine. He stressed the need for variety and yet accessibility and good, inexpensive wine. Wine was important. Wine was mentioned more than a few times.

"Well, the man's a wino, that much is certain!" Gerald snickered. He also noted that he hadn't been mentioned in the letter.

"Well, he knows me, Gerald, and you've been away." Ellen reminded him that it was she who'd waited in line at the post office and been waylaid by a hungry postmaster/journalist. "This letter, it proves our timing is perfect. Just the idea has the town buzzing." Ellen always had a positive spin.

There was also the barely veiled implication that Don was the arbiter of taste and influence in town, and perhaps without intending to, he laid down somewhat of a red line. *Please me, and it will go well.* Gerald slammed the letter down.

"This is an ultimatum! A veiled threat!" Gerald began pacing the kitchen. "'Listen to me because I know all, and you do not!' Inferring that we're invaders, shoving fancy down this provincial town's uncultured throat!"

Of course there would be a varied menu of accessible, well-prepared, and affordable dishes. Of course there would be bread, and of course there would be wine. This was a French restaurant.

Ellen was right—Don's letter confirmed that our new café was sorely needed in this epicurean wasteland. People were starving for something different, something of quality. But I could tell that Ellen and Gerald's doubts had resurfaced, as they looked at each other with worried eyes. They started thinking aloud.

Maybe they'd bitten off more than they could chew, not having anticipated the full impact on the local eco-structure or understanding the intense protectionism that existed? Motives were already being questioned, even before they'd begun. Maybe they didn't know what they were doing? Maybe this big move had been a terrible mistake. Maybe it would all blow up in their faces, after already having sacrificed so much. Maybe they were fooling themselves. This letter seemed to put them on notice.

But it was too late to turn back now; we were all in it way too deep. Gerald had finished his apprenticeship at Norman's, quit the Bay Area, and was living with us in the newly mortgaged house, now fully refurbished and outfitted for business. Our personal stuff crammed in upstairs, the restaurant and liquor license waiting to be signed, PG&E coming soon to connect a gas line to the gigantic twelve-burner stove now dominating the kitchen. The health inspector due any day now to give a final thumbs-up. Everything was moving so fast, and suddenly, this strange letter and disturbing wrinkle of possible rejection? They hadn't even decided on a name for the restaurant.

I reminded Ellen and Gerald of all the rooster dishes we'd spent so much time collecting and of our little pretend restaurant back in Berkeley. All the recipes we'd explored, the new foods we'd tried, vicarious travel to different countries, the experience of making something together as a family. Hadn't that been the whole inspiration and reason we'd ended up here in the first place, having had so much fun creating, serving, and then eating food in our little Berkeley bungalow? The whole act, a thrilling theatrical performance.

They looked at me as if I'd grown horns. Wisdom coming from my mouth when up until now, there'd only been resistance.

I acknowledged that this was indeed the real thing and a different circumstance. We lived in a very different place, we'd be making food for different people, but it could still be fun, right?

That did the trick. My parent's anxiety lightened somewhat, and there they were, smiling again. Of course, this was just stage fright. They'd been here before (both being actors), readying to walk out on stage and to be convincing. Gerald, the swashbuckling, singing pirate, and Ellen, the elegant fashion model. The electric charge of anticipation, gathering energy just before your big entrance. The fun was absolutely in the preparation of a magical experience and then a grand reveal. I felt a settling of nerves and realignment of focus.

These doubts were just ripples in the tiny pond. We would make this work. We could do this. There was a plan. They knew what they were doing. Prepare a magnificent performance and give a good show.

With a story in the paper, we could begin a dialogue with the community. They reread the letter and came to the exciting conclusion that Don was quite possibly (in his clumsy, well-intentioned way) a godsend. This wasn't a threat—it was a gift.

With someone like Don on their side, it could solve a lot of problems. With Don's encouragement (and free publicity), he and his wife would provide valuable inroads into this tight-knit community and perhaps a template for the ideal customer: skewing slightly older, appreciating something of quality, and able to pay for it. The bottom line was people were always going to be hungry and curious. Something new was just what this town needed.

But we couldn't just name the place what we'd called it when it was pretend. The Red Rooster was way too corny and dated a name. We'd outgrown that old place. This was a brand-new enterprise and needed something more appropriate, something that reflected the food, the locale, the simple ambiance of a farm kitchen, something unique and different, something French.

Pouring a glass of red wine from the open bottle, Gerald examined the label. "Beaujolais, a fun, fruity red wine!" His favorite wine and favorite phrase. Ellen and Gerald liked wine. Don liked wine. Then Gerald said it again. Ellen said it. I said it.

"Beaujolais."

"Beaujolais."

"Beaujolais." It was musical.

Ellen snatched up a piece of paper and slowly wrote in her long, curvy letters: Café Beaujolais.

CHAPTER 12

AUTHORITY OF ENIGMA

Gerald and Ellen interviewed a few people to be waiters. It couldn't be just anybody. They wanted someone with at least a modicum of experience and panache. They were asking for a lot.

I peeked through the window in the double kitchen doors as a parade of hippie moms showed up, all reeking of patchouli (or the lack of deodorant), one wearing a handwoven poncho with a baby hidden underneath, breastfeeding. Several nervous, inexperienced teenagers in dirty jeans with hastily handwritten résumés made an effort. There were a couple of older men in wrinkled suits, one with the price tag from Goodwill still hanging off the collar, the other (from where I was spying) pancaked with enough makeup for a candlelit performance. Was he trying to look younger? He had an absurdly long, twirled mustache, and a dyed toupee sliding sideways on his head—a Shakespearean bit player fallen on hard times.

After fruitless consultation with disappointing local job seekers, Gerald was apoplectic.

"What are we going to do? If this is the caliber of employee we can expect, then we're doomed before we've even begun." He opened a bottle of his precious Beaujolais. Ellen cut an apple.

They sat for a long time at table eight, going over notes. Who, among the flotsam, could be considered as a professional waiter? I felt their anxiety as the opening date approached.

We took a break from frenzied preparation and went to see an evening performance of *The Three Penny Opera*. A small theater had just opened on Main Street, the lobby painted with a bold black-and-white mural of Aubrey Beardsley characters.

Local amateur actors personified the cast of gritty Dickensian ragamuffins. Their earnest, cockeyed optimism and sometimes clumsy line delivery didn't seem like a play at all, but only slightly removed from the simple provincial life all around me. I'd seen many of these actors on the street, in the local grocery store. The play cast a spotlight on my ironic predicament, cast as miserable Oliver or poor David Copperfield in my very own dark melodrama.

The next day there was a knock on the front door. A short, neat man with a tight black Basque beret (just like Gerald's) was waiting patiently. I recognized him from the play we'd just seen and could tell immediately (even before he sat down to talk) that this man would be the Beaujolais's new waiter.

Jim Bertram was an artist with some experience working in a kitchen (he had been a bartender). Still, his qualifications were practically unnecessary, as the cool, easy manner in which he engaged my parents solidified his position. Jim presented the very ideal of the perfect waiter, and it took all of half an hour (and a few glasses of wine) for Jim to become the face of Café Beaujolais. I'm sure his beret sealed the deal.

There were a few more job applicants, and this time Jim, newly ensconced in his position, took the interviews. He hired a sweet young lady named Gayle who'd just moved to town.

We came to learn that Jim had been in Mendocino since the early 1960s and was associated with a tight-knit (but quarrelsome) group of local artists and considered somewhat of an eccentric founding father. He fit right in with our clan.

Jim painted an ongoing series of calligraphic brushwork. Modular canvases of various sizes in secret, nonverbal language resembling Sumi texts or alien hieroglyphs.

The polar opposite to that of everyone else practicing and selling in town, Jim's work stood out as unapologetically personal, an expressive pause in the constant push to paint the local landscape. All the seascapes and glamour portraits of water towers, Victorian architecture, the end-lessly reproduced caricatures of an easily recognized profile: the town of Mendocino laid out along cliff's edge.

Jim's work was unique and quiet, Zen-like, producing a sideways effect that meandered into my eye. I saw something and then, something else. Soon Jim was hanging his collected, painted runes in the foyer. He placed intentionally, one after another, squiggles and shapes leading me into the dining room. Indecipherable markings were seemingly saying something, coaxing an explanation but still mysterious, like some sort of spell. Jim presented himself as a mild-mannered artist, the perfect waiter, but I wondered if he may have also been a wizard.

One of the things I noticed about Jim's paintings (aside from his fix-ation on shapes) was the space around them. The area around squiggles worked just as hard as the shapes themselves. White space acting as a frame for the weird. I began to appreciate the composition of an implied authority all the space gave to his random squiggles. Even a chicken scratch (if it was anchored in a frame of white space) seemed somehow more important, and I couldn't help but associate Jim himself with the enigma of his work. Who was he?

My parents adored Jim, were hugely relieved at his arrival, and gave him carte blanche to build a method of service for the restaurant, and just like his paintings, he was discreet while also being quite attentive. Hovering just out of sight, he'd appear as if beckoned by a psychic teth-er, knowing what the customer wanted even before they did.

Notices began to appear in the local newspaper: staggered over a few months, small write-ups and quarter-page ads with the intriguing image of a floating, curlicue-handled soup tureen. Seeded by the newspaper, a gentle introduction to the brazen idea of another, second, restaurant. A small profile piece published a couple of weeks before the scheduled February opening revealed a juicy look inside the making of the town's new restaurant. What a scoop.

"French Café to Open in Mendocino."

Celebratory, encouraging, and remarkable in how it normalized the whole thing, painting the new restaurant as already a rousing success (instead of the untested and risky adventure it was).

On the evening of the café's grand opening, Jim coordinated the action as if he'd been tasked with herding marauding bison through a Hula-Hoop. Quietly handling the kitchen and juggling the components of service, between conversing with customers, he managed the event with a steely, understated professionalism. People came; they crowded in, sat, and ate food; it was loud, chaotic, and then…it was quiet. Jim made it all look easy.

Gerald and Ellen practically danced around the kitchen, tiptoeing at first, barely breathing; an order would come in, and they'd examine the small sheet of paper as if it might stand up and speak. A requested entrée was pulled from the refrigerator where it sat thawing. Prepared and frozen earlier, the labeled baggie was dropped into a pot of boiling water. I cut some green beans, and then Ellen cuddled them in a steamer, the entrée and vegetable ready at the same time. As the night progressed without complaint or mishap, Gerald, Ellen, and Jim began acting more like themselves. They relaxed. Gerald poured himself a glass of wine. New friends started coming into the kitchen to congratulate us but didn't stay long, as the dynamic of constant movement wasn't conducive to a casual chat. Gerald was too hyped up to pay much attention to any one person. There was a whole room full of paying customers.

Only late into the night, after all the diners had gone and we gathered around the family table, winded, somewhat in shock, staring at our blanquette of veal or herbed omelet, did we acknowledge the achievement. Our tiny team had made a miracle. Nothing broke. Nobody died.

"We did it!" Gerald raised his wineglass. He sounded almost doubtful still, at first, but then: "Huzzah! Huzzah! Bravo! Bravissimo!"

Jim drove a smart little Alpha Romeo convertible and would sometimes give me rides out to visit my friend Peter, who lived in a homemade geodesic dome in Albion. On those quick jaunts around the twisty
curvature of the coastline, Jim loved to speed up just as we'd near a
turn and hug the right edge of a cliff, almost showing off. I noticed his
Basque beret pushed back as he zipped around sharp angles, his little car
well within the lines, close to the road, never leaving the space provided
for an impulsive dash. Jim drove like he painted, like he worked a room:
quick, with a practiced, knowing style.

Buffeted by the air whipping past, our tentative conversations about
art, of high-concept theatrics, about what else I was interested in gave
me some confidence. When I'd play host out front, I noticed Jim's swift
brushstrokes flickering across the wall and could still feel the rush of air
past my head.

As Jim became more a fixture of our world, always a part of the
evening's service, sometimes showing up a bit early to hang a new set
of paintings or staying late to eat a family dinner, I began to notice the
counterpoint of his cool personality more fully. Next to Gerald, the only
other prominent adult male influence around the dinner table, Jim was
practically mute.

Like a watchful owl perched, sitting in his corner spot, Jim participated in our rowdy dinner conversation only if forced to. There was
always a lag between a question lobbed and then his thoughtful, halting
response. I could almost hear the gears and pulleys, a shuffling of papers as he made computational, hierarchal decisions as to how he might
answer. Again, the space around Jim was just as prevalent as the being
occupying it. He withheld himself. Sitting as I would in the middle of
the dinner table between Gerald and Jim, it could often seem like a
slow-motion tennis match.

"How in the hell can we make any profit if we're spending everything on advertising?"

Gerald railed about the exorbitant cost of the local paper's tiny ad space. "That little square costs about as much as a new kidney."

I took a bite of steak, played with the roasted potatoes rolling around on my plate, adjusted the intersecting fingers of haricot vert, looked at the napkin resting there on my knee. Wait for it, wait for it.

"Maybe I should wear a sandwich board and walk around town?" Jim offered quietly, with a slight smile.

Was he joking? The idea seemed absurd to me. Dignified Jim, debased, reduced to parading up and down Main Street with a cheesy Café Beaujolais sandwich board strapped over his narrow shoulders. All you'd see would be his beret and two feet.

"That's not a bad idea!" If Gerald got the subtle jab, he didn't acknowledge it. "Ellen will paint a sign, and, Eric, you can make a few rounds about town on the weekends."

That was not going to happen. I looked at Jim and caught his eye. He was kidding—why was I the only one who saw it? Then, he glanced my way again with a new look, eyes full of sympathy. *Thanks, Jim, thanks a lot.*

That sandwich board never materialized (thank god) as word of mouth and the tiny ad worked to help bring in people from up and down the coast. Café Beaujolais became an essential curiosity.

Jim was so much more than a waiter. An established figure of the local art scene (more or less a native son), he embodied the personality of Mendocino's emerging character as a hub for arts and culture, for the North Coast's allure, and now, for fine dining. Jim became as much a part of the restaurant as the food itself. His comfort level with the local populace—retirees, fellow artists, rough-and-tumble loggers, families, and hippie entrepreneurs—and the tourists all looking for relief and adventure and his ability to insinuate himself into people's personal space while simultaneously remaining an enigma created nothing short of magic. Jim was the perfect waiter, and it seemed, a warlock.

CHAPTER 13

101 NIGHTS

The restaurant Norman's gave Gerald the template for making gourmet food in bulk. Precooked, flash-frozen entrées sealed in plastic baggies, labeled, and then stacked one on top of each other in the freezer. Separate baggies of vegetables, potatoes, rice, then even smaller baggies of sauces, all labeled, frozen, stacked, ready to be thawed, then squeezed onto a plate, and voilà! A cost-effective, fast-fancy feast.

That lasted for about a month until a customer sent back word that they'd tasted the exact same dish recently, at Norman's. Gerald was mortified.

Gerald's apprenticeship at Norman's had taught him a few things about managing a kitchen, preparing food in an industrial setting, and then running a business. Still, the shortcut of preassembly, the trick of squeezing profit from reduced prep time, suddenly, was exposed as a lie.

Our restaurant, Café Beaujolais, was tiny, with only eight tables. Norman's model (deemed practical for a large, high-turnover crowd in 1969) was complete overkill and squelched any creativity from the personal touch, or for what the Beaujolais promised. There was no art in thawing out a petrified baggie marked: "12/2: Chicken Cordon Bleu." It became glaringly evident that quality food needed to be prepared in the moment, expressly for the customer, not be some glorified TV dinner.

The Norman's cookie-cutter approach wasn't going to work. Gerald needed to become a chef, not an assembly line cook cranking out one of a thousand dinners for some anonymous seat number.

Gerald's crisis of confidence gave way to catharsis, and with a leap of faith, he cast off training wheels and took on responsibility for a more honest creation. On that day, Café Beaujolais became Mendocino's fine-dining restaurant.

Gerald claimed one side of the kitchen, working out his new system between the butcher block and stove. Ellen cordoned off her opposite corner and began to bake various forms of bread and elaborate desserts. Not entirely out of the ordinary—back in Berkeley, they'd always had something on all burners—but this was at a whole new level.

Where sturdy American fare like apple pie or meatloaf had been the norm, now, steak au poivre and babas au rhum decorated our family dinner table. Everything the customers would eat, we got to try out first.

Causing a near riot of excitement whenever something we'd never heard of was presented, Gerald and Ellen built a repertoire of meals and vision of what an elegant, working French restaurant might look like.

Old *Gourmet* magazines, cookbooks, and stories about other restaurants were all my parents seemed to be reading these days. Julia Child's library on how to cook like French people and a small memoir about some old Pennsylvania fixer-upper were on the bedside table. The encyclopedia of French cuisine, *Larousse Gastronomique*, wore enough food stains to inspire an archeologist. A jolly, bald guy named James Beard (no beard, wearing a bow tie) prompted Ellen to suggest that I once again wear that little clip-on bow tie from a kindergarten photo.

"Look at what a celebrated gourmand he's become." She pointed to the latest bible open there on the blue prep table.

What was she inferring? That if I wore that ridiculous child's bow tie, I'd be more enthusiastic about deboning brisket? She was kidding herself.

Gerald particularly liked the high drama associated with horror icon Vincent Price (who also liked to cook). Bringing out a flaming, cognac-doused roast beast, Gerald would glare at us sitting around the dinner table with his wild eyes, snarling lips, a deadly knife raised high above his head, ready to stab.

"Dinner…is served!" To Gerald, fine French food was as much about the presentation and performance as the actual meal itself.

Ellen typed a list of ideas for a few small but critical structural changes to the house. What color to paint the exterior? Not the same blue as the house up the block, nothing impractical in an environment of corrosive sea air, a safe color that could complement the simple, boxy architecture of our home. They chose cream.

The picket fence out front needed to be fortified, a lattice enclosure along the side porch seemed like a good idea in the late-afternoon sun, and a lamppost in the style of New England vintage could hold the swinging business sign.

An elegant pair of heavy, wine-red velvet curtains and a coat tree in the front foyer. Franklin stove in the dining room for warmth. Striped wallpaper and placemats, candles and antique milk glass hens nesting sugar cubes on all the wooden tables.

Even more important than cosmetic details, Ellen and Gerald agonized over how much they could comfortably charge for an entrée, for a loaf of bread.

"What will induce someone to spend their hard-earned money on dinner, when they could just make it themselves, at home?"

This was a conversation we'd had many times back in Berkeley. Comparing what we ate around our dinner table to that of a restaurant meal. Not quite a fair contrast, since on any weekday, we ate like kings.

Conventional wisdom was to tediously measure the cost of all ingredients, divide by batch, calculate how many dishes were produced and then sold. But once they'd done the math, I watched color drain from my parents' faces.

"No one will buy a single entrée if we have to charge five whole dollars!" Gerald shrank at added-up results.

His frustration came from knowing just how much work went into making something special. Besides all the ingredients, time, and expertise, everything made was a unique work of art. Putting a price on something so precious was next to impossible.

"We live in a village. What villager will plunk down five bucks for a piece of fancy steak?"

It surprised me that they hadn't worked all this out long before we'd ever moved here. Maybe they'd had a discussion, but now that everything was so real, Gerald was panicking.

It seemed impossible, but it was necessary. They had to decide. They couldn't just give the food away but had to hammer out a compromise. Charge something more than a hamburger, less than a Fabergé egg. And it helped to put a number on something, legitimizing all their efforts. Bread and butter, twenty-five cents.

I was given a new project: paint the outside bathroom walls. Not just a coat of hospital white on every wall and ceiling surface but a series of illustrated murals reflecting the character of our new café. The bathrooms were located (for reasons of plumbing) down the steps from the kitchen's side porch. Any painting had to be done in the afternoon when the sun tilted into the small doors, so from twelve o'clock, I had approximately two hours before the tiny rooms would be engulfed again in shadow and arctic-like conditions.

Painting in a freezing cubicle with limited light was torture. Everything these days seemed designed as some sort of punishment, every chore meant to break me. My parents used any excuse to tie me closer to the restaurant.

I could barely feel my fingers but was determined to do this and do it well, even if my hands fell off. If I ended up with a pair of prosthetics, it would be my parents' fault. I knew I could draw, was getting better all the time, and this stupid exercise tested all my learned skills. Thinking back, that was probably precisely what my parents had intended all along.

Going pee, then washing your hands, you could follow the exploits of lusty French peasants cavorting across a flowering meadow, chasing sheep or each other, a pipe-playing country squire blowing hot air up a shepherdess's skirt, a buxom maid offering a basket of fruit to a hungry traveler.

Inspired by illustrators Alice and Martin Provensen, menus carried the theme. But instead of field workers, bewigged courtiers eyeballed each other over abundant wine, canapés, and a suckling pig.

A pervy customer once asked me if I'd ever eaten grapes off someone's chest before. Her husband swatted her with his napkin as I bussed her plate, struggling to come up with a suitable answer.

"I'm fifteen. No, I haven't." In reality, I'd certainly imagined more than grapes.

Ellen's hand-painted sign with the Beaujolais's signature curlicue-handled soup tureen was hung on the lamppost out front, a lit box attached to the fence displaying her delicate, calligraphic menu.

Every day was another chance for her to practice the art. If only she could keep all the letters in alignment, instead of them sliding to the right, mashing listed desserts (labored over in the kitchen) down into tiny insignificance underneath.

The nearby Noyo Wharf in Fort Bragg provided fresh fish straight from the ocean. An independent butcher in Cleon (north of Fort Bragg) always had whatever cut of meat Gerald needed. Abundant herbs and vegetables either from the garden out back or from any number of local farms, exotic cheeses sent from The Cheese Board in Berkeley. Most all the produce was gathered nearby, and what couldn't be found within a short driving distance up or down the coast was delivered from the Bay Area.

It was a given that Freed, Teller & Freed, the venerable coffee roaster in San Francisco (and a progenitor of Starbucks), would make a special delivery of French roast once a week. Our kitchen wouldn't be fully operational unless there was a Chemex of hot coffee on the stove.

Because the restaurant had been named Café Beaujolais, the red wine itself was featured as vin ordinaire, a bottle displayed as objet d'art in the foyer. Boxes were hoarded like Aladdin's treasure in the cool space underneath the back porch.

One of the reasons Gerald and Ellen had ultimately chosen Mendocino (besides the rustic charm of the town itself) was its proximity to several vineyards. Anticipating the potential of continued growth and a blossoming culture of gourmet sensibilities, they had the idea for the café to position itself as an advocate of good taste and champion of a wholly unique, local aesthetic. This vision proved to be prophetic.

One day, we kids took a trip with Gerald over the mountains inland to explore a new winery he'd discovered. In the sprawling, warm Redwood Valley, Fetzer Vineyards was a Hopperesque rolling landmass of gnarled vines surrounding a huge barn. They also had collie dogs. Gerald loved the Cabernet he tasted and became one of their first industry contracts, and we kids got a new puppy.

A bit closer to home, in Philo, Gerald and I visited another new vintner, whose name sounded, to me, like someone shushing you up. Husch vineyards were run by a young couple who fed us our favorite food, apples and cheese, on a picnic table while also serving us their first bottle of Pinot Noir.

Most all the local vineyards made it onto the Beaujolais wine list, complementing French, Spanish, and Italian wines, and Gerald was so proud to have curated his collection from newly available, local fields and new connections. Paired with choice meals, the small but potent list gave the Beaujolais an offering that signaled quality. Customers were intrigued and became better educated, and we kids snuck more than a few bottles from their wooden boxes for our own exclusive happy hour parties.

A short time after the menu had evolved into the dual offering of either a la carte or table d' hôte dinners, we got word that a restaurant critic had paid a visit, actually more than one, and always with friends. Gerald and Ellen had never known until it was requested that Café Beaujolais be included in a new regional restaurant guide.

Before Zagat's, *101 Nights in California* was a self-published venture promoting eclectic and small boutique restaurants in California. With an emphasis on owner-operated, fresh, local produce, and the personal touch, Café Beaujolais was the only restaurant from Mendocino included, the only place from the entire North Coast.

There it was, a lovely hand-drawn portrait of our little house next to a sample menu. This was real success! With only our genuine efforts, and surprisingly powerful word-of-mouth advertising, we'd been noticed. There'd been no money involved, only an enthusiastic industry endorsement. With that one small page, that simple drawing of our home, of Café Beaujolais reaching out from beyond quiet Ukiah Street, Gerald and Ellen were again both simultaneously thrilled and challenged. We'd arrived, and now, we were also exposed. We'd be paid more attention to, and we'd be judged. Girding themselves for the onslaught of tourists, they knew it would be hard work from now on. They imagined that with all the new popularity, it was both a blessing and a curse.

CHAPTER 14

AMERICAN GOTHIC

The café had been open for about a year, serving curious customers convivial French food with a pared-down, rough-around-the-edges aesthetic. Rustic dishes prepared with a bit of homespun joie de vivre, built just like the town itself.

Greeted by the cheerful Jules Chéret poster of a Parisian flower girl, the short foyer beckoned diners forward to the arched stage entrance. Marked by the heavy, red velvet curtains, the dining room was an understated formality of dusty pink–striped wallpaper and antique rosette chandeliers revealing the aura of contented well-being. Vintage prints of violets and a wildflower-strewn field hung in corners, subtle windows, reminders of the innocent, natural world left outside. Wooden floorboards creaked appreciatively under scroll-back chairs. The polished wainscoting gently encircled, paring the cherrywood frames of violets, of fields, of the tall windows themselves and the demure wooden mantle clock pointing its tiny bronze hands to five thirty, showtime.

People sat at comfortable, round wooden tables, warmed by the humble, squat Franklin stove and enjoying a leisurely two-hour prix fix dinner, or even a single bowl of soup. Serving themselves from the stoneware tureen. A slice of fresh bread, a nibble of pâté, a sip of local or imported wine. Savor chocolate broyage, filtered coffee, port, the soundtrack of a string quartet soothing. A typical experience at Café Beaujolais was to be transported into a bohemian utopia.

There was no dress code (we lived in the country), but people spruced up their chinos and jersey knits with a jacket or earrings. Even the hippie family splurging on a birthday celebration brushed their long hair and coordinated leather vests with prairie dresses. Kids wore shoes.

One morning, after I'd cleaned the ash from the dining room stove and arranged a new collection of cut logs, ready for the evening's service, the hidden bronze key to wind the mantle clock had pinched my skin. I'd looked at the soot, splinters, pitch, and some dried blood painting my hands. These were the hands of a servant.

Gerald and Ellen were occupied in the kitchen, crafting edible treasure for hungry tourists; my sisters were off somewhere riding horses with friends. I puttered around the house, feeling the aged wood breathe, my dirty hands tracing where turn-of-the-century carpenters had leveled, or missed. There was something so calming about standing silently out in the foyer, invisible in a corner, partially hidden by drapes, watching movement out there on the street. I contemplated my new life, of what had become…normal. This restaurant was my home. Even though I stood still out here, the noise and activity inside my head required me to act, to do something. Standing still seemed foreign. Running away was always an option, I supposed, but where would I go?

Through the set of long windows, I observed a raven scrutinize a leaf as it meandered along, tossed down the street by an unseen breeze. If I had wings (like that raven) I'd fly somewhere, anywhere, else. Flying was my favorite fantasy.

But there was nowhere for me to go. This was my home, and I didn't have wings. We lived upstairs. As evening diners enjoyed their pâté and port at polished round tables, our little family's stuff hung nestled in the upstairs rooms above them. I had records, art supplies, and books, the girls their clothes, sewing stuff, and jewelry; our parents shared a closet. Ellen and Gerald didn't need much in the way of a wardrobe to work in the kitchen; they always wore the same things.

The cushion of velvet silence in the foyer confirmed my morning success. There was nothing more to do; chores were done. I was just me again. Not Gerald's extra pair of arms and legs. Time stood still.

I looked at my cracked, bent hands, old before their time, like those of a witch, the crooked branches of a tree. Bony and stained by the morning's dirty jobs, the blood just a shade lighter than the soot. Besides cleaning up, cutting wood for tonight's service, I'd also successfully, efficiently, almost casually become a murderer. Huddled, hiding in the corner among the drapes, I could still hear Gerald's encouragement.

"It's not hard at all—now you try!"

He pointed to Wendy, the fat red hen pecking at my feet. He wanted me to kill her.

We had a motley collection of weird-looking chickens and ducks roaming the backyard, all of them on a constant hunt for snails, worms, any bug caught resting.

At night the chickens slept in the pen we fixed up, the ducks gathering around the little streamed well. It was Gerald's intention to raise the chickens for the restaurant and to somewhat re-create his childhood on a farm in Iowa. "There're certainly enough snails out here to feed a flock of chickens." He'd indicated the jungle now regrown all around. The newly straightened and cleaned-out coop with a fence of chicken wire housed the family of Rhode Island Reds. They'd lay eggs for omelets and then give their lives for whatever ornate recipe Gerald had in mind.

Abigayle already lay dead there on the ground, and now Gerald wanted me to follow his example. Grab Wendy by the head and swing her around like a rag doll, breaking her neck. We'd eat both of them for dinner tonight. This was a practice run.

He'd done it quickly as if it were easy, an annoyance, and he was impatient for me to "get on with it." But I balked. It was not easy! Aside from stepping on an ant, I'd never killed anything before.

"You eat chicken all the time!" he exclaimed. "Chicken's your favorite food. Where do you think chicken comes from anyway, the grocery store?"

Wendy came around for another go at the patch of ground near me, and Gerald grabbed her squawking then handed her over.

Holding her brick-red feathers tightly, my left hand closed around her head, and with a quick swing up and around, around, and around, I could feel the little snap, and she went limp. Now we had two dead chickens for dinner.

"There you go, Eric." Gerald complimented my swing as efficient and quick. "Got the job done."

He showed me how to pluck all those beautiful red feathers from Wendy's dead body, filling up a burlap sack. Two fat, naked birds lay on the butcher block.

"Now let's wash and then gut them." Gerald was enthused. I worried that my two sisters would be traumatized when they learned that two of our friends had become tonight's dinner. I never told them.

Watching that curled leaf slowly roll down the street now, I was not sure how I felt. One minute I was cutting wood, the next, swinging chickens. Everything had changed so fast. I was not a city kid anymore.

The crow flew off, the leaf forgotten, as two men walked up to the front door. They probably wanted to make a reservation.

"Hello, we'd like to talk to your parents if we could. We're from *National Geographic* magazine, doing a story about Mendocino. We'd like to include you in the article." One guy had several cameras hanging around his neck, and the other held a tape recorder.

I brought the two men through the dining room, got my parents' attention, and then let them talk. This was so cool! With the café up and running, now we'd be introduced to the world in a profile of this quaint little Victorian village, as a part of the environment. My parents might become famous, the café recognized as unique. I already knew it was special—I'd never been anywhere else like it, and I lived there.

Standing alone, looking around the room, I felt, as I always did, as if I were in three places at once. The quiet present of this morning, the Victorian past that still surrounded me, and the inexorable current pulling me toward the future. In a few hours, all these empty tables would have people crowding around; the logs I'd just arranged would be burning in the stove. I'd have to cut more tomorrow. I'd wash my hands of soot and blood. I'd go to junior high on Monday. There would be a movie at the Art Center next weekend. I'd eat chicken tonight (if it was offered). I'd listen to Sweet Baby James Taylor up in my room later. There was a gallery down on Main Street that would serve wine and cheese for the opening of my premiere exhibition of paintings in a few years. I'd make a million dollars and move to New York, the *National Geographic* magazine article encouraging more people to come to visit Mendocino, to eat at the Beaujolais, our town becoming a glamorous location for sophisticated vacationers.

I projected myself into an imagined, desired future, peppered with logical outcomes, grand fantasy, and possible results. Manifesting myself against what I saw around me, also knowing that everything always changed. So much had changed already.

The next day the photographer came back to hang out with us for a couple of hours. The girls were all spruced up in their fancy, homemade dresses, and we gathered together out in the foyer.

"The light's perfect out here," the photographer said. The late-morning sun, filtered by high fog through thick, lead-glass windows, cast our family in a diffuse fairy glow.

He got us all arranged like one of those old, formal, turn-of-the-century daguerreotype portraits. Gerald in the middle, looking very much like Henry the Eighth, comfortable on his throne. He has a satisfied smile, a glint in his eye. Greta sits at his feet, looking hopeful, exuberant. Kristin stands next to him, her small hand gripping the arm of the carved rocking chair. She seems angry, her eyes even menacing. Staring at the camera, daring the photographer to go ahead, take another shot. Ellen and I stand behind with our arms folded, protective of fragile spirits. Ellen looks bone-tired, distracted, her two long, gray braids hanging limp, her mind wandering. And there's me with that slight, questioning, flirtatious upturn of a thin-lipped smile on my face, the upside-down mop of hair growing like a plant, a tilted head that says: "I'm a model…but what am I selling?"

The portrait of a frontier family in the new world.

CHAPTER 15

GLAZED PERFECTION

I was addicted to bread. I'd become a breadaholic, and Ellen was unwittingly responsible. She enabled me by making the very best bread I'd ever tasted. Light years beyond Wonder Bread, even better than the famed sourdough from Fisherman's Wharf in San Francisco.

For the café, she baked hundreds of perfect little loaves, at least thirty a day. You could build a house from all the bread that came out of that oven. Ellen was a one-woman factory. Always tired and complaining of sore arms as she muscled big bowls of dough, kneading by hand, grappling with hunks, stretching, pulling, and pounding. She arm-wrestled like a champ and was an impenetrable wall of superhuman strength when occasionally she'd step between Greta and me, keeping us well apart to circumvent a murder.

Each table got its own fresh warm loaf of bread wrapped in a cloth napkin, presented on a little board along with a cute round of unsalted sweet butter molded into a thistle design. It was the first act once customers had ordered and were settling in, and when it was brought to the table, almost automatically, people would clap or squeal with delight. It was like getting a birthday surprise.

When little Kristin felt like helping (or just wanted to spend precious time with Ellen), they'd sit together at the blue table softening up the butter, then pushing gobs of it with tiny paddle-like knives into the small wooden molds.

After laying them all out in a row on a wax paper–lined tray, they'd then put the whole thing on a lower shelf of the refrigerator to keep cold, brought out to reach room temperature before serving.

Kristin took great pride in performing this small but essential detail, and it was just the right task for a little girl, we thought. We did also marvel at her intense concentration. You didn't disturb her while she was creating small butter thistles. I'd lean in to offer a hand, but she'd yelp and say: "Go away!"

She owned this job. Careful and precise, it was as if she were handling something extremely dangerous. Ellen and I exchanged many a glance over her shoulder while she handcrafted each one, paddling volatile, radioactive butter with pincer-like precision.

Ellen was always working and slept fitfully. She started alone early every morning, the first rays of the sun crisscrossing the kitchen to illuminate her makeshift baking pantry. She hovered like a shaman ensconced in her sanctum, surrounded by ceremonial tools. Bunches of dried herbs. Mixing spoons and ladles. Found or repurposed sticks and spatulas hanging on hooks, sprouting from jars, or doing double duty as bookmarks. Her mixing bowl ready, the cutting board clean, the family of bread pans oiled, lined up and ready, she would gather herself and begin the daylong process, which lasted until the café closed at ten, four days a week. Even on Sunday through Tuesday, our three days off, there was always something to do, something that had been put off.

But the mornings were sacred, and her ritual became the silent alarm for us kids upstairs. We'd be compelled to rise and follow the smell of the toast narcotic (still in our pjs) down to the kitchen and gather like junkies around the blue table. Ellen would greet us with hugs and kisses and our very own loaf of bread and a small bowl of honey butter she'd whipped up, and maybe there'd even be fresh strawberries she'd handpicked from the garden and then sprinkled with sugar.

Creamy-soft white bread, almost like cake with glistening tan skin that Ellen had brushed with clarified butter. She called it glazing. I worried on her behalf that it was a detail lost on anyone but her but was nevertheless impressed. Ellen always went that extra bit to achieve perfection. Perfect little loaves of bread, and I could have inhaled every one. The more I ate, the more I wanted; there was never enough. After I'd wolfed mine down, I'd look over at my two sisters chewing more slowly and feel my temper rise. Were they doing it on purpose? It was torture, and I'd have to get up, walk away, and calm myself. If they hadn't been my sisters, or so cute, I might have stolen their bread, maybe even killed to get it.

I could not fully wake up in the morning without my loaf of bread, and the world would tilt precariously off its axis when Ellen was so preoccupied as to forgo our morning observance. A dark crabbiness colored those days. Everything would be off, and it would all point to not having our individual loaves, the first act of the day. The hot bread, honey butter, and special ingredient of Ellen's loving attention were all intertwined. As the restaurant got busier, she was forced to spend less time with us kids and every waking moment, instead, prepare for the wave of business that was becoming the norm. There were fewer loaves of bread and more demands on our involvement. Instead of a morning greeting, our personalized loaf with requisite honey butter, we were more than likely woken up with the order to get firewood or help her mix a thousand eggs with a barrel of flour. The lightness of being that permeated our morning kitchen was all but snuffed out, and with success, came resentment.

At work, Ellen was a surgeon in an operations theater. She could reach up without breaking concentration, grab a ladle or proper-size container, and complete the procedure. If there had been a time-delay camera mounted by the side door, the home movie would reveal Ellen's stick-straight posture, eyes fixed to the mixing bowl, hair pulled back in a tight ballet bun with wild Shiva arms dancing all around. A human whisk.

Ellen's bread was the staple, the staff of life, that began our day and the experience of each diner at the café. The elegant finish was a dessert the likes of which had never been seen outside of a Parisian bakery, certainly not here in sleepy little Mendocino. Exotic confections with weird names like gateau, broyage, genoise, soufflé and sorbet, merengue, and mousse. Ellen produced an extraordinary assortment of pastries as well as all that bread. There was always something either going in or coming out of the oven. She never stopped, hardly ever slowed down. She was always spattered with chocolate, dusted with flour, or sticky with molasses. I'd sometimes wet a rag and slowly wipe off her fingers, taking my time so she could just breathe and we might stand there together quietly for a moment.

The café's patisserie became a moneymaker in the lean winter months when fewer tourists made the trip. The glass display shelves in the dining room were piled with big rounds of peasant bread, gathered kipfel crescents, or individual cups of chocolate mousse, and the hungry locals stormed in every morning when I unlocked the door at ten, literally emptying the larder. We were as busy as the post office.

With every new delectable Ellen concocted, we kids right away elected ourselves as official tasters, making sure that inferior product was not served, and through this process, chocolate mousse, quickly became a favorite. Like super-rich pudding, with the slight aftertaste of rum, amaretto, or coffee, it was a sweet tickle to be eating something chocolate that also sounded like something hairy.

Two thumbs-up every time, and we, along with the diners, became spoiled rotten. Ellen couldn't keep up with the demand for chocolate mousse. Always requested, demanded for special events; there was a backup bowl wrapped and waiting somewhere. I never found it, but the stock of individual cups kept mysteriously disappearing.

Lately, Ellen had been experimenting with a strange deviation from the clean, cakelike loaves that so far had been the required start to a meal. Whole wheat entered the vernacular. White bread turned into brown. The taste was something entirely different, and we kids weren't at all sure we liked it. It had a dark, almost nutty flavor. Our critical opinion actually gave Ellen and Gerald pause. Would the customers accept or reject these new loaves?

Fears were needless, though, as whole wheat bread quickly became the popular choice. My poor little cake loaves were less frequently seen in the kitchen, but I, along with the general population, grew to crave more and more whole wheat on little breadboards along with a tab of sweet butter and sometimes orange marmalade.

Ellen put wheat "berries" in, laced her brown loaves with millet and cornmeal, even went ahead and sometimes dumped in chopped-up nuts. She went crazy with whole wheat, but always, always the glazing. Whereas Julia Child's *Mastering the Art of French Cooking* had been permanently propped open, Ellen's new bible, *The Tassajara Bread Book*, now rested in Julia's place next to the mixing bowl, the position of honor. Julia took a break while the whole wheat–colored Tassajara book became smudged and bent with constant use.

On one gloomy afternoon, with rain clouds threatening and a cold winter wind blowing people off the streets to huddle near their stoves, in the café's kitchen, warm and humming with activity, there was another storm brewing. Ellen and Gerald were well into prep for the evening's service. Gerald had almost finished with his last-minute detailing and was enjoying a glass of wine.

But Ellen still had miles to go. The first batch of bread was done, gathered in a bin under the prep table. But another whole batch of bread still needed to be baked. The second and third seating would go without if she didn't pull it together in time.

It had taken her since early morning, all day until now, around three in the afternoon, to finish this first push. She was running late, and the shame of it vexed her. She'd been tired when she started with the sun; she was tired now and would be tired when she began again tomorrow, around five. Her resolve was weakening, her body letting her down, her goal of perfection and preparedness faltering. The anticipation of a busy night still ahead, her mood turned brittle, and a panic set in. How fast could she push this boulder uphill?

There was nothing to do but speed ahead; there would be bread on those tables if it killed her! Sipping cold tea, gathering strength, she washed all the bread pans and set herself to the job. She'd done this a hundred times before, and there was almost a thrill in the panic. It was routine at this point.

The game was: "Will I make it? Will there be perfect bread for every customer, and will yet another evening pass into history without anyone knowing of the struggle, to begin all over again when the sun rises? Or will this be the day that I have a nervous breakdown and run foamy mouthed through the dining room, right out the front door, and off the cliff?"

A last gulp of tea, and her second, third, or fourth wind kicking in, she set to work. Mixing bowl ready, tools clean, clicking into automatic, she was a machine. She would make it work like she always did. She didn't need the recipe, didn't need a break; she just needed two hours.

But to her dismay, as she began measuring out flour and scraped bottom, it was painfully evident that there wouldn't be enough flour to complete a dozen loaves, let alone three. Suddenly, everything would now have to stop while she made a quick dash to the store. We kids were still in school; otherwise, one of us certainly would have been pressed into making the emergency run. Gerald had disappeared. The lucky man was napping.

There was no getting around it; she needed flour and was going to have to go to the store herself. Shifting gears, she ripped off her apron and threw on a jacket. A scrawled note weighted down with the butter mold on the prep table dusted with flour; she flew out the door and into what was turning into a gully washer of a winter storm.

If she could fly like Mary Poppins, she would have, but her umbrella barely kept the rain off. It was raining so hard, pushed in every direction by gale winds right past flimsy umbrellas and completely through jackets. When Ellen made it back home, she was a dripping, miserable, drowned rat, soaked to the bone. Her cheap umbrella turned inside out halfway there, and she'd run back again through blinding rain. The only thing left dry was the small swaddling bag of flour clutched under her jacket.

Towel to her face and hair, wet shoes kicked off by the door, she put on dry clothes and once again set to work, now in bare feet. For some reason, she couldn't find any pair other than the sneakers she'd worn to the store. As she'd done so many times before with wet things (usually for us kids), she quickly wrapped the sneakers in newspaper and put them on the lower shelf of the oven to dry. The oven was on a low setting, waiting for bread, and the shoes would be dry in a few moments. She could resume her hurried mixing, and soon enough, she'd have toasty, comfy sneakers as a reward for this down-to-the-wire insanity.

When she had barely begun, flour measured and dumped into the bowl of risen yeast and a pinch of salt, the lights went out. Somewhere a power line had fallen, and the café kitchen went suddenly dark. The gas ovens luckily were still going, and she could still get the bread baked. Time was ticking.

Unfortunately, as the new batch of bread finally went into the oven, now turned up to baking temperature, Ellen's precious sneakers were left forgotten inside.

When I got home from school and unlaced wet boots on the porch, it wasn't warm, herby, toasty bread-baking smells that greeted me. All the doors and windows were thrown open. Ellen was crying, Gerald fuming. Our lovely, warm kitchen was cold and dark, reeked of a junkyard, smelled just like the dump. Someone had burned a rubber tire in here!

It was perhaps fortunate that because of the storm, many people canceled their reservations, some just not showing up. There would be plenty of bread, after all. The mysterious odor of burnt rubber was cloaked somewhat by more expected smells like chicken, beef, and coffee. Cedarwood in the fireplace helped. The lights came back on just in time, and those few who showed up were treated to perfect little glazed loaves of bread and the usual simple elegance of dinner at the café. It was a quiet, subdued evening, the wild storm having passed and run out to sea.

A new work of folk art had presented itself: an oven rack with liquified, melted rubber sneakers running throughout. Kind of beautiful, its random, hardened drip of rubber, glazed pink, smooth. Laces intact, they clearly used to be shoes, but now, they were something more. The irony was a testament to Ellen's tenuous relationship with perfection. Perfection was always achieved, but not without a few sacrifices.

CHAPTER 16

MAGICAL MYSTERY TOUR

I feel a tiny bit guilty leaving the restaurant and my parents, but also relieved, even jubilant. We were going to the river!

Our house was one of the first stops, and when Shepard Brother arrived in his rattling step van, we all grabbed our stuff and ran. A towel, fancy snacks from the café, maybe a tape deck, and the all-important stash bag.

Who knew what the van was originally used for; Shepard had painted it with all sorts of wild graffiti-like images, splashes of color and a few stuck-on flourishes. Now, it was a party on wheels. Any time I saw his van drive by (or parked on the street), I immediately got all the vibes. For me, it was a magic carpet ride to and from the woods and river to that special place where only us kids existed.

"It's like the *Magical Mystery Tour*," I offered. That stuck, the Beatles reference perfect. Picking folks up, passing joints around, we ventured toward the mystical spot at the end of the road. Primed and ready for a day spent lounging butt-naked, floating in our own idyllic sanctuary, the designated spot at the end of a long dirt road the perfect getaway: removed from the world, work, school, any responsibility, parents, the foggy coast, from time itself. Where we were going didn't have many rules or even a deadline; we could stay out here all day long if we wanted, forced to leave only when the sun finally receded behind the curtain of trees. Even on those rare occasions when we lingered past twilight, we knew the paths by heart, could recognize leaning tree limbs, the shadow of the big van waiting to take us home.

Our friends from school, Sean and Annie, siblings Kelly, Michael, and Sean. Meadow, Shannon, and Lynka, Jeannie and her brother Craig. All were waiting on their doorstep or at the end of their dirt road. With my two sisters and me, that was thirteen kids all piled in, hanging onto straps, lounging in the back, straddling the motor casing upfront, or leaning out the open passenger door.

Someone put in the tape of local band Cat Mother. Cued to our favorite song, theme music for this magical moment, all of us singing along, bouncing in rhythm with the riffing guitar and van.

"Well, you can smoke it, you can eat it, you can mix it with your beer. You can hang it on the wall, and you can hang it in your ear..."

Excitement rose as I watched the gnarly scrub of manzanita and moss whisk by, banks of azalea and rhododendrons. The gray cast of morning fog began to lift, then brighten and finally disappear. The glorious sun dappled the narrow two-lane road beginning to curve now, descending down into the Woodlands campground, the road narrowing even farther, now dirt. The trees were thick shafts of bright sunlight directing our way.

The farther from the coast and into the woods, away from the various dramas of home, even as the fuzz of pot and music jangles, guilt still tugged at me. Anything could be happening back at the café, but I was out here having fun. Just last night, Ellen had stepped outside to swing newly washed lettuce in the strainer, her movement both shaking off the water and frightening a skunk on the back porch. She'd spent an hour soaking in the bathtub full of tomato juice while Gerald grumbled about falling behind. There'd been nothing we could do, just keep going. Ellen had been so miserable, Gerald extra cranky. *Drive faster, Shepard!*

He steered the van around ruts (or not), bouncing and swerving. Us kids yelping, laughing, singing, hanging on for dear life. Here was the fallen tree that stopped all traffic, and Shepard pulled over in a cloud of dust. I could smell the warm pine needles and water. Now we were just a short walk away from our perfect little patch of paradise.

We didn't even call it skinny-dipping because to swim without a bathing suit was expected, was normal. Who cared? We relished the freedom from convention and labels in the nakedness of our free spirits. We were born again, brand-new, blithely dismissing anybody's insecurity or shame. There was nothing to be ashamed of. We were all the same, uniquely different, but also matter-of-factly, fundamentally all the same.

I looked at the girls' breasts and simply took note. It was the boys' dangling penises that I had to be careful and not stare at for too long. I'd developed a practiced mental distancing that had become second nature. It helped to know that none of the boys were remotely interested in me. It was not a big deal anyway; we were all just kids.

With the motor and tunes turned off, the wild bouncing ended, a serene quiet enveloped us. Then: blue jays warned of intruders, we laughed as we all leaped out and began our short march to the preferred spot: Lillie's, just down the path.

My secret wish was that no one else would be there, that we'd made it out early enough, that this special place would be all ours without any controversy, without any need to share or to be shy. That was usually the case; only occasionally we'd disrupt a couple of teenagers drinking beer or making out. When our happy group arrived, towels were thrown down, and clothes were ripped off, and it became obvious. This was our beach.

I knew next to nothing about our chaperone Shepard Brother except that he seemed to have a lot of free time to hang out with us kids, he was a good driver, he had a guitar, and he wasn't a perv. Long, brown hair, a handlebar mustache, jeans, boots, and a leather belt (the generic uniform of a hippie dude), he reminded me of the student teachers back in the Bay Area, wrangling all of us wild children. He reminded me of Jesús.

Shepard was a jovial big brother with endless amounts of energy to spare for our crew of ragamuffin kids. Available and present (but also simply just hovering in the background of my experience), he and his colorful van were synonymous. They were the same being.

After a day spent in various languid states within the gentle caress of nature, we begrudgingly trundled back into town. The sting and charge of a day's vitamin D tingling our blood, our skin bronzed and taut, the dust of sand and road clinging, the chill of fog the only thing compelling us to put our shirts back on. It was only then that I once again anticipated what disaster might have happened back at home while I lazed the day away.

A long, hot shower in the newly tinged tomato-red tub was the ultimate luxury, a civilized equivalent to throwing my naked body in the river—and it was a reminder that life was all too real.

If some responsibility didn't distract, maybe we could go back out there tomorrow? Not wanting to be left behind, I found it a tough decision even if I was deep-fried, even if I knew there might be trouble on the horizon. The water so cool, the air sweet, the palpable quiet, trees and birds and solace of friends so healing. The euphoria of being included and delivered into an easy remove seemed almost criminal. This couldn't last. It was too much fun.

CHAPTER 17

ROCK SOUP

The big, bubbling pot of colorful, fragrant veggies parked on the back stove burner gave weight and solace to the kitchen. An anchor for the eye, the large stainless-steel pot was always hot, with a curl of steam issuing forth like a thermal spring. Primordial and constant, the delicious subliminal message of security and comfort permeated our late mornings and seemed to warm up whatever else was happening.

We kids could tell what time it was by what smells were lingering. For instance, the delicate tang of leeks announced that it was not only soup au pistou (our favorite) but that it was ten o'clock-ish, and from that point on, the game was afoot and preparation for the café's evening performance had begun in earnest. A quiet, serene sense of calm and well-being permeated the house. We knew that our parents' burden and the general mood had been made significantly lighter. Things were well in hand, and it would be smooth sailing into the long day.

Knowing that once in the pot, all those vegetables just cooked themselves, we could walk away to tackle other, more involved, tasks, and there were always other tasks. We all had sets of chores, as well as the surprise lists and dreaded blurted demands that came from harried parents as they took on the mantles of chef and pastry cook. But for now, the light-green flavor of our morning kitchen broadcasted a new day, sweet and light and still quivering with potential. Soup was an essential start to the meal, and this big pot full of a cheerful, colorful first course advertised a good time, satisfaction guaranteed—a propitious place to begin.

Many other dividends radiated from the back burner. The fact that I'd taken any interest at all in helping out without having been coerced, threatened, or blackmailed set in motion a ripple effect. On weekends especially, home from school, when my two extra hands were available, I was put in charge of the opening act. Soup preparation gave rise to a growing sense of camaraderie and confidence, and confidence was something I sorely needed.

Entrenched in a teenager's low self-esteem, skulking about with a mass of oily hair sprouting from my head like a curly mushroom, a battlefield of zits warring for space across my face and arms that seemed too long and to have grown extra joints, I was a monster. Stretched tall and gaunt, I wore oversize sweatshirts to camouflage the skeleton rattling within and squirmed with despair over the loss of my former, more manageable self, who'd almost overnight transformed into a sullen, ill-tempered ostrich.

Surmounting the constant fear of failure was itself a Herculean act. Patience for new ideas or challenges, in general, remained shallow, and if the project didn't produce almost instantaneous gratification, an obvious result or praise, it became toxic.

Brittle, irritable, and petulant, protective of my fragile hold on security and excuses not to try, I was my own worst enemy, until the miracle of making soup for the restaurant became an unexpected way in.

The routine adventure of collecting all the needed vegetables and herbs from the backyard garden, however, involved first facing down an ugly personal demon. It was a test of willpower and patience, and just expending the effort of getting my hands dirty was enough to tempt the beast.

In the raw, uncomfortable slog through mud and cold, thorny bushes and messy wilds of the backyard garden, my growling discontent seemed to grow into full-blown Beelzebub possession. I stomped around in a whorl of hurt, spinning drastic fantasies of a trapped alien, or of a doomed jungle adventure, where intrepid explorer Michael Rockefeller lost his way in the strangling primordial forest, to then be captured and eaten by cannibals.

I perpetuated similar horrors against poor, helpless carrots. Ripping them out of their beds by their leafy green heads, kicking dirt lumps of potatoes from the ground, and then cursing them for scattering (as I then had to bend over and pick them all up). Out here alone in the yard, I ranted and railed. Snatching handfuls of silver thyme, ripping off hunks of basil, tearing up sprouted leeks, yanking green beans from tangled vines, and finally, grabbing at ripe tomatoes from within the protective cage where they tried to hide.

Along with the pile of looted vegetables, I wrangled the spiteful and cantankerous creature who had come to inhabit my body. And by the time I made it back from my bloody little safari, I was far less grumpy, and I was more surprised than anyone when eventually, after many attempts, I became quite good at the job. The results of my jungle exorcism blossomed into a restaurant staple.

It was more than vegetables that received a makeover; my whole attitude changed as I grasped cause and effect. I began to look again at my place within the scheme of things, spinning a new analogy from my rough, garden harvest and recalling an old story of how, in hard times, an impoverished community came together and donated what they had to the family soup pot. Well, I had a family, I had a soup pot, and these were indeed hard times, at least for me.

Washing everything in the sink, then arranging the pillaged trove of fresh vegetables on a prep table, the palette of cheery, primary colors together looked like a collected, fallen rainbow, and I couldn't help but appreciate their simple, innocent, and ornamental beauty. Pristine and glistening tomatoes, scrubbed, dayglow-orange carrots, happy little rock potatoes with their skins rubbed off in places to reveal tender tan lines, every green bean a character in my personal melodrama. I married all these innocent vegetables together, all newly clean, and now ready to be sacrificed to the hissing soup cauldron.

I learned by doing it over, and over, and over again. Practicing the art of efficient and correct preparation became a point of pride and calming meditation of sorts. Marshaling focus, following basic instructions, and building a pattern, I learned how to get better at something and, in turn, moved the rest of my experience forward as well.

Along with all the veggies thrown into that pot, the beans and herbs, water, and pinch of salt, all my wants and worries, imagined dramas and failed attempts, the rocks, twigs and bugs, pints of blood, chopped-off fingers, the eye of newt and toe of frog, lizard's leg, and owlet's wing, it all got mixed in, stirred up, transforming into something else. My witch's brew of ugly and nutritious ingredients became something amazing. A hearty meal in itself. I learned how to make the perfect soup au pistou.

At the time, I was too dumb to grasp what was happening, of how everything was connected. Still, literally from the ground up, from con-cocting and then feasting on my particular version of rock soup, I be-came the caretaker of my own success. I joined the family business instead of fighting it.

CHAPTER 18

CHARLOTTE'S HANDS

She had such perfect, petite, soft, little girl hands. Perfect for holding with tender care as we walked around town and ideal for cupping next to my face, so I could be closer to heaven. Pillowy soft little cherub hands, like resting on a cloud, and Charlotte's hands were also perfect for pressing down onto a sheet of stiff cardboard.

Ellen had a new recipe for lady's fingers and came up with the idea of turning my Charlotte's perfect, graceful little doll hands into dessert. The cardboard kept the shape of her digits, and Ellen could use the pattern as a stencil for cutting out perfect Charlotte's Hands to be baked, decorated, and then devoured.

We experimented with several finishing strokes, implemented just before presentation to customers. First, Ellen placed a large doily over each hand and applied a light sprinkle of powdered sugar, instantly transforming each print into an elegant Victorian glove. Down our short assembly line, pale-pink buttercream frosting was piped onto each fingertip and a seasonal bracelet or elegant ring of ripe raspberries, baby strawberries, or blueberries (all from the backyard garden) were individually placed in quickly improvised repeated patterns. If there was an abundance of berries, Charlotte's Hands came enshrined within an oval berry frame.

There was also the weird sideshow quality of Charlotte's Hands. Served on a laboratory-white plate, each dainty, disembodied pastry hand had a mummified quality. Powdered, cracked meringue preserved under the dust of sugar. A Victorian doll's gloved hand recently excavated. It was Ripley's Believe It or Not, Marcel Duchamp's Dada dessert. Featured with a small illustration on the evening's menu tacked out front and requested whenever it wasn't, Charlotte's Hands became a favorite, and because she had supplied the template, helping to cut out, decorate, and then eat plenty of broken "fingers," and because she was my girlfriend, she became a member of our family.

The rest of Char, however, was not quite so dainty. At fifteen, she was already a woman, a fully formed blond bombshell, and the same soft little hands that inspired cookies, the same hands I caressed with fondness, I also found, to my delight, were great for all manner of not-so-delicate tasks.

We'd stand about the kitchen innocently cuddling, carrying on a conversation with Ellen or Gerald (who were always preoccupied, oblivious), and Char would have one of those perfect little cherub hands down my pants. Mine would be up under her shirt, pinching a nipple—just two teenagers in love.

It was our secret, dirty joke that Charlotte's Hands were the hit of the season. That Ellen had turned Char's hands into an edible work of art only further animated our fledgling affair. Enshrined with berries, dozens of Charlotte's Hands cooling on a tray were a performance piece, Warholian and surreal. Customers got the pastry version. I got the real thing.

We were beasts in heat when not masquerading as angels, and once behind closed doors, our true natures manifested. Clothes ripped off, and chairs knocked over, lamps broken, we wrestled each other almost in desperation as if keeping hands off any longer would result in cataclysmic destruction.

Our lovemaking was like Odysseus on the high seas. The greatest adventure ever told, and once a course was set, the discovery would be life-changing, the stuff of legend: typhoons, lightning storms, and mythical, mind-numbing melodies. I couldn't remember my name. All I wanted to do was to touch her again!

A bonus was that as I carried on with Char, the nagging shadow of my inner freak (the dangerous, unnamed feeling I had, the guilt of having messed around with boys) seemed to disappear. I was normal, after all. I was banging a girl, and not just any girl but a powerful, Shiva-like deity in human form.

Char was the smartest person I knew. She was a brainiac. Her mind went places I could only imagine. A blond, blue-eyed Renaissance woman who seemed to ace everything she tried. Crunching numbers, reading classics of literature for breakfast, she performed in a flawless bell-ringing choir. She even moonlighted as the assistant camera on a hit TV show.

She was beautiful, funny, creative, and deadly serious. She debated openly the female species evolving beyond any need for men with her intellectual, feminist mother (including at one of the little round Beaujolais tables while eating a salad I'd just tossed), and she reminded me of the powerful Bene Gesserit sisterhood from the sci-fi epic *Dune*, beautiful, alien, and secretly in command of the universe. I began to feel somewhat like mating stock, and it was strangely exhilarating. Even though I was not her equal in the brain department, I did have something that she didn't have, something she wanted. I had a wiener, and I throbbed.

I was also lifted and transported away from the fact that I might be a hideous pervert. I was, after all, the Chosen One of She, She of the golden mane and graceful heavens. She who knew all and somehow found it pleasing to love me. It was a high compliment, and I was encouraged, thinking I might not be as stupid as I thought I was. Because why would someone as smart as Charlotte mess around with a dope? I felt enlightened, encouraged to explore avenues of thought, agreeing with her that toxic masculinity was the scourge of the planet. I worshiped her body and loved her right back.

But I was always so busy with the restaurant: arranging tidepool swirls of almond crescents, harvesting vegetables from the garden, hand-washing the never-ending conveyer belt of dishes, polishing glasses and silverware, folding napkins, refilling salt and pepper shakers, cleaning bathrooms, confirming reservations, chopping wood. So much fun.

The splinters in my hands were an irritating reminder that whereas I used to be the crown prince, now I was a kitchen grunt. I'd look at my scraped, raw hands sometimes and marvel that Char let me touch her.

"C'mon kids! Let's decorate Charlotte's Hands!" would come yet another enthusiastic call to the kitchen. It was difficult to resist Ellen if she announced the task with a smile in her voice. But it would most likely be Gerald's default method of banging on the stairwell wall three times with his fist, demanding, that got us moving.

"Eric! Come now!"

It was usually me who'd be drafted on a moment's notice to decorate a table covered with Charlotte's Hands. Contrary to their interruptions, I'm sure my parents were thrilled that I was so enamored of this powerful woman. So beautiful, so smart, so well-appointed, and so female.

Despite my fondness for Charlotte, I anticipated the day when she'd leave. Charlotte had a career path; she was destined to press buttons in a nuclear facility, chart the stars for NASA, or hold diplomatic titles at the UN. Char's superhuman qualities were no accident. Her father was a professor at UC Berkeley, and her mother painted abstract illustrations of mathematical equations, and Char's older sister was working on a PhD. It was only a matter of years before Charlotte became president. I was a terrible student with a future in wine sales and laundry bills.

The more I learned about her and spent time in her world—an inconceivable world of wealth: even though her parents were divorced (her sadness about the split only adding gravitas to her aloof, celestial stature), Char and her mother lived in a charming Craftsman bungalow in a fancy Berkeley neighborhood and, as well, had a summer cabin north of Mendocino—the more I felt outclassed and naive, and over time I found it increasingly ironic that the closer we got, the stranger it became. She was fascinating, charming, and yet terrifying, and I often felt as if I were playing with a time bomb. Stroking her hair or kissing her face often created static electricity, and it was only a matter of time before one of us exploded.

Projecting the end before knowing how it would happen, I envisioned Char possibly evolving into something like the Dark Phoenix from X-Men and destroying all in her path, or she'd just stop calling. She'd wake up one morning with the epiphany: "Oh my god! What have I done! I'm hanging out with...I'm fucking a...himbo!"

She'd rush to the shower, scrub off the feeling of loser, then fly to Hollywood to film a documentary of Amazon women who secretly run the government with superior intelligence and sex appeal.

Something else entirely happened.

Ellen models for I Magnin catalog.

San Francisco. 1954.

Twenty-six-year-old Gerald.

San Francisco. 1952.

Baby Eric. San Francisco. 1955.

Ellen, baby Greta, Gerald, and Eric
at the Greek Theatre. Berkeley. 1960.

Gerald reads The Red Balloon
to six-year-old Eric. Berkeley. 1960.

Eric paints his adventures in drag.
Berkeley. 1960.

Random ideas *Perfect!*

Name displayed on sign at gate-/just inside fence.
at right angle to street- name on both sides.
Hanging from lamp post. Light-a reproduction of old gas light. NNIXX

White picket fence. 'Service entrance' marked on the gate to the right.

House painted xmmxxy smartly (more research on color and kind. Nothing
that might be considered by the towns people impractical. Blue might be
considered so, because it does not hold up under sea air and rainy conditions.
The type of roof suggests a soft mf or cozy or informal color. The house is
not an elegant Victorian house - more country styled or cottage type. I think
of if as a Grandmother house. The house nearer the schoool which is painted
a cream and delicately trimmed in blue would be ideal for our house, but
because it is so near, we had better not copy it.nx

A light needed at door,-gas light type. Perhaps a little shelter should be
built over the entrance door and platform,-and light could be on side of doorway instead of overhead. Door should have old fashioned handle and window
panes to copy windows in entrance hall. Menu posted under light.

Entrance hall should have coat tree and umbrella stand and perhaps hooks
for hats, coats, etc. Door mat nxxk outside xmxxxxxxxm door for wiping feet.
Floor should be bare and sanded and smooth - perhaps a hooked rug (round) xxxxm
inside door. Wallxxpaperxm perhaps of mattress ticking. Crisp, white curtains
at the window. Old mirror on wall to right of door as you come in. Picture at
far end of entrance hall, with a table for two under it. Under windows pxxmx
could be a bench of old design.The electric heater will have to be removed
and the wall patched. The double glass doors should be removed to allow more
space. Perhaps in winter time a kerosene heater will have to be placed in
entrance hall. Music and good smells greet you inside door. Another menu
posted.

First dining room should be warmed by Franklin stove, buxin burning either
wood or coal (preferably oak logs). Fixxxdixingxtxbxxx Dining tables covered
with linen mats and set for dinner. Wall paper of small design - red color.
Ceiling and floors bare polished wood, likewise woodwork at windows and doors.
White muslin drapes tied back. Shades of fabric with design compatible with
wallpaper. Chairs of natural color, hand polished wood, odd chairs of country
fixxmx kitchen flavor, likewise tables. Lighted by candles,fireplace and one
overhead light.
Xxxxxxdxxingxxmxm
Second dining room decorated the same. Hutch used for glasses, and nxxxx red
wines xx which have been bxxg brought up from cellar earlier, and wine baskets
and other table setting things as extra napkins and mats and silverware.
Coffee service can occupy corner just inside 2nd dining room by stairway wall.
Three tables in this room. Rather than proposed sliding glass door,
another door with window panes like front door (maybe Dutch door).
Both dining rooms should have a mirror each and pictures
(old victorian mirrors + pictures). 2nd dining room may
need more light - maybe a lamp on the hutch. A tub
of flowers should be outside on platform leading towards
toilets. Doors to kitchen should be swung open
to stay, rather than swing constantly, unless kitchen choices
are too loud.

Ellen and Gerald's notes for improvements

to the newly purchased property. 1968.

French Cafe To Open In Mendocino

by Don Burleson

A new restaurant will open in Mendocino Saturday, Feb. 22.

Cafe Beaujolais, a dream in the process of coming true, will serve its first meal to the public on Washington's Birthday at 961 Ukiah Street.

The dreamers? Jerry and Ellen Pitsenbarger, of Oakland, who bought the home of Florence Swartz last summer.

The dream? Operating a small, comfortable cafe in the French manner; a family enterprise devoted to the enjoyment of fine food and good wine.

The French countryside is dotted with delightful, unpretentious eating places, operated by owner-chefs, serving exquisite dishes in quite, relaxing surroundings.

Ellen and Jerry, artists both, feel that the cooking and serving of food is an art. Circumstances made it possible for them to test their creativity. Wisely, they are moving slowly.

At first, Cafe Beaujolais will serve only on Saturdays and Sundays from 5:30 until 10 or 11. Jerry is still retaining his position with an Oakland firm and will commute for the weekends to Mendocino.

Who will do the cooking? Both. This will, however, spoil no soup. Each has specialties at the range, each will be able to fit his talents to the total repertoire. Jerry has a way with sauces, Ellen with sweets. Each has a list of main dishes,

French vintages says of Beaujolais: "— frequent, friendly, vigorous, healthy, unsophisticated —." Again, "It leaves the head clear, the palate inspired, and is a perfect foil for honest and fastidious cooking . . . "

California wines also will be available, and the Pitsenbargers plan on serving 'house wine' which will correspond to the vin ordinaire of French bistros — a plain, good wine which will either be served as part of the dinner or for which a nominal charge will be made. These matters are flexible until their experience points the way.

Dinners will be served in five courses. Arriving at the table the customer will be presented with a generous tureen of rich soup and a loaf of Ellen's home-baked bread. When everyone has had his fill, the main course will arrive. At present this will vary from night to night, but only one such dish will be offered each evening. Steamed rice will be the usual starch, accompanied by a fresh vegetable. In the French manner, a tossed salad follows the entree, with dripped olive oil and wine vinegar. Then will come cheese and fruit, followed, as a second climax, by a sweet and French roast coffee.

What sort of dishes will be served? Supreme of Chicken, for instance, which will be chicken breasts with Mornay Sauce. Or Scallops and Shrimp

the fruit and cheese to bring a rising tempo for the exciting ending — all topped off with the satisfying chord — a superb cup of after-dinner coffee.

Who are the Pitsenbargers? Jerry was born on an Iowa farm where the daily round of starchy sameness drove him to seek variety as soon as he learned there were other cuisines. French cooking hooked him. He's a composer, but the market for musical compositions is limited, while that for good food, he believes, holds more promise for a man to "do his thing" and get satisfaction. It is infinitely more promising when husband and wife can create together.

Ellen was born in Memphis, raised in Texas and studied dance in Wisconsin. She was working at the University of California when their chance came to achieve their ambition. She moved to Mendocino in time to place their three children in school last September, and has been working on the conversion of their house into a restaurant. Jerry would drive up each weekend, labor arduously, then drive back for his five-day week in Oakland.

Mrs. Druscilla Clark, Ellen's mother, was persuaded to leave Minneapolis and join the family. She found a rental just a step down the road, and is now making curtains "and wonderfully wry comments" as she aids in preparations.

Because of the limited space

Don Burleson's first promotional article. 1968.

Pitsenbarger family: Eric, Ellen, Kristin, Gerald, and Greta. 1972.

Photo Credit: Doug Gieble

First advertisement in The

Mendocino Beacon. 1968.

Ellen's hand-lettered Thanksgiving menu.

1975.

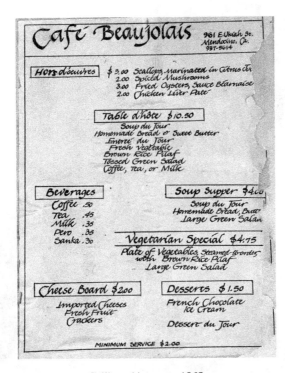

Calligraphic menu. 1968.

Ellen in her pantry. 1972. Photo Credit: Doug Gieble

Gerald and Ellen hard at work. 1972.

Photo Credit: Doug Gieble

Gerald prepares dinner. 1974.

Front foyer. Paintings by Jim Bertram. 1972.

Front dining room. 1972.

Gerald and Eric sitting at table eight. 1972.

Photo Credit: Doug Gieble

Jim Bertram. 1972.

Water tower. Mendocino 2021.

Greta. 1972.

Photo Credit: Doug Gieble

Eric in the foyer. 1971.

Photo Credit: Doug Gieble

Kristin. 1972.

Photo Credit: Doug Gieble

Kristin, Greta, and Eric in the shed. 1972.

Photo Credit: Doug Gieble

Gerald and a glass of wine on Bolinas Beach. 1967.

Driftwood bench above Portuguese Beach.
Mendocino. 2021.

Elizabeth and Eric at the prom. 1973.

Eric, Ellen, and Gerald on the headlands. Mendocino. 1974.

Queen Anne's lace on the headlands.

Mendocino. 2021.

Ellen and Gerald. 1972. Photo Credit: Doug Gieble

Mendocino. 2021.

Greta, Eric, and a picnic in the new VW. 1968.

View from School Street. Mendocino. 1971.

Pitsenbarger family on the headlands: Ellen, Kristin, Eric, Greta, and Gerald. Mendocino.

1972. Photo Credit: Doug Gieble

CHAPTER 19

PILLOW TALK

The quiet streets of Mendocino were fully realized, life-size stage sets. There was an immersive, surreal quality of walking around an open-air museum, back and forth through time. Any corner acted like a frame for what or who may catch your attention and, then, magnified. Against the dulled surface of turn-of-the-century glamour, any contrasting activity instantly became iconic, and sometimes, the mundane was transformed into life-changing.

For me, the sensation of skipping between centuries often resulted in sharp irony. One foot in the past, another in the present, meandering toward the future. A specialized existence, living in several places at once.

Watching tourists wander around taking pictures of your home and then get into their cars and drive away, back to the real world, could be disconcerting. There was the feeling of being left behind, of being invisible.

For me, the ordinary was transformed into mystery and theme-park reverie. The fog, the isolation, and simplicity of Mendocino only enhanced the overwhelming experience: that of a waking, somewhat melancholia dream. It could mess with you.

In the fall, while Charlotte was at school in Berkeley learning how to harness her superpowers, I enjoyed a weekend scholarship at the Art Center, throwing pots and wasting expensive tubes of acrylic paint.

The Art Center for me was sacred and had become a place of infinite possibilities. A complex of studios named after local artists, several main galleries, a theater, and small apartments scattered over several acres. Marked by trees and gardens, connected by paths, guided by sculpture, the Art Center was a hub of subdued activity and focus, a laboratory and proving ground. I spent so much time here, the Art Center had become almost a second home. Walking through a small, open field, down often empty streets, past familiar gingerbread buildings and fallen-down wood fences; from the café to the Art Center (on the opposite side of town), it became a pilgrimage of sorts.

I'd been one of the first young students to be given a yearlong scholarship studying fine art fundamentals. Life drawing, painting, sculpture, pottery, weaving, even animation—it was all offered to me free of charge with the cost of materials my one expense. As a dishwasher in the restaurant, I found my wages were spent quickly, but the immersion of creative ideas and practiced skills became the reason I got up in the morning.

Finishing studies in the pottery studio, after a day spent pushing clay around on a wireframe (attempting to sculpt the perfect figure of a man), I took my time walking back home. While fantasizing about becoming a famous artist, I also wallowed in epic loneliness. It lurked around every corner. No matter how many times I followed the same streets, I always ended up in the same sad spot. My life existed somewhere in an ideal future, somewhere just out of reach. I was a ghost.

My hands felt and looked like desiccated, cold, wrinkled mummy hands (handling clumps of wet clay sucked all the moisture out). I could see every line, every dent, and every wrinkle. What an ugly dessert these husks of human hands would make. Even Ellen's sweet buttercream frosting couldn't help these clay hands taste any good. Only Charlotte's Hands were dessert. I missed her.

I was all alone on the street and feeling the emptiness pressing in around me. Weeds underfoot, the familiar sway of a fallen-down fence following the wide-open street, only a parked car resting, a solitary crow pecking at something. Nothing moved except my stiff, cold hands. Warm water and dirty dishes seemed like a good idea.

Then quite suddenly, the appearance of a solitary figure walking across the street made me forget all about dishes. The incarnation of someone straight out of my fantasy world. A character I'd only imagined, someone I'd been writing about. Entertaining myself with a tale of adventure and magic, starring my alter ego: the hardscrabble medieval waif Grebe.

Named after a little diving bird, who responded to danger by diving rather than flying, Grebe was a kitchen grunt, just like me. I'd always been encouraged to "write about what you know."

Living in a run-down castle, bullied by surly knights, pompous courtiers, and a drunken cook, Grebe had a secret life; he studied the dark arts. In my story, a pet dragon, grizzled, tantrum-prone father figure of a wizard, and mysterious secret pathways through the ruined castle (only a small boy could maneuver) filled page after page of lengthy description. I was going to write a weighty book to rival *The Once and Future King* or *The Chronicles of Prydain*.

Grebe was described as: "Lithe and mercurial, with shoulder-length black hair framing a keen face of focused curiosity. Mouth in a perpetual half-smile (as if everything were slightly amusing); his flinty blue eyes also hid an epic loneliness and a bitter soul."

A clever, mischievous, sometimes vindictive lad, Grebe told a story all about giving power to a marginalized kid existing on the periphery of castle life, and there he was, walking on the other side of the street, right out of my id.

That raven's blue-black Prince Valiant haircut, fine-boned features, the slight, smirky smile, arms swinging in a vintage red velvet blouse, tight blue pants that hugged his butt and flared a bit over the high platform shoes as they took stealthy steps over uneven ground. There was something very different about him. He certainly wasn't from around here. I'd never seen him before (except in my dreams). He was the most exotic creature I'd ever seen, and on that empty street, he stood out like a dark fairy prince.

So, right there, without any fanfare or warning, the freak resting deep inside of me suddenly woke up, took over, and together, we walked right across the street to waylay this person. I felt compelled, I needed to look more closely at him, to admire his beauty, and perhaps, perhaps, to be noticed myself.

Who wouldn't notice the only other person on the street suddenly make a beeline for you? I had the cruising technique of a dump truck. A bit startled, Grebe looked right at me and locked me in his steely, slightly amused gaze, and I think I said something like: "Hello, I haven't seen you before," which was a lie.

Oddly, his name wasn't Grebe. It was Ray, and I learned that he was visiting from San Francisco, staying with his older sister who had an apartment at the Art Center.

Right there on the street, I gave him the thirty-second Reader's Digest synopsis of my entire life. As I admired his perfect hair and the tapering of his slim waist, I also observed (as if from a powerful telescope stationed on another planet) the hunger deep within myself begging to be let out of its cage. I tried to calm my heartbeat and to hide the epic loneliness.

I must have asked Ray to come over to the café for a bite to eat or just to visit sometime because while I was out front washing windows the next day, suddenly there he was, standing in the street watching me wipe at the antique glass as if I were performing in a sideshow.

I remember feeling excited, a bit cautious, and even oddly, frightened. Ray's recognizable frame reflected in the old windowpanes appeared ghostly, and as I turned around on the ladder to look at him, I felt a moment of instinctual warning.

He just stood there silently posing, and I had a long moment to assess exactly what it was that I was seeing. A storefront mannequin propped up there on the street in front of the forest of blackberries. He wore a different pair of pants today, a slightly lighter shade of blackberry purple, but just as tight.

He seemed so stylish, so sophisticated, and yet so strangely remote. It was difficult to gauge in his body language, difficult to tell whether he was shy, scared, or even challenging me. There was also a slight mocking quality in the way he just stood there, quietly staring.

I felt it again, a warning. There was an off quality about him. His eyes. That smirk. Was that the look of a showoff, a cornered cat, or a dangerous predator? I had a distinct feeling that what I was seeing was not quite real, was still only a reflection. He was a figure more of fantasy than real life.

I dropped the dirty rag into the soapy bucket with a big *sploosh* as my eyes traveled over the vision in front of me. There was a big, shiny belt buckle right above the lump in his crotch. His mile-high platform shoes were like stylish, shiny horse hooves.

Touring the restaurant, he remained quiet. He just followed me around, like a shadow or a skulking cat. I introduced him to my parents, who looked up, said hello, and then continued with their food prep, too preoccupied to notice my tongue hanging out.

The tour went quickly and was over too soon: the dining room, backyard and garage retreat, my room upstairs with all the James Taylor, Elton John, and David Bowie albums, and some of my colorful drawings of flowers, of elegant 1920s flappers, and of scrappy Grebe himself.

I told Ray about my stupid story, and he looked at the sketched caricature of himself, no comment. No comment was his reaction to everything I'd shown him, to my entire world. Standing next to Ray's fitted colorful clothes and perfect hair, I felt like an unkempt hick with the oily mushroom growing on my head, sloppy sweatshirt, messy room, and culturally insignificant entertainment choices.

Ray was carrying around what looked like Mary Poppins's Persian carpetbag on a strap. Sitting down on my bed, swinging one slim leg over the other, he plunked it down and began to unload a pair of sparkly rainbow socks, an assortment of wire bracelets that clanged together like a Slinky, a small record (a forty-five), and a bag of multicolored Pop Rocks. He poured me a handful.

"Here, put a bunch in your mouth. They explode," he said, squinting his steely-blue eyes.

Thankful that he was finally sharing something of himself with me, I popped the whole bunch in my mouth, expecting the candy sweetness. Ray downed his handful as well, tossing his head back, mouth open as if in ecstasy. The Pop Rocks fizzed and popped and exploded just like he'd said, and it was almost too much. I wasn't sure if I liked it. The foaming sizzle of artificial sweetness filled up my mouth with an audible blast, and as I contained my confusion, Ray gulped hard, licking his lips like it was the best thing he'd ever tasted. I swallowed more slowly, relieved that my stomach didn't burst open. I watched Ray wipe the edges of his mouth with a pearlescent, manicured finger. His tongue turned green, blue, and pink. He then handed me the record.

"Put this on," he said, almost daring me. "It's my favorite song."

The song was "Pillow Talk," and as the disco beats and cooing whispers of Sylvia filled the room, Ray suddenly started pulling all the wire bracelets over his slim wrists and got up, posing in the full-length mirror, dancing around as if suddenly channeling Salome.

Raising his elegant swan arms, swirling around, and pushing at the air, bracelets clanking, his big shoes scrunching up the throw rug, he turned around and around, becoming a wild, spinning, clinking dervish. I just stood there entranced (a spare crackle of Pop Rocks fizzing to late life in the back of my throat), listening to Sylvia moan about what she's gonna do, of what she's gonna teach me. And then, Gerald started banging on the stairwell.

"Eric! Come now!" he yelled.

The spell was broken. Ray yanked his nasty record off the turntable, jerked his two arms once over the open bag emptying all the bracelets in. And without even saying goodbye, he threw the bag over his shoulder, opened my bedroom door, clomped downstairs in his high heels, and was gone. I heard the screen door slam as he made his getaway. It was like the air had been sucked out of the room, almost as if I'd been dreaming, and then startled awake.

Did that happen? I looked around at the evidence that said yes. The rug was all turned around, the record player was still on, and there was a crumpled, spilled bag of Pop Rocks on my bed, a few sparkly candies lying in the indentation where Ray had been sitting, and there were the pair of shiny new rainbow socks he'd forgotten. Part of Ray was still here.

Gerald was banging on the wall again, so I went downstairs to do whatever it was he wanted. Standing at the bottom of the stairwell next to him and his butcher block, listening to him bark like a drill sergeant about "getting the wood chopped and the bathrooms cleaned before five," there was a grounding quality about his familiar bluster.

The glitter and fizz of Ray's presence fell away, and I could breathe again. The cold outdoor bathroom with paintings of frolicking peasants, the backyard and woodpile, the rusty ax, and the wet grass were welcome, familiar friends, things I could relate to.

CHAPTER 20

RATTLING THE CHANDELIERS

As I was absorbed backstage in the kitchen prepping, cleaning, fetching, and organizing, my gregarious younger sister Greta decided that she wanted to be much more public with her participation.

She determined that she'd be a great waiter, and our parents gave serious thought to the idea, encouraged that Greta wanted to be a part of the venture (as opposed to my constant foot-dragging).

Being only fourteen and untrained in the nuances of service was only a minor hitch, as we'd all come to learn that once Greta set herself to a task, she made it her own. The glamorous theatrics of presentation, an opportunity to wear some of her handmade outfits, and the reward of tips at the end of the night were all the inspiration she needed to step into the role.

However, dignified gentleman waiter Jim Bertram had more than a few reservations about the recruit and of suddenly being compelled to accept the owner's smart-aleck tomboy daughter as his assistant. This was an unexpected wrinkle. I wouldn't doubt it if Jim bitterly felt himself placed uncomfortably on a slippery slope (perhaps even contemplating employment elsewhere) as Greta was so eager and assertively confident yet hopelessly naive.

Just a kid and she was already a threat. She was a force of nature, and Jim had not signed up to be the mentor that she'd obviously need if they both (and if the restaurant) were to survive. Jim also pointed out that Greta was way too young to serve wine.

Transitioning from a wild, muddy, horse-riding hippie chick into an efficient, clean, food server was going to be a challenge and would undoubtedly become a bit of a spectacle. Likening Jim to Professor Higgins training the ignorant flower girl, we all placed bets on just how fair a lady Greta could be.

Jim's coworker Pam had mysteriously quit one night, leaving a plum job and a huge vacancy on the dining room floor. She'd just taken her apron off, thrown it on the blue table, and left, and I always wondered why. It was never spoken about. She'd been irreplaceable, and then she was gone.

A charming and cheery, strikingly tall, elegant Amazonian, Pam sometimes had to tilt her head so as not to collide with the rose chandeliers. So careful to place and then retrieve plates, avoiding customers' oblivious gesturing hands, engaging and efficient, Pam had also been a sweet counter to Jim's brittle sharpness. It shocked us when she left. She'd been like a member of the family too. Now that she was gone, with her conspicuous figure leaving a hovering impression in the space she'd once occupied, it would take someone with an equal amount of verve and capacity to assume the position. Greta was to become that person.

When Greta first made her intentions clear, Pam had generously given her every encouragement. She'd taught Greta all her tricks, giving her confidence, until the day she left. It was all the other stuff that Pam didn't talk to Greta about that she'd have to learn on her own. It would all become clear soon enough.

Greta had no experience, was not a physical specimen, was hampered by her youth, but had every bit as much energy and gumption and could fill a room with her presence. She'd looked up to Pam (as we all had, quite literally) and been impressed by how the big lady jockeyed through a night without disaster and felt a sisterly bond.

Jim's first assistant Gayle had also left after the first year (Pam taking over). Now it was Greta's turn. Greta had watched how it was done, she knew up from down, and now that there was a job opening, she demanded to be given a chance.

It had been through Greta's noticing of Pam, in her larger-than-life gesture and definitive action, her big heart and grand display of advice, that Greta felt emboldened. Greta was just as large as Pam in her own way; she'd come galloping into the dining room fresh from jumping horses over logs on the beach. She'd survived those untested handicaps, so waiting on tables would be just another obstacle course. Our parents were no match for Greta as she made her case (and there was no denying, with Pam gone, they now needed a new waiter), so Greta was given the job.

There was quite a bit of trial and error, plenty of hand-wringing and improvisation, but we all lived through it, even though gentleman Jim, whom I'd thought (in his infinite knowledge of all things proper and gracious) would have at least given Greta some support, instead was rather a discouraging, obfuscating curmudgeon.

Grumbling and groaning, he would scold her for not doing this or that, for not being perfect, and impossibly, for not being him. Greta's education on the floor became a learn-by-doing exercise, or rather, one that was learn by not doing. She remembered Pam as the benign source of encouragement and Jim the hard wall she bounced off.

She was introduced to the way things worked:

Greet and seat customers after crossing their names off the reservation book, give them menus, talk about the specials, pour water, take their orders, deliver bread and drinks, pick up appetizers and deliver, greet new customers, cross them off the book and seat them, give them menus, talk about specials, pour water, give them bread, greet more new customers, seat them with menus after crossing their names off the book, talk about specials, pick up empty appetizer plates, replace silver as needed, take orders, deliver drinks and bread, pick up entrées and deliver, refill water and drinks, take orders, greet and seat customers, cross them off the book, pick up appetizers, refill water, acknowledge new customers and find menus, ask the first table how their food was, deliver menus, pour water, deliver appetizers, refill water, take out bread, talk about specials, deliver more bread, seat new customers, cross them off, pour water, pick up appetizers, deliver menus, replace silver, more butter, more bread, refill water, describe Beaujolais as a fun, fruity red wine, relay specials, relay request for no salt on an appetizer to the kitchen, look at new customers huddled in the entryway, ignore the phone ringing, pour water, deliver entrées, find a new fork for the person who dropped theirs, tell Jim that table five wanted a different bottle of wine, the one he'd just opened tasted like vinegar, seat customers, look for menus, grab a falling glass before it hits the floor (or don't), refill water, ignore customer's upraised hand, deliver menus, talk quickly about specials, acknowledge that, yes, there is indeed beef in the boeuf bourguignon, quickly cross off new customers from the book, take orders, pick up empty plates, replace silver, pour water, replace a napkin, greet new customers, turn away others without reservations, menus, water, bread, answer the phone, put on hold, quickly sip a glass of water, pick up entrées, seat new customers, find menus, talk specials, describe a wine and point to Jim, answer the phone, take a reservation for tomorrow, pour water, take an order, greet customers, deliver appetizers, deliver menus, pour water, talk about specials, answer phone, take a reservation for later that evening, deliver entrées, take out bread, seat customers with menus, spit out specials, answer the phone with cancelation for five minutes ago (thank god), sip some water, take orders, clear plates, deliver bread, more butter, pour water, talk wine, another napkin, take order for dessert and coffee, clear plates, deliver entrées, pour water, answer phone, put on hold, gulp a glass of wine, pour coffee, find cream and look for sugar, take an order, pour water, take a reservation for next week from the person on hold, greet customers, seat, water, specials, desserts, take one more coffee to the table who previously didn't want any, pour water deliver menus specials phone water bread wine entrées plates appetizers entrées dessert water phone silver take order wine water bread customers appetizers entrées dessert clear plates deliver check…and breathe!

Greta felt like she'd joined a three-ring circus.

It didn't help that the dining room also seemed to be laid with booby traps that if she were not constantly alert, could sabotage her normally functioning body. Bonking a cabinet door, knocking over a chair, dropping the phone, cutting herself with a steak knife, or even sending her elbow into someone's face. Everything she did had the potential to further disrupt the smooth flow of things, if she were not vigilant. She had to become a robot, to retrain herself to move differently than she did in real life; this was not real life. This was a restaurant. Running through a maze of competing details, the slalom of anticipatory choreography had to be just right, or it all fell apart.

Greta learned a new respect for the personalities of many an inanimate object. The biting bread knife and the slippery ballpoint pen that went flipping across the room as if magnetized by someone's face. Her main antagonist, the haunted water pitcher that never seemed to pour water into glasses but instead splashed lumped up ice cubes onto diners' laps. Many extra napkins were folded on Greta's shifts, raising the laundry bill.

"I swear to god, you create accidents on purpose, just to give me an aneurism!" Gerald accused.

Some nights we wished he had just spontaneously combusted, but what happened later was almost worse.

Through observation, repetition, and determination, Greta became a seasoned pro. One moment she was just my annoying little sister and the next, a respected, glamorous, and well-paid member of the team. A decorated, war-weary, rhinestone-wearing lieutenant. Buoyed by her youthful energy, toughened by the nightly humbling, she grew up.

She also called Jim out on his hoarding the lion's share of pooled tips at the end of the night.

"I worked just as hard as you, so I should get half the money."

Jim's head almost exploded, his sputtering response unconvincing, but he gave her another couple twenty-dollar bills.

As Greta would hoist her fistful of dollars at the end of the night and regale us with entertaining stories of people whom she'd just fed, I listened with growing scorn at just how far she'd come and, by comparison, how far I'd been left behind.

"Those people on table eight kept asking for more bread and tried to talk me out of charging them. Three loaves of bread. No way." She'd gotten to play bad cop.

"When I took the bread off the table, they grabbed my arm and said OK, they'll pay." Gerald was scandalized but also, I think, glad that she'd stuck to her guns. We needed every penny. Giving away the farm was his greatest worry.

It was obvious to everyone that Greta was channeling Christopher Robin's Tigger. Even though she practically lived on horseback, she acted just like a scrappy alley cat with nine lives. Always taking chances, careening wildly in midair sometimes, but always landing on her feet. She increasingly walked the tightrope between the kitchen and dining room with practiced ease. Weathering the heat of a chef under pressure, demanding customers, or Jim's dismissal, she blithely brushed off drama as if it were an inconvenient gnat.

Shoveling down my dinner, I'd extricate myself at the end of service and continue my clean up in the kitchen. I just couldn't stand to be around the glinting starlight that emanated from Greta's side of the table. I'd rather wash pots and pans and take out the stinking garbage than listen to the glories of Greta's successful conquering of yet another opportunity I seemed to have missed.

Batting flies away from my face, I tied up the garbage bags and shoved them into the cans out back, in my mind's eye, dropping them down on top of Greta's gloating smile. Damn her for doing so well.

But underneath the sibling rivalry, I did have to acknowledge that

I was also rather proud of Greta, since not only was she taking on this hard job (and relieving me from doing it) but she was showing us all how to do something new. Quite unexpectedly, Greta single-handedly was breathing a much-needed gust of purifying air into the corrosive atmosphere that had come to linger behind the scenes.

Trouble was brewing as the restaurant became more popular. The stress of trying to keep up, to maintain a high level of service and the unique nightly experience, was taking its toll. Discontent and chronic fatigue chewed at the edges of everything. Greta also began continuously clocking Jim on his surly behavior, turning the tables on him. She didn't respond to his bullying, and secure in her position as the owners' daughter, she gained more control over her own service and the dining room in general and, slowly, managed to limit Jim's unquestioned authority. He began to cede his young assistant the space she demanded, ending his constant criticism, becoming less of a dictator and a more willing coworker. Greta, the lion, had tamed the lion tamer.

Gerald had started to drink lots of wine, Ellen grew sullen and would retreat, and Jim would simply disappear. He could escape. He didn't live here.

Yet somehow Greta was motivated to jump into the center ring and attempt to fix a thing. Her gung-ho attitude injected a much-needed jolt and kept the motor running. She inspired us.

Watching my firebrand sister take charge, mastering the unsettling, mystifying power plays that wracked our little world, I was, as well, encouraged to try harder.

There was hope and promise in the brash faith she showed in her innate abilities that only seemed to grow stronger. Like the revisiting spirit of can-do independence our parents had wielded at the very beginning of this whole enterprise. She reintroduced us all to what was most important: our enduring love for one another, and for making it work.

My resentment and envy were scrubbed away and replaced with new interest. More than just doing a job, it became our mission: saving our family and the café, irrevocably intertwined. If Greta could do it, we could all do it.

Besides running a restaurant, we all had our hobbies. Ellen and Gerald were in a musical group who met once a week. Jim was an accomplished painter with a studio on the other side of town, I had my drawing and various theatrical incursions, little Kristin was into knitting, and Greta (besides riding horses everywhere) taught herself how to play the guitar, sang like Aretha, and was becoming a seamstress.

Greta's studio was her bedroom upstairs, and when she wasn't serving food or mucking out a stall, she was writing lyrics, practicing chords, singing along with Chaka, and sewing with her heavy, antique, peddle-driven machine. Sewing at night for Greta became an act of defiance and of self-preservation. Sneaking even one quickly run hem, guitar riff, or belted-out verse, even if it disrupted the subdued quiet of the dining room just below the floorboards, was worth it.

She played with fire, and she knew it. Business as usual for Greta. During any evening shift, she'd be working on a new song, rehearsing a troublesome phrase, or creating jean skirts or lace blouses, a new wardrobe for school, presents for friends, or a blazing-red satin prom dress. Rushing quickly up and then back downstairs to check on customers, she drove Gerald crazy.

Greta had nimbly taken on the job left by Pam, had become a good employee succeeding beyond all our expectations, but she was also, still, Greta. As she gained in confidence, she also was becoming an even larger, broader version of herself.

Around seven or eight o'clock, it would start. Diners would pause over the large porcelain bowls of soup Greta had just carefully placed in front of them, their spoons lifting in anticipation of that first delicious sip, and then suddenly, the roar of a freight train came barreling overhead, or a ghostly, soulful voice drifted from somewhere unseen. When Greta would come back down to check on her customers, they'd be wiping up spills and whispering about whether this old house was haunted. Gerald was furious.

Encouraged to do and be anything we wanted by our daring and creative parents, Greta (the prime example of daring) was unquestionably her father's daughter and by taking on the job, found herself boxed in by paradox. Singing and sewing and leaping headfirst into a challenge were naturally her things but faced with the imposed limitations of her new job, a conflict of interest emerged, and Greta pushed the envelope.

"Greta! No sewing or singing during restaurant hours!" Gerald yelled up the stairwell for the umpteenth time, implying violence if she didn't comply. She heard him, would stop for a bit, poised for the orchestral camouflage of the evening's soundtrack below, then start right up again. A quick flare of horns or timpani cued Greta to quickly run a long skirt hem or strum that complicated fingering of her guitar.

"Greta! Stop now!" Gerald was always desperately exercising authority, laying down the law, the thin red line, a new limit, or an ironclad rule that Greta always skipped right over, intentionally broke, or completely ignored. She had Gerald's number. He needed her.

Her taunting reply: "Bouncing is what Tiggers do best."

Ignoring or pacifying with false promises, flirting with predictable rebuke, she would recklessly follow her muse, and it became almost a sport to see just how long it took after a heartfelt verse or thrumming run of the sewing machine peddle before Gerald once again turned colors and yelled upstairs.

"Greta! Be quiet!" Poor Gerald, his job was never-ending, and I found it so weird that every time Greta did her thing upstairs (igniting Gerald's ire), his own yelling defeated the purpose, almost encouraging her.

It took many nights of illegal activity, commenting customers, and teasing Gerald's boiling point before she finally traded in that Victorian foot peddle for an electric (slightly quieter) Singer machine. But even that was only a Band-Aid solution.

The freight train was downgraded to a scooter, and on any typical evening at the Beaujolais, while one could enjoy a bottle of warm, red Châteauneuf-du-Pape, be served a perfectly cooked leg of lamb by a Botticelli youth in red satin, you could also be then surprised by the occasional, haunting run of scales or vibrating one-point-two-magnitude quake rattling the rose glass chandelier globes overhead. Greta was creating a masterpiece.

CHAPTER 21

ASTRONAUT

I was finally alone and in total control of my spaceship. Humming along in third gear up the slow rise of Little Lake Road, directly into the haunted forest. Alone and free to imagine that the approaching alien landscape of lichen-encrusted pygmy trees would remain dormant and not attack as I drove by.

With my force field on high, I'd soon be safely past the woozy gloom emanating from this ancient thicket. It was how the gnarled trees trapped unwary travelers, by putting you in a trance, lulling you into a hypnotic stupor, and then snatching you unawares. Who knew what happened after that?

I would not become another victim. I was on a mission and couldn't allow myself to be trapped by the unseen forces. This road, just like all the other roads around here, exactly like the dump road I'd learned how to drive on, had two narrow lanes and swerved around a few slight hills, skirting past the deformed trees hunching alongside.

After you left the coast, the rising ridges of mutant scrub oak, manzanita, cypress, and sage all made for an otherworldly terrain, and it was easy to fantasize as to their true nature: as goblin shrubs, hungry for anything warm.

I turned a familiar corner where everything clumped together and revved the gas. I heard Gerald's disembodied voice bellow, "Shift! Shift!" as he held on with one hand, gesturing madly with the other. He would not approve of me going so fast around this corner, but he was not here, and I couldn't let the reaching vines ensnare me.

Learning how to drive in the VW bus with Gerald as instructor had been a layered lesson in survival. Enduring his barrage of shouted direction while also staying focused on the road, on staying alive, listening and reacting quickly to his commands, subverting my defensive instinct to squawk back obscenities.

"NEVER take your eyes off the road," he barked.

I was never perfect even when I made the correct maneuver, not as fast or efficient enough. It was like riding around with a gorilla in the passenger seat. Gerald's big hand swatting mine away from the long gear shift. The tilted beret on the back of his head the only clue that he was still my dad.

Eventually, after endless dump runs, the grinding of gears, nerves, and lectures, I finally scored a driver's license. The calmer instructor from the driving school gave me high marks.

But Gerald's tough love teaching had left an impression, and even with the joy of independence, I still felt a sting if I didn't fully mesh with the vehicle. I understood that even though I could drive back and forth on my own, I'd never be quite as good as Gerald.

The lingering tang of rotten garbage and a ringing rebuke always seemed to accompany me on a drive. No matter how fast or how far away I went, I was never that far away from another dump run or Gerald with his glaring eye under arched eyebrow, judging my every move. All roads were a dump run.

Gerald gave his approval at my new driver's license (even as he continued to offer critique). Now, I could be trusted and sent off on unaided shopping errands. I'd become a courier, his pair of extra hands.

Still, any time we were in the car together, even if he took the wheel, he'd demonstrate the art of driving. Just as it was in the kitchen, I was always the acolyte, Gerald the master.

The art of driving: A simultaneous press on the gas and release of the clutch, of listening for the correct pitch of gears that signaled a necessary shift, the anticipation of a curve and downshifting and the imperative of signaling with your turn indicator. Even now, alone on this lonely road, his presence lurked there in the passenger seat, judging my hand placement on the steering wheel, the weight of each foot on the pedal. He was still correcting my hands, poking at my legs, almost yelling.

"Not tight enough! Gas and clutch! Shift! Shift! FEEL the car."

As I reasserted my grip, the car remained steady on the road and zoomed past the predatory pygmy bramble. I noticed rusted mailboxes at the beginning of small roads that then disappeared into labyrinthine trails of handmade hobbit homesteads.

Off-the-grid buildings made from scrap wood bleached as white as the nutrient-starved soil rose like skeletons over the elfin trees. Some had towers with stained-glass windows, some were built on stilts over goat pens with baroque plumbing apparatus elbowing off into the thicket, rooted into cement cisterns. A lone teepee or yurt plunked down among clawing fingers.

Weathered barns were leaning groggy into wet fields, the listless weather vanes pointing at some unspecified direction. An isolated water tower guarding ruined, moss-covered pens; the fences fallen to press tall grass into emaciated scarecrows. When the fog was high, it was as if a curtain had been drawn back from a long-dead world.

Eruptions of violet and plum-red rhododendrons masked the occasional blank face of a prefab suburban ranch house or sad, broken trailer left to slowly melt into the silt.

Retirees, communes of hippies, farmers, and state forest rangers lived out here. People needed a horse or four-wheeler to get over some of the ruts and treacherous mud swamps that occasionally revealed a drowned deer or tractor.

I knew people out here who braved the bewitchment of the forest, existing under a wave of constant fog. It was astonishing to me that they could even get out of bed in the morning as there was always the feeling of being swallowed, of being buried alive.

But when the sun came out, once I'd driven past the fog belt and the lid popped off, it was a revelation. Warmth and light bringing out a cacophony of euphoric nesting birds, the bright-blue sky, and maybe a suntan.

Today wasn't going to be one of those days, though, as the whole world seemed enveloped by gray soup. Everything blurred in suspended animation as I whisked by in my blue shuttlecraft.

It didn't matter. I just needed to collect the prize waiting at the end of the road pronto and then fly back to our café kitchen. The day's prep already underway, this dash up the hill past otherworldly landscapes was a crucial last-minute bequest. Gerald's demand to appease Ellen, whose handmade salads would be naked without the final ingredient: a garnish of organic alfalfa sprouts.

A minute but vital detail that gave Ellen comfort in the satisfaction of being correct and complete. Without it, her design and her many efforts toward perfection would all be forfeit, and Gerald would lay blame on someone for falling down on the job. It would be me, and then it would be Ellen, and I couldn't let that happen.

The day's delicate morale already threatened, Gerald was acting out and Ellen had retreated to her cubby. A familiar, melancholy foreboding had crept up from beneath the floorboards. Palpable, even as we went about our duties with no one speaking, plodding along with nose toward the uneven path of readiness ahead. The uncomfortable silence was only broken by the phone ringing or Gerald suddenly, erratically breaking into a dramatic phrase from *Carmen* or *La Traviata*, his tenor cracking into melodrama.

"Don't you like my singing?" he'd accuse the charged air around him. "I won a national contest with this voice! And look at me now, a has-been who never was."

He was an amazing singer and could have been famous in his youth. But that brush with fame had been a very long time ago. It was ancient history since he'd decided to decline an offer from the San Francisco Opera and, instead, go on tour with Billy Graham. He'd told me once that this decision was his worst mistake.

"*You* were a mistake, you know? I never wanted to be a parent."

I'd just happened to be standing there and was an easy target. A crude excuse, maybe because his hands hurt, he had a headache, was behind in his prep, worried about finances, was conflicted about his choices, and maybe could sense his own family's resentment.

I didn't want to believe him, but it stung, nevertheless. I reminded myself that he'd also told me many times that I was his greatest pride and joy, and he had indeed, been such a great father.

Times had changed. His pride and joy was now an indentured servant and my father had become a bully.

"Fetch sprouts! Begone! Vamoose!" The mighty hand of Zeus was pointing to the door. Thunder would rain if I hesitated. Ellen was on her own, and she was vulnerable. The fate of the world hinged on my dash into the twilight zone.

Just a pinch of these special sprouts gave the bed of greens a floral finish and a subtle crunch and, to me, also added the exotic flavor of space-born hydroponic weirdness. Grown in long, inverted tubs, the squiggly, wormlike alfalfa sprouts looked like dayglow topiary, the nursery at the end of Little Lake Road secretly a laboratory for space food.

I could imagine the gardeners floating about in sterilized white zip-up suits snipping off little bushels of sprouts with their laser scalpels, quickly securing the delicate alien life form in plastic baggies, then stapling them shut for an interstellar journey, or to sprinkle on top of Ellen's salads.

One baggie would sustain a Mars-bound astronaut a whole month if chewed correctly. Releasing the powerful enzyme and proteins, they worked their small miracle. But wolfed down unchewed, these same sprouts could have the opposite effect. They'd, in turn, consume your brain like a virus, and you ran the risk of being transformed into a different kind of vegetable altogether. I always chewed my sprouts, hoping for the best.

This necessary errand to retrieve a few baggies of alfalfa sprouts had, somehow, the potential to shift a crucial power struggle going on back home. It felt as if by my retrieval of the golden fleece, I might save the restaurant, if only for a moment.

The ridiculous urgency to complete a thing, to be perfect and to avoid reasons for complaint. It weighed on the gas pedal as I drove into the strange, murky world at the top of Little Lake Road. Those salads must have sprouts!

Upon passing the driver's test at sixteen, I'd summarily been lumped with a weekend's worth of driving up and down the coast, was shown maps, given instructions, phone numbers, even a few warnings.

"Don't miss the turnoff just before the sign. Don't go past the small house on the right, or you'll have to turn all the way around, and you'll be wasting time. Don't drive fast down those long dirt roads, or you'll throw the axel. And don't look at the squash lady's lumps."

I made all the mistakes and then understood why. I had to miss that turnoff then turn around and stare like a frightened horse at the poor squash lady and all the lumps that rode up and down her spine, across her shoulders, and into her neck.

Down a long, winding dirt road at the end of Albion ridge, behind a curtain of scraggly trees, her little front yard was full of colorful, misshapen gourds.

She'd laid out selected squash preordered by Gerald over the telephone. Yellow, green, oblong, squat, and covered in bumps, they all looked as if they might have been harvested from her own body. I remember how lovingly she spoke about the display as if they were her children. I drove way too fast back to the main road.

Becoming the café's pickup and delivery service (sometimes on a moment's notice), I was often interrupted as I lay cocooned with a book.

Commanded to pick up groceries from the market in Fort Bragg, begrudgingly I'd leave poor Frodo Baggins hanging upside down in a giant spider web to go get duck breasts from a farmer out near Comptche or weird, flowery mushrooms gathered by a hippie family who lived in a treehouse. Each sojourn, each shopping trip a small adventure, fueled with a rising sense of urgency, even panic. Checks were written, Gerald sighing deeply as if it were a gold ingot he was promising, signing the paper with blood.

"Don't lose these or give them to the wrong person and ask them to wait until Monday to cash this."

I'd tuck the hastily written checks with Gerald's voluminous scripted signature in my shirt pocket and wonder: how far could I get on fifty dollars?

After reaching for his new best friend the wine bottle on a nearby shelf, Gerald took a long swig from our namesake vintage. He enjoyed his wine, he enjoyed it all day long.

He smacked his lips. "Ahhh! The fruit of the gods."

The fruit of the gods had become the poison that was slowly transforming Gerald from his generous, funny, theatrical bombast into something else. He was still the chef, still our father, but he was a different person. Ellen floated like a ghost behind her pantry table.

There was some relief driving into the carnivorous, reaching forest because at least I knew what lay ahead for me. What haunted the café was pernicious, formless, and scary. The finances that allowed Café Beaujolais to operate at all were in disarray.

There was never enough money. The color red tinged any talk of menu planning or of even opening the door. Audible groans accompanied what used to be a thrill for them. Gerald drank his wine.

"We can't afford dish soap, let alone rum for the tarts!" Gerald told no one in particular. It was perhaps an exaggeration, but it made a point. He would just stand in front of the butcher block, dented dark red from cutting up meat, and stare at the marks. I worried that he might consider some sort of ritual sacrifice. He'd written a short operetta at one time about Abraham's dilemma and his eventual capitulation with God. Perhaps I should just keep driving?

My parents were artists and only human, and even in success, they struggled. Despite the popularity and status of being a top restaurant, even with all the accolades and reviews, the movie stars and government bigwigs that dined in our little house, these days it was always the lack of something that motivated operations, and lately, both parents seemed to be running in fear of something.

There was a monster living in our house, and somehow, it was the monster running the show. It clawed at them throughout the day, hounded their every move, telling them what to do, and then pulled them down each night into a sea of paperwork and unpaid bills. There wasn't enough money and I sincerely doubted that there would ever be enough sprouts.

"Everyone will know what a phony I am," Gerald lamented to his bloody cutting board.

"We're failing. Our standards are slipping." He'd sip more wine, then whoop as if he were falling off a horse, holding on to something to keep his balance.

Whisking around corners, passing slowpokes on the two-lane road, I shifted into fourth. The world outside was dangerous, the atmosphere toxic, but I was safe as long as I kept going. Almost there, my deft handling of the VW proved that even if I was scared of everything, seeing danger around every curve, at least, at the very least, I had control over the car.

I knew that these stupid sprouts were only an ephemeral fix. The ugly, runty trees only weird looking, and the fog, just fog, the nursery not a secret lab. There was no golden fleece. I drove through the nursery's front gate and slid into a parking space (exactly as I would maneuver a shuttlecraft from the USS *Enterprise*), bumped gently the railroad tie and turned off the motor, pulled the emergency brake and sat for a moment in silence; the onboard computer spoke to its counterpart within the nursery, reading code and exchanging vital information. My emergency ration of superpowered sprouts was waiting.

CHAPTER 22

RAINBOW CAMP

I didn't see Ray for months. I'd look for him as I walked around town, to and from studies at the Art Center, hoping for a chance sighting at the grocery store or post office. He didn't magically appear on the street or outside the restaurant (like the last time). I began to wonder if maybe I'd dreamed him up, projecting so mightily my fantasy character into reality. Was I crazy?

But he was real. I still had the glittery rainbow socks he'd left behind; I could still taste those Pop Rocks.

After spending such a long time looking, doing double takes (was that him walking around the corner? disappointed when it wasn't), waiting, anticipating, and wondering, I guessed that Ray had left and that I'd probably never see him again.

I shrugged, continuing my routine. Art classes, school, the restaurant, walking around town. What else could I do? This was my life. It had been a flashy, one-of-a-kind meeting, something entirely out of the ordinary, and now my life was sliding back to normal, but it wasn't. It wasn't normal. Something had changed.

I felt the pull and attraction in what I remembered of Ray but was also oddly repulsed and even somewhat relieved not to see him. There had been an off feeling about him that bothered me, and by not seeing Ray, I avoided what was beginning to feel a bit risky.

Ray had opened the door to something dazzling, strange, and scary, the thrill of danger only accentuating my attraction. I recognized that feeling.

When I was a kid back in Berkeley, my neighbor, Charlie, and I had rendezvoused in the backyard shed, in the dank basement of the house, even bent over in a large wardrobe stored in the garage. Touching and being touched by Charlie was the most excruciating pleasure, and it being infused with jeopardy (the chance of being discovered) and of knowing somehow that it was wrong made it all the more exciting.

When Charlie suddenly decided that it was indeed wrong, he landed a painful karate chop to my neck. That ended that, with parents talking, me crying in my room, Charlie avoiding me. I saw him years later standing outside a movie theater. Our eyes met, and I saw something flicker.

What Ray presented challenged everything; it was like observing a new life form. His stylish mix of masculine and feminine without any pretense or affect; he seemed gay, but then again, maybe he wasn't. Ambiguous and yet not ashamed or shy in any way. He didn't sneak around (like I did) or pretend to be something else. He was completely open about it; he even seemed to advertise the fact. Unapologetic, he was proud of who he was. This (to me) was very different.

The more I thought about it, the more confused and frustrated I became. It banged up against the knowledge that being gay was a terrible thing, was ugly and wrong and even sick (my parents, bullies at school, and Charlie's karate chop had told me as much). Being chased home from grammar school by a large kid in class, slapped around at the front door of my own house, called Dirty Faggot and Little Pansy. Shunned by the world and punished for liking other boys would be the fate of someone like me, like Ray.

But Ray didn't seem to care. He was none of these things, and he hadn't seemed afraid at all. I'd sensed defiance. His daring, assertive confidence and swagger encouraged a second look. Did I see what I thought I saw? In my memory of that first sighting of him, he was at once both graceful and steely strong, walking down crooked Little Lake Street like a prince.

I was a moth drawn into the lovely, shimmering light, knowing all too well that I would probably get burned, that something horrible could happen. I might die, but I couldn't help myself.

And nobody knew my fascination. No one knew that while I went about my day, always in the back of my mind (and then suddenly blazing right in front of me) was the vision of Ray, and of what lay beyond that door, of what all that scary information was saying. Who was I, and what was I becoming? It stabbed in the pit of my stomach, wanting to see Ray again, while I also was terribly apprehensive of what would happen when and if I ever did. I felt crazy.

School or art classes during the day, dishwashing in the evening, I'd walk around town, peruse the bookstore, the galleries, follow the narrow paths along the bluffs, around tide pools, end up at my spot on a cliff envisioning mysterious, sexy mermen swimming freely in the wild surf below. Was that a bare chest, a strong, fishy tail? Was that long, flowing hair I saw among the seaweed?

Ray was gone, but I still had the rainbow socks, and after so long of his not returning to claim them, I decided he'd forgotten, so now, I guessed they were mine.

One morning I decided to wear them to class. Even well under the length of my jeans (hidden as I walked), it felt as if I were parading down the street wearing a clown suit, or bull's-eye target. I could feel the synthetic lurex fiber grating the soles of my feet, reminding me of what a subversive act this was.

Simply wearing a pair of rainbow socks was a rebellious yet safe way of being gay, while also, not. Fooling everybody, the sheen of a glittery rainbow peeking out from the rolled-up denim cuff, was my secret, transgressive statement. Pretty, practically invisible, and somewhat dangerous. Only I knew.

My art teacher, Hilda, saw me squeeze drops of acrylic onto the palette from the new paint sampler I'd purchased. Acutely aware of how expensive these new tubes of paint were, I wanted to use them sparingly (this was only an experiment and would never be a masterpiece). I thought, once I was more confident, I'd use a bit more, but one tube cost as much as a whole evening's work.

Hilda tssked and took the small tube of red from my hands and squeezed the whole thing out!

"Don't skimp on your spontaneity," she encouraged the class. "USE your paint. There will always be more. You need your paint NOW. Let's see what happens when we cover the canvas!"

She mashed my new, expensive sable brush into the red and then yellow, wiping in abandon up and over and all around the now messy orange canvas. She'd used my one small canvas as an example of spontaneity.

"Experience the sense of freedom, of letting go. Let the paint tell you what it wants to do." The paint had told her to waste all my alizarine crimson and cadmium yellow.

"Nice socks, Eric."

My heart stopped. Everyone looked as I sat there (mad about the waste and plunder of limited materials). What could I do? People were admiring my new socks. Not supposed to be noticed, but now that they were front and center, I stretched my legs out to reveal the length of a rainbow. It was strangely exhilarating.

"Freedom in all things," Hilda declared. "Let inspiration flow from your every moment, from the mundane, from the unnoticed." She walked around the room and picked up someone else's brush, jabbed it into paint, and slashed blue across the canvas.

"Now look at these two canvases." She drew our attention to the blue slash and then to my red-and-orange mess. "Look at the relationship. There is none, and yet..."

She pointed to my socks. "Eric chose to wear rainbow socks this morning, because why?"

My face was burning.

"Uh, the colors?" someone offered.

When I got home (my paint completely gone and canvas gessoed), there was a note stuck on the front door, addressed to me. It was from Ray!

"I came by to see you. No one answered the door. Staying with my sister."

I raced back to the Art Center. How had I missed him? I was just there!

I knew which apartment his sister lived in, but no one answered. He was out there somewhere, somewhere in town. I had to find him!

I power-walked down the street, looking, looking. I walked into the new hippie restaurant the Uncommon Good, the Gallery Bookshop, Dostal's Clocks. I looked in the bank across the street, down to The Hotel and looked in the lobby (not expecting him here), into all the little shops and galleries up and down Main Street; I even looked quickly in Dick's Place and then back down to Alfonso's Smoke Shop. Nothing.

I walked fast back into the middle of town, past the little red Chinese temple, across the open field by the post office, up and down the grocery aisles of Mendosa's General Store, the pharmacy across the street, The Sea Gull restaurant, the tacky clothing store and all the other tourist spots, The Corners of the Mouth health food grocery, nothing.

Where was he? I was staring at people, looking hard at their faces, between them to see if Ray was behind or walking around the corner. I felt like we were just missing each other by moments.

Back to the Art Center grounds, looking all around, knocking again on his sister's door, nothing. He'd disappeared again. I walked up the hill to the high school, looked in the playing field, searched the tree line (was he walking out there on the Headlands, along the bluffs?), nothing. I could feel him, see him. He was right there, and then he wasn't.

Out of breath and frustrated, I trudged back home, having spent at least an hour walking the entire length of the town, covering all my usual haunts, anyplace that might hold any interest for someone, for someone like Ray. He was elusive. It only added to his mystique.

My feet were on fire, receiving a vigorous acupressure massage from synthetic sock fibers. Sparkly rainbows or not, these socks were coming off the minute I got home.

As I picked my way down School Street, past the middle school (giving a precursory glance into the grounds) and approaching the Beaujolais down the hill, I saw him. There he was. Ray was waiting for me on the front step.

He had a new record he wanted to play for me.

"This is the best!" He turned the album over in his smooth hands, showing me the stylized illustration of a flame-haired woman. I'd never heard of *The Divine Miss M*, and Ray kept talking about how this album was the "soundtrack of his life" as he casually followed me into the front door, past Fleurette, as we'd come to call the Chéret painting, into the dining room where he fell slouching in a chair as if he lived there.

No hello, no explanation of where he'd been or what had been happening in his life, asking me how I was, of what I'd been doing, if I'd missed him, or where his rainbow socks were. He just pushed the album into my hands with excitement, and I saw that he was wearing pale-pink nail polish.

The kitchen was warm, and my parents were working, barely noticing me as I scooted into the family room (where the stereo lived). I turned the volume up, just past the twelve-oh-five position (louder than usual, but not too loud).

I was reminded of the Andrews Sisters, of a subterranean cabaret, some smoky bar somewhere in an imagined dance hall. The singer, a bit of a floozy, breathing heavy, belting out these retro-tinged songs evoking another era. She seemed a bit melancholy and resigned to her life, but the music was also sweet. There was a romantic yet sardonic edge; I liked it. Music I wouldn't think I'd like, but it tickled something. Was this how Ray felt?

When Bette Midler sang about her hustler boyfriend, Ray got up and started dancing. Prancing back and forth across the length of the dining room, turning sharply to throw me a look, holding on to one of the scroll-back chairs, mouthing the words:

"I'm in love with a down-home man. Simple lovin', I can understand. I've been hustled by the best of them, and you ain't nothing but a crazy man. Hustler!"

Ray posed, using the chairs as props, leaning back onto table eight, his hand on a hip then back against the wall. He was wearing tight blue pants that showed off his protruding bulge. His paisley shirt was opened down to the navel, and I could see tiny black hairs on his chest. Gold chains around his neck, a slim crucifix, glinting single stones in his perfect ears.

"Hustler! Hustler! Hustler!" Bette kept singing as Ray kept lip-syncing, posing, showing me that he'd memorized all the words, and all the moves.

We hadn't talked about what he did in the city. I knew next to nothing about him (even though he was aware of my own story). He'd only told me that he had to get away, and that was why he was up here in the first place. Had to get away from what? A hard city life? And then it suddenly hit me. Hustler. What was Ray telling me? Was I projecting something onto him, again? Was Ray a...hustler? Was he a... hooker? A whore? Ray was a male whore! I didn't know there were such things.

"Ray, I have to ask. Are you a, a hooker?"

He turned his perfectly manicured hands over to reveal the obvious (to anyone but me).

As Bette moaned about being blue, Ray told me that he only worked the nice streets and that the money was good, that he was clean, that he had repeat clients, that he was always in demand. I must have been staring, my mouth open.

"It's not a big deal." He shrugged. "It gets boring."

Boring being a hooker. My mind was racing to imagine what that must be like, to walk the streets, and to solicit men for sex. Ray, having sex with strangers, for money. Getting paid for it. Not a big deal, he said. His nice clothes, perfect hair, nails and jewelry, his reserved manner, and then sensual dancing. What kind of mindset did you need to have to walk the streets, to have sex with strange men, and to purposely put yourself in such danger? How did you become bored with being a hooker? The knot in my stomach had tightened, and alarm bells were clanging. My fascination with Ray had changed. I was afraid.

I panicked, scrambling to find a way to finish this visit in a hurry. I kicked off my shoes and started pulling off the rainbow socks.

"These are yours," I offered. "When I didn't see you, I figured you'd forgotten them, but here…" The poor socks were all scrunched and had lost their newness. They looked like oily puddles in the street.

Ray just looked at the well-worn rainbows lying on the floor between us. He could tell that something was different.

Bette sang about how "you've got to have friends," and Ray looked a bit hurt, like I'd said something mean. I saw doors closing in his eyes, his body language changed, and he sat down, still not taking the socks.

"I left the socks for you. They were a present."

And suddenly I felt guilty for rejecting him, because that was what I'd done.

"Oh, I, I love them. Thank you." And then I said it: "You scare me, Ray."

And then he looked almost triumphant, as if I'd given him the highest compliment. Standing up again, he reached over and gently gathered up the pummeled rainbow socks, put them in my hands, chuckling.

"It looks like you've worn them ever since I was last here."

I nervously explained my quick walk around town, wearing them to class after holding on to them for months. I remained barefoot, and we just stood there, listening to the song.

"What do you call this kind of music?" I asked. It was pop music, but it was also not. I couldn't put my finger on it. I was so confused. I wanted to kiss Ray but also run as fast as I could. But I couldn't run, since I lived there.

"It's called camp," he said, cocking his head as if it were obvious.

"Camp? Like in sleeping bags and pup tents?"

Now Ray was laughing at me. "No, it's a style of music, of cabaret.

It's supposed to be cheesy but also sophisticated. Kind of like turning something upside down."

"Oh, you mean like ironic?" I got it.

Ray was like that. He was camp. This music that illustrated his world, the way he dressed, acting both male and female at once, the hot and cold, sensual, flirtatious then distant, the dangerous, anonymous life he led and then his choice to seek me out, a naive person. He wanted this intimate moment right now, he wanted to be my friend, but that too would soon disappear.

Then "Boogie Woogie Bugle Boy" was playing, and it was Bette's version of a favorite Andrews Sisters song. Camp. I got it. Reverence for something old while also putting your own spin on it. Ray was like that, and I guessed I was too.

CHAPTER 23

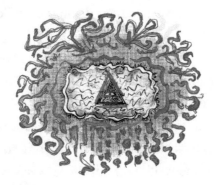

THE DUNWICH HORROR

In a small town, when a big movie company moved in and wanted to use your home as a backdrop, it was a big deal. A film starring former child actor Dean Stockwell was the event of the year, and suddenly almost overnight, Mendocino went from a sleepy artist's hamlet to a bustling factory town.

Trucks and equipment crowded in where only open space used to be. Strange faces and pushy people clogged the grocery, and the café was booked every night with the film crew dropping big bucks for the very best Ellen and Gerald could provide. Everywhere I looked was a sign of foreign activity. The picture-postcard landscape and tiny streets were clogged with impromptu campgrounds of arc lights, piled cords, and sandbags, people lounging, people smoking in canvas chairs, cameras pointing in every direction.

There was no one area where the film centered as the entire town had become a backlot. The bookstore, the Art Center, the bluffs, my secret eucalyptus grove—turn any corner, and there they were, casually disrespecting sacred ground. Even walking to school was detoured by roped-off signs and guards with walkie-talkies. Yesterday I lived there, there was room to think, but today they were filming, so go away. Even though I knew it was a boon for the local economy, it nevertheless felt like an invasion, and as I washed their dishes at the Beaujolais, I leveled a curse. Stupid tourists!

Based on an old H. P. Lovecraft story, *The Dunwich Horror* was about occultist shenanigans unleashing a horde of demons and turning the earth into an unrecognizable limbo.

As I looked around, this scenario felt oddly familiar. With my life so recently and drastically changed, relocated from comfortable city life to this wide space in the road, with all these bossy people swarming, I once again felt off balance. Was the truth right under my nose and my worst suspicion true? Could the calm and serenity of Mendocino all be a charming facade for something darker, something hideous?

All the signs said yes. The slightly decrepit, pickled Victoriana, creepy fog, foreboding weather, endless expanse of ocean and angry surf crashing against forlorn cliffs, trees clawing the air, listless citizens wandering as if called by some otherworldly force. The atmosphere of repressed angst and violence roiled just under the quaint surface. You couldn't ask for a better place to film the end of the world. I wondered, was Mendocino secretly a doorway to hell and were the end of days right around the corner? Of course not. But what if they were?

With everything going on in the world (the Viet Nam war and continuing violent protests, the specter of nuclear annihilation, even the Beatles breaking up), it seemed almost plausible. The world was crazy. Who knew what could happen? I went even further and asked myself if this moviemaking was coincidence, or somehow, impossibly an allegory for actual fact? Were these strangers and this "movie company" here in town filming a documentary?

When the ad showed up in the local paper for extras, I decided that instead of just waiting around grumbling about the apocalypse, I'd get out of the kitchen, face my anxiety, and join the show. I'd go undercover and find out what was really happening. As part of the action, I'd also make a bit of extra money and experience moviemaking from the trenches, and maybe I'd also expose the terrible truth: that Mendocino was evil.

And maybe, just maybe (remembering my reading of old Hollywood legends), I might also be discovered along the way. Hey, if it happened to Lana Turner, plucked from obscurity, it could certainly happen to me, a teenage kitchen grunt. In my overamped magical thinking, I considered that perhaps by becoming a star, I might also, somehow, even prevent Armageddon. I needed this job. The world's (and my own) fate might depend on it.

My friends Sean and Annie and I lined up with everybody else and were instantly cast as regular people who'd become the newly possessed. How clever, I thought, since most of us were stoned by 8:00 a.m. An army of hippie-dippy succubi.

On the day of the shoot, I was up before the sun, too excited to sleep and way too early to pick up Sean and Annie, who lived together. I waited in the idling car as they came stumbling out of their house clutching coffee cups, disheveled and complaining that this had been a mistake.

"Jesus, did you even go to sleep?" Sean teased. "Remember, we're extras. That means background noise. The chances of us being plucked from obscurity are a factor of negative point zero." Sean always found pleasure in dowsing cold water on my enthusiasm.

Annie chimed in. "They'll probably cut the scene."

As I drove out of town, they nestled together in the back seat half-asleep, cranky until I offered up my alternate take on the possible true purpose of this film, pointing out that we already lived in a gothic horror movie. That got them chuckling.

They could relate, as everything was always up for ridicule. Sarcasm tinged with vague pessimism was a shared language between us. They talked about escaping Mendocino all the time, the second they turned eighteen. What would I do when they left? Who would I be able to complain about the world with?

Halfway there, Sean lit up a fat joint, and responding to my look of surprise, he explained matter-of-factly: "We're getting into character."

I went ahead and took a couple puffs—what could it hurt? We'd been completely stoned when they'd cast us, so for all they knew, this was completely normal. It was normal. Possessed by the demon weed.

When we arrived at the graveyard location, I was out of my body with caffeine, adrenalin and Maui Wowie. I followed Sean and Annie as if watching the three of us from above, hearing the crunch of dirt as we stumbled forward. I concentrated on not tripping over my own two feet, now suddenly grown three sizes larger, dragging like cinder blocks.

We ended up waiting around for what seemed like hours, all of us extras clustered together along the side of the road like cattle, trying to keep warm, pacing back and forth already completely bored, engaging in uncomfortable chitchat, waiting for any instruction, for anything to do. We were here to act like demon people, so set us loose! I had a headache, and my hands were numb.

Looking at the group, it struck me that the casting director was either a genius or just by dumb luck had netted a particularly gnarly crew of hardscrabble locals who could have either just risen from the grave or worked in a local gallery.

Sean remained his usual cool, unattached self, the slits of his eyes a badge of stoned perfection, Annie's perpetual sneer blunted only slightly by lack of sleep. Even bored, I maintained my very uncool exuberance, hyperalert to my visible fantasy of being discovered or for any sign indicating the film's true meaning.

When someone finally came over and herded us all over to the spot where we'd act possessed, I couldn't feel my face, saw sparkles in the chill air, but I subverted discomfort into method. Demons didn't care about feelings.

The scene we were involved in was a chase. Mr. Stockwell was to come running up over this small hill with us zombies lurching behind.

"I wonder if we'll get some artistic direction?" I mentioned to Sean, only half-kidding.

"Don't overact" was all he said.

That stung. Nobody got me.

Moments later, the director yelled at us through a bull horn.

"Demon people! I want you to walk awkwardly over this hill toward the camera! Arms outstretched, stumble a little, you can moan if you like! I want to see some wild eyes and sadness! Look as if you're fighting a battle inside your head! Remember! You've been forced against your will to follow Mr. Stockwell!"

This was it! I'd always thought that my most expressive features were my eyes and hands, and now the director was giving me license to use these natural tools to project my newly demonic nature. It was now only a short ramble over this hill toward the future, closer to the truth and my amazing new life in front of the camera.

Props people started pumping fake smoke all around us, the instant atmosphere wafting between tombstones, hunched trees, drifting over the hill. B movie nirvana. I could feel the war begin to rage behind my eyes and the terror rise at being taken over by a malevolent force greater than my own. I was no longer in control.

My soul was restless and damaged, the horror driving me mad. An itchy combination of claustrophobia and ravenous hunger. I wanted to escape. I needed release from this purgatory, wandering in a void in search of some peace, in search of redemption, in search of revenge, in search of fresh meat.

Annie practiced her arm reach, shoulders slightly askew with an expressive bulging eye twitch. I turned to Sean and put my hands around his throat, gritting my teeth and snarling. I really wanted to pet his long brown hair and kiss his pretty lips, but I'd settle for strangling. He was Annie's boyfriend after all.

The makeup people had applied bits of dark-colored smudge to our faces and hands. Our eyes were accentuated, and I thought that Annie, in another life, could have just as easily been a silent film star as a zombie. Her big, watery eyes projected a deep sadness. When she stared wide-eyed at me, her eyes said: "I know you have a crush on Sean, but he's mine."

"Action!" the bullhorn echoed over the hill. The bunch of us started moaning and stumbling, lurching, and reaching for the limping Mr.

Stockwell, who was way ahead of us zombies, easily avoiding us.

"And cut!"

We were left milling about on the hill between the trees. I had long legs and was standing farther down, closer to the camera, than my friends. There was a big hippie guy next to me. He stank, had big hands and lots of ratty hair, a beard with twigs and leaves stuck in it.

"You in the front, the big guy! I want you to hunch over a bit more and amble more like an animal!" the director called out.

No direction for me? I was standing right next to him. Hadn't the wild-eyed searchlights of my craven soul, the grasping, groping hands of a young man taken before his time garnered any notice at all? I had literally thrown my demonic presence at the camera.

I could feel the beast within me writhe in fury, my guts in contortions. Stupid director. I wanted to lash out and snatch the pumping heart right out of this guy's chest, gobbling it up in one messy bite. Along with the anger, I felt a momentary wave of pity and compassion for the poor man. He didn't know what he was doing or what unholy forces he'd unleashed.

He hadn't fully observed my obvious, shivering, demonic behavior. He was distracted, dismissive. Was it the big stupid guy next to me who wasn't doing anything, just lumbering down the hill with gravity in control? I resolved that I would turn the volume up a bit. I had an agenda, and I wouldn't be overlooked.

The director wanted something more animalistic, a hunched, injured ape? I could do that. I felt the thing inside me instantly transform into a feral, rabid, knuckle-dragging neanderthal. Prickly hair crawled along my back, the brow over my bloodshot eyes thickened, drool pooled at the back of my throat.

Everyone ambled back behind the hill for another take. Glancing at the big guy who'd elicited comment from the director, he seemed nonplussed, even a bit irritated. He reeked of alcohol and what was that? Piss?

"Action!" The moaning was louder this time. A woman was wailing, pulling on her long, stringy hair. Wow, people were getting into this. I sent forth a guttural, gurgling cry and rolled my eyes back. My right cement foot dragging behind, the left arm a gnarled stump grabbing at the air with my right hand (now a mutated claw), the last two fingers curled under. I shambled down the hill like Igor, even barking a couple of times. A completely over-the-top zombie stereotype.

"And cut!" I had made it a bit farther down the hill, again next to the big dumb drunk.

"That was good," called the director. "Let's do that again, and you in front, the skinny guy with the big curly hair! No barking!"

Since I was so far down the hill, it took me a bit longer to get back up, Sean and Annie already mingling with the other zombies. Were they avoiding me? The cold air felt good on my hot face. Perhaps barking wasn't the best idea after all, but it was so convincingly savage and strange, and strange was good for a zombie, right? After all, I was no longer human, and the possessed did things differently. This director, disappointingly, knew nothing about demons.

Criticism at such an early stage in my new career dug deeper the farther up the hill I got. Chagrin was a feeling I'd certainly gotten used to, but this didn't make any sense. Maybe I simply wasn't cut out to be an actor after all.

But what would I do? I tried desperately to quiet the familiar despondency, the spiraling apathy that curdled any new ideas. Was I going to be stuck forever as a kitchen drudge in this backwater town while Sean and Annie moved on, escaping the curse? I knew in my heart that I was destined for something better. I wanted to come crashing out of this prison and scream at the world, "I am THE most convincing zombie! This is a goddamned fucking Academy Award performance!"

Annie was snickering when I finally skulked up to her and Sean.

"I've never heard a zombie bark before."

"That's the whole point," I responded. Thinking, what was the point again? Was this about being a zombie, about being possessed or trying to become something different, and where was the evidence of prevailing evil I'd sensed? Was it right under my nose? I knew that something was going on, but I couldn't quite wrap my head around it, and it, like Dean Stockwell, was just beyond my reach. Not quite visible but like a siren song pulling me forward. I had felt…compelled.

This whole exercise was suddenly tiresome and overwhelming and no longer fun. The high worn off, I was freezing and wanted to go home, or I could just go ahead and walk off the cliff that I knew was behind us. I could hear the sea roaring.

"Action!" called the director.

I was a different kind of zombie altogether, and I wasn't acting this time. Walking with a halting, wholly unenthusiastic shuffle, eyes staring coldly ahead, I think I moaned. I was gnashing my teeth.

"And cut! That was great. Let's do this one more time, and then I think we've got it." The director seemed pleased.

As I walked back up the hill for the last time, I reran these last moments along with the other two takes. It was the dead part of this latest performance that had worked. No mention from the director meant it had been successful, and my spirits revived somewhat. Dead was dead after all. I was not supposed to be in control of my own body.

This last time, I stayed close to Sean and Annie, who were so completely over it by now that they just walked down the hill as if on a short stroll across town to the record store. I put my arms up with a slack-jawed moan, but I was as well ready for this frustrating exercise to end. I longed to retreat to my room where the idea of stardom and barking zombies could exist without criticism.

The world I'd spun for myself was, so far, so much more satisfying, the subtext of all my fantasies muddling together. I concluded the world (and neither of my two friends) shared this vision or didn't understand. Was I wrong? I would just have to show them.

CHAPTER 24

THE D. B. W.

What was it about adolescents? Why was I always so fucking angry? I struggled to keep my bad mood in check and maintain composure. One minute I was fine, the next a snarling werewolf. Loping along (bell-bottoms dragging), fists clenching, unclenching, wanting to rip out throats, punch old ladies, lock myself in my room, or run off a cliff. I was a mess.

Everything was so frustrating, overwhelming. If it weren't for all the amazing food and love for my family, I might have considered jumping in front of a logging truck.

I knew why I was mad. Nursing my grudge at being ripped away from Berkeley, sentenced to a life of drudgery, and now, my parents wanted even more. They wanted me to become them. They were grooming me to become a restaurateur.

I lived in constant dread. I could see that Gerald was dead set on me eventually taking over the family business. It was my legacy.

"You'll become a fine chef, just like your papa." He cheered me on with a jovial wink and raised wineglass. There it was. It had been decided. That I could barely flip a pancake these days without a panic attack never factored into his decision.

Perfectly happy to gorge on pastries and pâté but stumped by the opaque cooking or baking process and amount of know-how (stuff talented adults knew how to do), I was freaking out.

My proficiency was limited to slinging lettuce or peeling potatoes, and I could see that it took more than basic kitchen skills to pull off multiple orders of perfectly steamed salmon fillets, let alone balance the books. I felt like a deer in the headlights, that logging truck barreling ever closer.

I was completely unprepared and knew that I would fail miserably, only this time it would be the last time because it would be the end of everything. It would be painful, it would be ugly and embarrassing, and I would probably die. At least I'd be out of my misery.

I still struggled in school (math shit), and I couldn't hold a paring knife without either getting nicked by the sharp edge or Gerald's criticism. I was just making it as a kitchen grunt, so how in the hell was I going to become a master chef? This was Gerald's fantasy, not mine.

Any early enthusiasm for creating an event out of our family dinners had vaporized. That had been fun, but this was different; this wasn't fun at all—it had become relentlessly hard work.

I struggled to whip up a rue or efficiently debone a chicken (or twenty), I couldn't cook rice without it becoming plaster, and I apparently didn't know how to efficiently deflower broccoli or melt chocolate without supervision. The thought of putting on a chef's apron and inheriting Gerald's many responsibilities was ridiculous. It was horrifying.

Gerald constantly worried about whether anyone would come to eat (all the prep and food, time and money wasted), and if they did show up, he worried if they'd even like it. If I were the chef, most likely they would not.

It would take a lifetime to catch up, but I didn't have that long. I was sixteen, and the handover could come at any time. I'd wake up one morning, and instead of asking me to chop wood, Gerald (with great solemnity) would place his soup ladle in my hands and demand an avgolemono. I had not studied the finer points.

"There's no avocado in avgolemono, right?" No, there was not.

Worse, Gerald could keel over dead onto his butcher block from stress (Ellen fading away soon after from a broken heart), and it would be up to me to make ends meet. It would be a very short career. We three kids ending up in an orphanage, as wards of the state, or on the street.

I could never be Gerald, yet there I was, being forced to slowly march into a tar pit. The sleepless nights, the drudgery, the blistering arguments, and the cold walls that went up around my parents, the sinking into drowning debt. I knew that there would never be enough people, enough money, enough time or patience or room for any more mistakes. Gerald had declared (in barely concealed desperation) that absolute perfection and unparalleled success were the only way forward. It was all or nothing. It had only been three years, and both Ellen and Gerald were fed up, they were exhausted, their enthusiastic spirits fading. They seemed injured; they were damaged.

That bottle of half-finished red wine next to Gerald's chopping block would be mine sooner than later, and very soon, I would be the one watching Café Beaujolais (my parents' dream) fall apart, and it would all be my fault.

Resentment and dread grew daily (like mange), and I skulked about with the weight of the world. Those waves crashing and booming against cliffs signaled the melodramatic finale of my colorful but short life.

But when I got far enough away from home and "the Beauj" (as I called it at school or hanging out with friends), oddly, the wolf retreated, and I found myself quite human after all. I became just me. The full moon curse evaporated, and the tenacious root of humor found its way through angst.

Humor had always been my expression of choice. Even in a deep funk, I could find something funny in just about anything, and once again, this acknowledgment saved my life. Away from home, my house-servant, master-chef predicament was reduced into the abstract. From a comfortable distance, it seemed ridiculous. Chains fell away, and I emerged wearing my signature, comfortable clown nose.

I possessed a special knack for skewed insight and, sometimes, the inclination to take the joke to the next, lower level. There was always a way I could insert a posh English or heehaw hillbilly accent over whatever news I had, turning a conversation into a statement or lopsided observation. Plus, raunchy expletives shoved into a title or rhyme, while also sounding like Jeeves the butler or Mrs. Slocombe, cracked me up. It was silly. People laughed, and I liked getting this kind of attention.

Readin' Ellen's elegant French menu like it wuz from a nasty white-trash truck-stop diner wuz just funny to me. The self-deprecating reference (me, a skinny, white, hippie kid pretending to be a sophisticated potty-mouthed gourmand, speakin' French and talkin' fancy). It was a dig at our very real, attempted reality.

I often made note that the front part of my cerebellum had evolved a special node just for toilet talk. My wry character, being both serious and then ridiculous—people were kept guessing. Who was he? They had to look twice, and I liked that; it felt powerful, and acting like a fool allowed me to embellish my life while providing a much-needed pressure valve.

Out of the kitchen, the liberating venue for my original wit blossomed into lurid color at the Headlands School. Created by concerned liberal parents, this all-ages school was a utopian experiment in freedom of expression. Named after the promontory hugging the far western edge of Mendocino, the school and its wild grassy fields framed our physical world and created for us the analogy of untamed weeds, free to grow however we chose. We three kids were enrolled, and I vowed to try harder, to learn something this time, anything besides food service. I wanted to fit in, but it had to be something I was actually interested in.

"Teach the children well." The Crosby, Stills, Nash & Young quote was handstitched on a colorful banner that hung over the balcony. All the fundamentals plus a reasonable tolerance of everything else young minds might ponder.

The Headlands School was housed in the theater building of the Art Center. Named after mysterious benefactor Helen Schoeni, it was a large box with a simple stage, seats, and a ceiling of skylights that during the day baked everyone inside like ants under a microscope.

There were apartments on the second floor for students of the Art Center, and occasionally, someone would hang over the edge of the balcony and banner, observing our wild goings-on.

All this space, an actual stage, the lights, odd props, the few painted sets shoved up against a wall, a walk-in closet full of costumes. It seemed only natural that we turn our experiences into drama.

Curled up and faded, tacked to a support beam (barely noticed in the hurly-burly), Shakespeare's quote "Life is but a stage" spoke to me. With a dramatic flourish (not unlike my actor father), I pointed out the quote and drooping banner. They meant something; they were there for a reason.

This was the perfect opportunity for me to stage my reinvention. My big idea? The just-wrapped *Dunwich Horror* movie shoot and frustrating morning I'd spent imagining a glittering, now-aborted movie career. It still felt raw, and I wanted to tap into the disappointment and turn it into something else.

Spinning the whole experience on its head with a cathartic send-up felt like the right thing to do. They hadn't chosen me, so I would blow a mighty raspberry and make something myself.

It was about a week after the movie company had left, returning Mendocino to its near-abandoned, hushed, ghost town aesthetic. I'd been pondering which way to go, what to do, how to deliver my special brand of humor. I wanted to reference the movie somehow without simply copying. It needed to be original, it needed to be clever.

One evening I hunkered down, flipping channels on late-night TV. Past all the stupid Westerns, dull action, and cheesy romance shows, I landed on something that almost reached out of the screen and shook me, slapping me in the face.

I couldn't believe what I was seeing. Dark melodrama with clichéd, busty women portrayed as either blissfully cheerful or constantly in peril, harangued by smarmy, louche playboys in eye-rolling, sexist pandering and then, a grisly murder most foul.

Jiggly, odd-angled camera work and way, way too much fake fog. It was like some twisted Molière farce in leather and lace. Black-and-white, campy, and overwrought, with sinister lurking vampires, ghouls, and the random farmhand. And even though it had been clumsily dubbed, I could tell instantly that, of course, it was Italian.

Transfixed, I realized that what entertained me was the gross exaggerations of stereotypes and crude production values. It was weird and so silly, and if anything had even a whiff of silly, it rocked my world. I had a nose for it, and this movie stank to high heaven.

This was it! I'd found my loadstone of inspiration. What's more, I was convinced that the symmetry of this midnight epiphany was more than just coincidence—it was a sign. I'd found the perfect vehicle to translate my teenage numbskullery. I had stumbled upon and found my niche. I'd learned what it was. It was called camp.

Relief flooded over me. Everything was solved. *This* was the beginning of my brilliant new career: not as a lowly, two-bit B movie extra or as a clumsy chef de cuisine for my father's flailing restaurant. I would become a film auteur.

Awaking at dawn on the downstairs couch (covered in crushed kipfels), I had been transformed into a schlockmeister.

The script practically wrote itself: Italian sci-fi monster movie musical with wacky, slapstick silent film histrionics, dramatic lighting, revealing costumes, and in-your-face fourth-wall audience participation. This would be an event. High art! Shakespeare would be proud.

And renaming *The Dunwich Horror* as *The Dumb Bitch Whores* was almost effortless. I did think twice (more than twice) about whether I'd crossed the line and was just too offensive, but it matched so beautifully and delivered such a verbal punch.

It was offensive (awful, the more I thought about it). Insulting and crude, derogatory, even mean, and by using this title, I might even hurt someone. I was asking for trouble. I'd be placing a target on my back. But it was also obviously absurd, and absurd was my mantra.

Tiptoeing forward, I examined my sixteen-year-old moral compass for any past trauma that may have triggered this possibly misogynistic behavior.

Did I secretly hate my mother? Why did I feel it was OK to disparage women this way, and was that indeed what I was doing? I didn't think so. All the women in my life were sage, interesting, and essential. Ellen was a goddess, my sisters cherubic, fierce individuals, any girlfriends I had were friends, fascinating people. Nope, I didn't hate women at all and couldn't point to anything, except for the fact that early on I'd been spoiled rotten. Maybe that was the problem.

I was a brat, grown used to getting my way. Entitled, coddled, and cherished, told as a kid that whatever I did was wonderful, even when I wasn't. Now at the crossroads of becoming a young adult, blaming my parents for yanking me out of childhood and for daring to dictate my future, now faced with the glaring limitations of how little I actually knew, I'd landed on what was safe. I did know how to make people laugh. This was an act of defiance, of rebellion and survival. My hubris won out. Everybody and everything were up for ridicule. Nothing was sacred.

I took an awfully big chance and went ahead with the nasty title, expecting a lecture, censure, even banishment from my teachers or punishment from parents, but it never came. I never heard a peep.

And the joke began to take on meta significance. The stage of my life set with symbolic props, a script, and willing avatars performing in my existential catharsis, with the entirety of the universe watching through the skylights of the Helen Schoeni. This was a test, but what did it all mean? This was school, after all, the school of life. Wasn't anyone going to stop me? It *was* funny, wasn't it?

My glee in realizing that there were no longer any limits (except what I placed on myself) to publicly utter dirty words, encourage sexually aggressive women, paint men as threatening but fumbling monsters, and explore adult themes only fanned the flame.

I concentrated on skewing cliché, exaggeration of damsels in distress harassed by hairy, snarling creatures from the black latrine. My intention was for a quality smut performance.

But deep into rehearsals, anxiety again took hold, and I had serious doubts. What was I doing? I must be crazy, had gone too far this time. I was delusional, depressed, full of rage and rebellion. I realized that everyone would never look at me the same way again. But the die was cast, and the show must go on.

Girls lined up, jumping up and down with arms raised. "I want to be a whore!"

I was a bit surprised at their enthusiasm and had a flash of guilt. Was I introducing a dangerous element into these young lives? Would my actions today result in any one of these innocents blossoming into a bona fide hooker? I was a pimp rounding up my harem. Casting would be tricky, but I needed whores.

They all got the job, but I reminded them that they had to practice. This was more than just lounging around with makeup on. They had to show up for rehearsals and scream on cue. They had to say *shit* and *fuck* and mean it. I was assured by the squeals of delight that not only did I have a cast of dedicated whores but that I'd made inroads into being popular.

Everybody was having so much fun that the terror of being punished took a back seat. Or maybe it was what drove us. We were breaking so many rules I lost count. *Shift it into high gear, people—we may never get another chance!*

To offset the underlying seriousness of the subject matter and to make obvious the lampoon, I cast myself as the madame of the whorehouse. Writer, director, drag queen, buffoon. The ultimate act of sacrifice. A nod to raucous English pantomime. See, I informed the universe. My idiocy was based in tradition. This stupidity had roots. I wanted everyone to know that as I was making fun at others' expense, so I also included myself. Eric as big fat Italian mama barking commands at her ladies of the night.

"Get out there and make-a more money! Mama needs a new Mercedes!"

Waving my hands in the air like I was throwing pizza, a Christmas tree of jewelry jangling.

The twist was that when the johns became monsters and truly threatened their lives, the whores fought back. With Crazy Mama encouraging the girls to "Kick-a their butts!" petite, angelic girls, rouged up and wearing various degrees of old lace and ripped silk, became a ninja army that surrounded the beasts and beat them into submissive pulp. To pump up the action, we choreographed elaborate fight sequences that involved tag-team judo and karate. Girls beating up on boys. It wasn't difficult to get everyone to practice. Synchronized faux martial artists with cheerleader moves, *The Dumb Bitch Whores* turned out to be anything but.

There would have been people up on wires if it were possible, flying through the air to land a superhero punch, and we did try to throw a rope around a beam and haul somebody up, but I put the kibosh on that. I'd seen what happened when little girls were put in precarious situations, and I didn't trust the Helen Schoeni to hold anyone up.

This was a new building, and already there were signs of instability. The front glass doors were falling off their hinges, wood paneling peeling up from behind molding. You couldn't sit in aisle five when it rained.

Instead of high-tech effects, we mastered the art of illusion. Large movement and exaggerated reaction. The final tableau: a mountain of squirming, tiny legs in ripped stockings with monster arms flailing. The fight sequence a highly choreographed vaudeville.

Monsters vanquished, the happy hookers gather to lift the smallest girl onto the mountain of defeated and battered boys.

The principal prop we saved for the climax. A grotesque, green rubber Frankenstein's monster's head poked with nails, gouged with scissors, kicked around, and displayed in corners since being discovered. He'd seen better days, the green pallor faded, looking supremely tired. We gave him a proper send-off.

It was *Beauty and the Beast* with a sharp, nasty left turn. With everyone cheering, the little trollop in training triumphantly raised the green monster head up. Her one big line: "Viva la revolution! Long live the hookers!"

When one of the girls got shy, I would motivate them with a sense of competition. Who could scream the loudest and look the sexiest while kicking monster butt?

My army of whores disrupted any quiet time in the rooms next door. Art Center instructors complained of blood-curdling sounds coming from our laboratory. Some of the boys playing monsters began to lose interest (as they were getting regularly trounced). I wanted to rehearse until every detail was right, but I could see their point. No more dress rehearsals, it was time for the performance.

With everyone more or less ready, we set a date. I made up posters. The screamer headlines proclaimed: "More Terror! More Horror! More Whores!"

No one had to suggest that I restrict a bulk mailing to only families of kids attending Headlands School (though a few mysteriously ended up stapled to phone poles around town).

On a select batch, there was an anonymous critic's quote: "SIN-sational! It will SHOCK you to your core! Whatever you do, don't bring the children! Wait, we are the children."

As monsters roared and hookers judo chopped, the audience whooped and cheered. *The Dumb Bitch Whores* was an unqualified success. I wasn't flunked or expelled or dragged off to solitary confinement. I didn't receive an A either (as there were no grades) but was instead complimented by laughing parents and winking teachers.

"I thought I'd piss myself when she said: 'Oh my god! It's so big and hairy!'"

The relish of so many chances taken, of a creative endeavor fulfilled, of entertaining strangers and dodging bullets was my big reward. It softened the disappointment of not seeing my parents' faces in the crowd. They were, of course, too busy.

CHAPTER 25

SLEEP OVER

My biggest mistake and regret involved listening to my dick. When he spoke (and I weighed the options), there was no contest. I was a dickhead.

After my last encounter with Ray, I'd come away with way more than expected. Learning about camp, about style, about a particular urbane cynicism, I'd also been reacquainted with the warning: that talking to strangers was risky.

I'd also learned that because I was single-mindedly horny, ridiculously ignorant, and lonely for a kindred spirit (whatever that was), I'd allowed myself to be seduced by something beautiful and scary. Suddenly lost in uncharted territory, I'd invited Ray right in and been this close to getting my hand bit, or something more. Ray was a wild animal, and I was his prey.

Still afraid of him, of his harsh life, of what he represented, I was also now afraid of what was happening to me. I'd also pondered the thought: did I need to become a hooker?

As naive as I was, I knew I was privileged living within a loving family. He didn't seem to have that, as he'd always been on his own.

No, I didn't have the guts. I wasn't that desperate or cold to do what he did, to be the way he was. I loved my version of life more, but something was missing. Ray had something I didn't. He knew who he was, while I was still figuring it out. I thought about him all the time.

I'd spent so much time tamping down any outwardly display, anything that might expose my secret, that when chinks began to appear, I almost didn't recognize myself. Who was I? Could I let down my guard and just be myself, and what did that feel like, to be completely yourself? Ray was showing me how.

I needed to put the puzzle back together, to retreat and find my center. I needed more information, and I needed to reconnect with Charlotte. Char was my one true friend, she knew me, she cared about me, she was my girlfriend, there'd been harmony, I had been more myself with her than anyone.

But I hadn't seen her in months and months and suddenly, acutely felt her absence. I missed her. If she'd been up to Mendocino or their family cabin, she and her mother hadn't called. They hadn't come to say hello or dine at the Beaujolais in what seemed like a very long time. I'd begun to wonder, was something wrong? The gap (since I'd last seen her) suddenly seemed shockingly wide. So much had happened. I was almost a different person.

I finally called to ask if I could come down to visit her in Berkeley, but instead of the usual encouraging yes, she seemed hesitant.

I understood (she had commitments), but I also sensed some genuine doubt in her voice, as if she didn't want to see me. This was weird and set off alarms.

Did she know already? I hadn't told anyone about the feelings I was experiencing. No one here in Mendocino knew, neither of my two sisters, certainly not my parents, no one. I didn't really know; how could she know?

Unsure if Charlotte would be able to help shift my confusion or provide any answers, I hoped that a familiar face, my one true friend (and my old city, Berkeley), would jog equilibrium back into place. I was hoping for a miracle.

I'd come for the weekend, and she'd make time, but it felt like I was imposing. Even though she'd eventually said yes, it felt like she'd really wanted to say no.

On the long bus ride down to the Bay Area, I worried that somehow Charlotte had received a psychic telegram telling her that I was gay, gay, gay and that she was also dreading this meeting, scrambling for something to say.

I envisioned a messy breakup, Charlotte meeting me on the doorstep, not even letting me into the house.

"Go away, I never want to see you again." I was putting words in her mouth. "I've known for a long time; that's why I don't call you. We're not lovers anymore; we're not even friends. I can't stand to even look at you." The door slammed and locked in my face; window blinds dropped. What would I do then?

I was making this long trip just so she could tell me to fuck off, and it might be another long, sad trip back home, with nothing gained but a broken heart. But I had to know, and I had to tell her.

I took the Greyhound bus down in the early morning.

Even with this drama playing in my head, the closer we got to Berkeley, I began to feel a strange volcanic charge building. It pressed out, expanding in all directions.

Recognizing landmarks of buildings, signs, and roads, the ocean and sway of trees, I also acknowledged that this feeling had been growing, burning deep inside for a long, long time, since I was a kid, and now, it was ready to explode.

It felt oddly like excitement, like rage and even joy. It felt like fire!

This fire lifted my spirits when I started to freak out. It burned past doubts and my terror of the unknown. Sitting straighter in the cushioned bus seat, I took a deep breath and opened my eyes wider, taking in the landscape rushing by. I saw what I was. I was angry.

Not angry at Char, not angry at anyone in particular, but I was angry. A righteous anger at all the ways I'd been tortured for feeling this way, told that it was wrong, that I was broken. That it was a bad thing.

I didn't feel broken at all, in fact (even in this confused state), I felt so not broken. I saw myself clearly for the very first time. This was me. This was the truth, and it felt good. I was gay, but I wasn't Ray's kind of gay. It didn't have to be that way. I would be different.

And I was ready (almost ready, I thought) to defend myself and confront any blowback I'd get. This time I was ready to fight, and this was new.

"So what? So what if I am gay?"

Doubts were replaced by a steely conviction as I rehearsed how it would feel to say the words: "I'm gay, but I still love you."

I did also have to ask myself, what was that? Being gay and still loving a woman? It sounded silly, but it was true. I loved my mother, my two sisters. Char was my best friend (had been my most intimate friend); she knew things about me; she had also loved me, and I was (after all) still me. I looked and acted the same. Except now I was different, and it was the different part that might change everything.

Maybe things were different, but they were also simply more, not less. I was more real.

This was the real me, and wasn't being real and being truthful a loving act? I had to trust that Char still believed that it was. Everything I'd come to know about Char was that she prized honesty; we had that in common.

But when I finally made it off the bus, onto BART, walked the blocks to her house, sweaty and dazed, I still had no speech. With each step, I kept having to reconvince myself that it was going to be OK. I practiced how to be a confident person who just so happened to be loaded with a bombshell.

I had nothing to say that might make it any easier, nothing but the unvarnished truth. It was all I had. It would have to be enough. I owed Charlotte the truth, but whatever happened next, I couldn't predict.

Char (and her mom) were serious, thoughtful people. Char's own mother was gay. Even disappointed, they might understand, and this could end up not being such a big deal, after all. I might even receive guidance on what to do next, on how to tell my parents. I might get some advice and some adult congratulations; Char's mom might even take my side (if her daughter was too upset).

That didn't happen.

When I knocked on the door, Charlotte let me in, hugged me; her mother said hello and offered a glass of water. It was as if we were seeing each other after only five minutes, not many months, apart. It was going to be all right.

The friendly welcome, however, had the unexpected effect of disarming my fiery argument. The fight I expected didn't seem like it was going to happen, so now what? I still needed to tell them. But I didn't right away. I chickened out.

Charlotte had planned a small dinner party and invited someone over, a new friend I hadn't met yet. I didn't know any of her other friends from Berkeley, and I could tell that this dinner was important, that she was even a bit nervous. Why was she nervous? This was her home. I was the nervous one.

"Eric, do you have a friend you'd like to invite over for dinner?" Charlotte's mom asked. "Anyone here in Berkeley?"

The only person I considered my real friend was Charlotte, so no, but then I remembered, I'd met someone up in Mendocino, and I'd wondered how he was doing, and he just so happened to live right across the bay in San Francisco. I had his phone number.

I could still feel the heat of his presence, the lessons I was coming to terms with, the reason I was down here in the first place.

"His name is Ray, and he's...very interesting" was all I said.

Charlotte and her mom exchanged a look and encouraged me to invite him over. Dinner was at six.

Suddenly, the ground started moving faster and in a very different direction than I'd thought it would. Ray was on his way. I needed to tell them.

We hung out, listening to jazz, chatting about what we'd been doing, Charlotte working periodically in Los Angeles filming, her mom in the studio painting. I was experimenting with acting and working at the restaurant, of course.

We talked about our artistic process, what inspired us, any insights, frustrations, and what we wanted from our lives. Still, I didn't tell them.

As I listened to Charlotte and her mom describe their activities, I saw myself in a stark profile, facing an empty void. The fire had been snuffed, replaced by my familiar stabbing fear. I needed to tell them.

"I've allowed fear to call the shots," I said to the living room. "Fear tells me that whatever I do, I'm a fraud. I don't trust myself."

Charlotte's mom confessed that she too still had difficulty believing that she was any good. I found that hard to believe, since she was a dedicated professional, selling her artwork, making money. But she said that it was all quite normal and that she'd gotten used to it.

"Doubting oneself is the constant companion of a real, working artist," she encouraged. "Patience and stamina help. The inner critic is always going to nag."

The fire sputtered to life, and I thought, I must be on the brink of a breakthrough because worry, doubt, and fear of failure were my guiding principles.

And then it just happened. Charlotte changed the record and asked me to describe Ray. What was he like, how long had I known him, what made him my friend?

Looking down at myself on the couch (the living room suddenly a giant stadium with me in the spotlight), I started speaking but couldn't hear the words coming out of my mouth.

My face was hot, feet cold, heart racing, palms sweating. Lights were flashing. I went blind for a moment. I said something about how I'd first seen Ray on the street one afternoon, thinking he looked so much like the fictional character I'd been writing about. I described our two memorable encounters, the music he'd played, the Pop Rocks, the rainbow socks, my learned concept of camp, how handsome I thought he was, and that I thought that I was probably gay. I left out the part where I'd learned Ray was a hooker.

Charlotte and her mom again exchanged that look, but they didn't explode and kick me out. They didn't get angry or start crying. Char just looked at me with her serious blue eyes and said, "I know."

In my shock and relief, I blurted out, "Wait, how? How did you know?"

But looking at them both lounging in chairs, comfortable in their house, it was obvious. Charlotte and her mom had known for a while.

"Oh, I just figured," said Charlotte. "It began to make sense. There was no one thing, but many things, y'know?"

No, I didn't know.

She went on to describe what she'd perceived as a cooling of passions we'd first experienced. She realized that it was even uncomfortable and naturally, no longer the right fit.

She described it so matter-of-factly as if it were simply a normal shift in the way things were. Not a big deal, not a heartbreaking, life-changing, disastrous, hurtful, disgusting, or awful thing. This was normal.

Charlotte's mom went into the kitchen to start dinner, and while I sat on the couch rearranging my life, Charlotte made a quick phone call.

"Let's take a walk," she said. "Let's go meet Michelle."

I guessed that Michelle was the friend who'd be coming over for dinner. She lived a few blocks away, and we could just bring her back to the house.

This lovely neighborhood of comfortable Craftsman bungalows and leafy trees, the tended gardens of roses and bougainvillea, deep-green ivy draping over fences, starlings chirping pleasantly in the late-afternoon sun all wrapped around me as we strolled up the block. The world gave me a hug.

But even as the pent-up anxiety evaporated, there it was again, the void. Where all the fears had been just moments ago, primed for upheaval, a quivering space still pestered me. There was something else.

As we walked, Charlotte told me that she was far from upset. In fact, she was relieved since she had realized over the last few months that she too was also gay and that Michelle was her girlfriend.

That was her, waiting at the corner as we approached. I'd thought it was the figure of a man, the way she stood, hands in jeans pockets, a plaid shirt, her dark hair cut short. Charlotte introduced us, and Michelle gripped my hand firmly, shaking it once, then put her arm around Charlotte's shoulders. Charlotte was her girlfriend.

The void quickly filled back up with angst and confusion. Charlotte was her girlfriend. I had been replaced.

The walk back to Charlotte's house was the longest four blocks of clipped, forced conversation. Charlotte in the middle as Michelle told me how they'd met. I should be happy. Happy for Charlotte, for myself, for the freedom and opportunity this represented, but I wasn't. I was heartbroken.

It was a different house we returned to. Charlotte's mom had laid out nibbles, and with the three women casually chatting on one side of the table, I sat on the other stuffing my face with crackers and cheese.

Michelle fit right in; she was already a member of the family. I could see that this was the chair she always chose, her arms upon the table, leaning in deference toward Charlotte, their hands touching. Whenever I raised my head from the plate of rearranged cheese cubes, I caught Michelle staring at me with her sharp, green eyes. Eyes sliding from Charlotte back to me, down at the table, Charlotte, then me. The conversation between our glances an assessment and a challenge.

Charlotte is my girlfriend.

I wore a tight smile, mouth opening only to let in cheese, working that cube like a pearl. Then the doorbell rang.

It was Ray, and I was never so happy to see anyone. He looked only slightly uncomfortable but stunningly handsome. His jet-black hair shiny and straight, now a bit longer, just touching his broad shoulders. He wore a pale-pink bomber jacket, his carpet bag slung next to slim hips. He was wearing those tight blue pants and platform shoes, and he'd brought flowers.

There was a chair on my side of the table, and he sat close, his left knee pressing my thigh, rubbing back and forth as if to say, "I know how you feel." When I looked over at his face, he slowly turned to look at me, still inscrutable but with a gleam in his eye.

There was that fire again. It radiated up from my groin, flowing down my arms and sparking out of fingertips, pounding heart, prickling my face. It was a brotherly encouragement and invitation. There was no question. He liked me too.

Somehow, we survived dinner, and when Charlotte took Michelle outside to say goodnight and Ray gathered himself to go as well, Charlotte's mom suggested he just spend the night, since it was late. He could sleep in the guest room adjacent to Charlotte's. I would take one of the two twin beds in Charlotte's room (as I always had when visiting), now in another life.

Pent-up and restless, I lay there in the dark listening to Charlotte breathing; she was asleep. I was wide awake, throbbing, and could feel Ray (through the doorway in the next room); he was waiting for me. I wanted him, and he wanted me. He was lying there, so close, probably in his underwear.

After torturing myself for a few hours, I got up and tiptoed through the door and sat down on his bed. Yes, he was awake, and he pulled me down. We had sex right there, with my ex-girlfriend in the next room.

Afterward, I slunk back into my other bed, triumphant, jubilant with passion and relief. I had found myself! With Ray, because of Charlotte, through so much indecision and doubt. Past fear and worry, the indescribable, terrifying, newly recognized, and now, wonderfully realized self. All of this, this secrecy and the stumbled-upon breadcrumbs toward what was real. I had arrived. Charlotte was still asleep, the house quiet as I silently whooped.

The next morning, I noticed that Charlotte was already up, and when Ray and I descended the stairs, there she was, at the dining room table sitting close to her mother. They were cold statues staring at me.

"My bedroom is right below the guest room," said Char's mom. "I didn't get any sleep last night because of you two."

My heart froze. Discovered! We had been so quiet, but I guess not quiet enough.

"I'm extremely disappointed in you, Eric." She didn't even acknowledge Ray.

"To do this, in our house, with Charlotte in the next room. This is a violation. This is unacceptable, and I want you both to leave. Now!"

Ray's bag was at his feet. He just grabbed it and in disgust, not saying goodbye, just walked out, not even closing the door. I heard him sucking his teeth. He was gone.

I had only brought a jacket, and as I automatically shoved my puppet arms in, the cold morning air outside pulled at me. Closing the door behind, I stood for a moment on the porch, facing the void.

CHAPTER 26

BARNUM & BAILEY'S
COLOSSEUM DEATH MATCH

I t had become clear to me that every single item in the café kitchen mattered. Every little thing was there for a reason, personally chosen, and had almost taken on a personality of its own from constant, active use.

The family of knives, from cleaver to carving, were surgeon's tools, medieval torture devices, or dragon's teeth—now repurposed for boning salmon, angling a julienne of carrots, or separating the skin from garlic cloves.

Arming dueling Musketeers, gouging eyeballs, or chopping hands from heretic monks remained options, but in our little kitchen, these daggers and cudgels performed more selective, simple functions.

My favorite abalone-handled paring knife (named Sting, after Bilbo's famous blade) could seriously damage a burglar in the dead of night, but Sting was mostly used for peeling peaches or removing the heads from strawberries.

Whisks, spatulas, rolls of twine, and the meat mallet (carved crisscross grooves made for pounding either pork chops or faces) hung off hooks, clawed from repurposed jars, or lurked in drawers.

Life hinged on each ladle, spoon, olive fork, box of wax paper, vial of saffron, package of sun-dried tomatoes, wine opener, and dish of salt being kept in constant rolling awareness and, once used, cleaned, re-packaged, dispensed with, or replaced to the very drawer, cooler, rack, nook, or cubby it came from, to where it lived, to be then made available once again.

It was expected, for instance, that Sting, after paring down an oblong truffle, be immediately cleaned and repositioned upon the magnetic knife board (point up) with the other bayonets and cutlass. It was a bla-tant act of disregard, defiance, potential flashpoint, or death wish if that knife was left unattended, misplaced, or uncleaned. You were begging for trouble.

It was something I could agree with Gerald on (as knives were dan-gerous in the hands of little girls, pirates, or trolls) and needed to be han-dled with great care. But it was also all the other stuff, like toilet paper and toothpicks, dish rags and matches that Gerald could lose sleep over that made me pause. He got as worked up about the last roll of paper towels as a knife left on the tabletop. Somebody had been lax and made a terrible mistake if the toilet paper in the outside café bathroom was not roll out (with a backup perched on the tank).

"You're no son of mine!" would come the verbal grenade, his point brought home with a whack of the butcher knife. The guilt of not being as obsessed over toilet paper sinking in, I had to wonder if I was in-deed his offspring. The father I remembered was more a playmate than an executioner.

Wherever the knives were, toothpicks or toilet paper, Gerald always seemed to know and a sure way to get my ear chewed off was to forget something as important as toothpicks. If that little antique box of tooth-picks in the foyer was low (if I noticed but didn't replace or add to the list), then I was a saboteur.

Make up some lame story about how the box spilled into a puddle of grease and there wasn't enough time to go get more toothpicks today and Gerald gave me the look. Eyebrow arched (like Mr. Spock as French chef just before Pon Farr), he not only clocked me at light speed but I'd wasted his time. Time was gold in a restaurant, and I'd squandered an entire sovereign.

"While you make jokes, you could be cleaning up this mess!" His eyebrow lashed, finger jabbed.

There was a psychic string attached to every spoon, frying pan, and toothpick in the kitchen, and they all ran back to Gerald. Like a wary spider hovering at the center of his web. Tug on a string or pick your teeth after dinner, and the eyebrow went up. He knew.

If anyone noticed that the kitchen was getting short on guest checks, celery, coffee beans, or toothpicks, that fact should be confirmed, vocalized, and then written on the big obelisk of a blackboard hanging over the refrigerator.

The looming blackboard was like Gerald's disembodied, omnipresent black eye, scrawled upon and watching. The busy eye of an angry god. Visual evidence of needs and wants and emotional fallout. In the beginning, we used to draw messages of encouragement to each other, but now that the café was a full-time business, the blackboard yelled.

"Toothpicks are low!" Everyone's head turned to the board as Gerald scrawled big letters: TOOTHPICKS.

Cave painting sgraffito of battles waged against celery and toothpicks and the passage of time, and there was never enough of time. Lists showed either the acute lack or sudden abundance of time. Lists reminded us that even though work was endless, we were inching forward, moving inexorably toward the end. Dinner would be served; people would eat and then go home to their beds. I would also get to sleep.

"Sit down, eat up, pay up, and then get out!" Gerald would bark at a lingering guest check, still hanging on the line if they'd overstayed a reserved two hours. A relaxed meal in the café had its limits.

The blackboard indicated that we needed celery, baking soda, vanilla extract (and yes, toothpicks), which also then guaranteed a necessary, imperative shopping trip. There would be a break from the kitchen.

Someone would get to escape out into the world.

Observing sights to and from the store, I noticed flowers blooming, leaves turning, houses being repaired. I recognized people who were customers, people I went to school with, people who only looked familiar but whom I had never met. Clouds were charging elephants, seagulls dive bombers; the wild grasses in fields and along roads were longer or newly mowed, dried up, built over, leaning left or right, sprouting cows, horses, slow-moving tourists, or statuesque, international orange land surveyors. The trees were always bent here, sparse at this break, the curve in the road too sharp for a misleading speed limit. Grocery shelves presented the possibilities for Hamburger Helper, a Manwich, or turkey pot pie.

In the kitchen, we existed in a bubble, but outside, time changed. The sun rose and set, tides moved in and out, and there would always be another box of toothpicks. I would happily erase the board when I returned.

Sometimes I quickly drew chalk pictures on the blackboard to illustrate something (making more obvious the need). Beautifying the mundane, but once again naively implicating the luxury of time. Time spent drawing was time wasted for fulfilling a need.

The indulgence of mindful play in the drawing of celery—I couldn't help myself in reintroducing subversive visual markers of joy found in the toil. Because a drawing of celery was more than celery; it also said that, *yes, I'm paying attention, I'm using the precious coin of time to draw and force eyes to acknowledge the moment. Bucking the system, yes, I am a saboteur. We need celery? There's your celery!*

Each item marked off or erased was also an opportunity to communicate with one another. Sometimes it was the only time, and we chose our words carefully.

"I'll get the celery, Gerald. Nice drawing, Eric." Ellen was always the diplomat; just the sound of her voice created calm. "Looks good enough to eat."

Oh no, she went too far that time, complimenting me for an indulgent drawing. Gerald sensed mutiny.

"I hope the celery is as good in the refrigerator as it is on that board." He gave me the look. Note to self: a backhanded compliment or not, it was us against him.

With every word, we were acknowledged, lifted, pinched, or stung. It all depended on what time it was, who said what, and how much wine Gerald had guzzled.

I looked for his bottle of Beaujolais by the bloodied butcher block, half-empty and it was only three o'clock. Mashed paper towels, some cooking sherry, and a small pile of steak fat. It could go one way or the other. Ellen drank tea and kept her end of the kitchen neat and tidy.

Our many codified reports and summary of missing salad forks or abundant napkins spoke of how we were dealing with the moment and what might be inferred from the exchange, in how we should proceed. You could read a lot into: "Someone stepped on a tomato! It looks like murder!" Gerald might die mysteriously in his sleep.

Lists were always being made and juggled like small, sparking meteors tossed between gods. Hands in the air, words, visual reference, and description, synesthetic or emotional import communicated either by a blurted gesture, scribbled abbreviation, or raised eyebrows, the Rosetta Stone blackboard getting passed over if the information burned.

"Now is now!" the pointed finger said. "There is no time to write! Just do!"

Announcements barked over the hubbub of an evening's excitement, with an expected acknowledgment punctuating. An automatic call-and-response composition that reverberated throughout the day. I'd taken to employing several stock sound effects that gave a personal touch.

"I need shallots for the filet mignon," Gerald spat over sizzling steaks.

A clean blackboard meant that shallots were there somewhere, and my neanderthal grunt acknowledged. Making a show of shifting my hump and loping like Igor over to the cooler, an obvious, guttural "Ungh!" meant Gerald's' shallots were forthcoming and that I was his servant.

God forbid someone should forget something, neglect to write it down, announce the lack of, or lose the chalk. An empty blackboard translated into a well-stocked kitchen, some well-earned peace of mind, and a bit more sleep in the morning—or heads would roll come dinnertime.

A new batch of thinly sliced shallots magically appeared on Gerald's prep table accompanied by the exclamation of brass horns. "Tadaaaa!" I was suddenly a hero, the attentive son, a worthy second-in-command. Every act made toward the success of an evening confirmed full entry into the Gerald Still Likes Me Club.

Sometimes, when I had an exorbitant amount of time to spend, I'd notice that those two wobbly wire whisks Ellen used to whip up egg whites or crème fraîche also made perfect alien antennae. Rising animated from behind my head, radar beeping (in reaction to the radioactive chocolate broyage laid out for tonight's dessert). Ellen's laughter was worth any momentary pause in the white-knuckle ride toward five thirty and dinnertime.

So much care was lavished on every detail, and timing was everything. The laborious all-day buildup to service culminated as Jim or Greta brought in that first order. The kitchen doors creaked as Greta scribbled. Gerald took a breath as if for a high dive, wiping his hands on the blood-stained apron, craning his neck to examine the tiny letters on her check.

"How am I supposed to see anything if you write like chickadees?" he yelped. "Write bigger. Like a child, so I can see. Instantly."

She ripped it down, wrote again quickly:

TABLE # EIGHT. 2 SALADS, 1 FILET MIGNON (MR), 1 SALMON (W) w/ RICE, (NO VEG), 2 BROYAGE

I got it, large-print projects, there was no time for decryption. Once that check was presented, the clock was going, and time weirdly, simultaneously stopped, then sped up again, ticking down to this crucial moment. The civilized conversation between customer and server, soliciting a delicate, sometimes emotional, choice based on the menu, personal anecdotes, quirks, and expectations all boiled down to a scribbled cartoon, translated into dinner. The circle of life.

It was a practiced, deliberate pattern, each plate of food built in a descending, layering repetition, each becoming small paintings of color and texture.

Ellen washed the salad greens and caged them in a folding basket; then out on the back porch, she swung around her propeller right arm to throw off water. Leaves were patted dry in a cloth, placed into a metal bowl where she lightly salted, tossed with a drip of vinaigrette. Then a small heap was gathered up in driftwood tongs and delicately placed onto a plate.

When the time came, Gerald painted an asymmetrical swatch of peppercorn sauce across the wide dinner plate. Jabbing tournedos with demon Barbie's trident (a long-handled fork), he positions two pieces, fanning them slightly to show the pink framed by a blackened edge.

A big, leaky spoon with holes punched through it spilled a few baby potatoes next to a construction of slivered carrots. Bound for a different plate, salmon was lifted gently from the pan of shallow water with the fly swatter spatula and laid gently over splashed lemon sauce, basmati rice was cuddled, then there was the finishing pinch of minced green herb.

That was the signal that plates were ready (demanding) to be delivered. If the little hotel bell got dinged twice, that meant someone was going to get lectured.

Art wrangled from thin air and dirt; the plates radiated a tantalizing aura as they rested for a moment on the blue table. Their edges were quickly wiped, then collected and carried out to the dining room; to do over, and over, and over again.

The café kitchen looked and smelled like a kitchen, with a stove, sinks, a refrigerator, and a freezer. Cupboards and drawers full of stuff, the shiny blue table in the middle, pots and pans hanging, the large blackboard hovering. Operating like any restaurant kitchen, it both fed our family and the nightly crowd, but this kitchen was also the cleverly disguised center ring of Barnum & Bailey's big top.

Gerald, the quintessential ringmaster bellowing above the din, mighty Zeus raising his quivering right hand ready to lash out in a deadly smack. It was all for show, but his predictable behavior set the stage for our circumspect roles.

Ellen balanced high above the fray, juggling the world from her precarious tight rope; Greta attempted acrobatic daring either on horseback or out in the dining room; Jim, the elegant big cat tamer, cracked the preverbal whip; while I, the listless, disgruntled clown, prepped vegetables, washed dishes, and dragged out the trash while lobbing wise-ass jokes.

Managed panic and spontaneous solutions were constantly, sometimes frantically, applied backstage by our family circus troupe. Fire eaters, sword swallowers, freaks, and midgets running back and forth between the lions, tigers, and bears.

Upfront (just beyond the magic threshold of the two swinging doors) remained a serene sea of calm and harmony; a total fiction.

Occasionally diners would catch a glimpse of the action when one of the swinging doors got stuck. *Who are those crazy people?*

CHAPTER 27

NORMAL

E llen was always the first one up, even before the sun sometimes. She sipped lapsang souchong and read Anaïs Nin quietly at table eight or, if it was not raining, out on the back porch in the pale morning light. Then, pulling her handwoven poncho and teacup close, she strolled around the yard, accompanied by her tortoiseshell rescue cat, Buttons.

I watched them picking their way past a wave of low-hanging Cecile Brunner roses or ducking under stickery purple bougainvillea. Sometimes getting caught, Ellen exhaled in exasperation. I heard her. I was awake. Meticulously freeing herself from the purple needles, she continues her garden circuit, with Buttons leading the way.

I was also an early riser, learning to listen for a robin's song (or Ellen's gasp at being bitten by roses). From the small window of my garage hideaway, I watched her, and Buttons, slowly maneuver through overgrown grass, stopping to admire a cluster of daisies or a shock of wild orchid. Ellen leaned down to consider a stem's length, Button's nose kissing the flower's face.

She gathered a few curated, dew-covered blooms or long, wispy weeds while Buttons explored the underbrush (disappearing for a moment) then scampering back out in front once again, her tail directing.

Standing up in bed still encased in my mummy bag, I watched Ellen sample a new strawberry from a small patch and pluck green apples from the old tree elbowed over the path. Pouring out the cold tea, she narrowly avoided Buttons bounding up the porch steps. It was breakfast time!

Ellen brought the outside in, laying out her morning forage on a checkerboard tablecloth. The family of bud vases, mason jars, and vintage coffee cans awaited arrangements, but first, Ellen completed the morning ritual by placing a small piece of old salmon on a plate for Buttons.

Sometimes Ellen indulged herself with a hike along the cliffs or down to the beach, coming home with armloads of Queen Anne's lace or rattlesnake grass, her socks fuzzy with burrs. Smoothed, curved pieces of driftwood filled her blue satchel or back pockets. Washed up from a faraway Japanese forest to become favorite, decorative utensils. I've picked up wiggly magic wands and naturally forked tongs, offering Ellen a new trophy when I joined her on a predawn beginning, but she graciously refused anything that couldn't be repurposed toward practical use in the kitchen.

I was the one who made the coffee, and if I was smart (a team player and aware of the day to come), I'd have ground the beans, ready the night before.

Waiting in its filter, the dark French roast expanded and released nutritious caramel perfume as I poured in boiling water. When the drip was steady and clean (filter balanced, no grounds escaping, the Chemex filling up and a level reached), I felt a rising tingle of anticipation. We had a large beaker full of plenty, and I got the first cup.

After lighting a fire in the front dining room's little stove, I sat with Ellen next to her pastry table as she measured out flour from her large ceramic crock. Muffins? Kipfels? Bread or buns, cake, roulade, or tart? A gob of butter, the red baking powder jar, chipped salt, and pepper roosters from Berkeley brought down from their high roost. My sandy eyes took in what was on her table to explain what she might be making this morning.

"Eric, will you please find the gruyere cheese in the cooler?" Ellen nodded to the narrow cupboard behind me. I reached from her table to the cupboard door. "I'm making cheese biscuits for breakfast," she said.

There was the cheese wrapped in brown paper on one of the old Victorian shelves, tied with string, tucked behind a flat of brown eggs.

Greta clomped downstairs, barely acknowledging me, her curly chestnut hair mashed into a strange shape on the left side. She was unbothered by my raised eyebrows and went right for the shelf to grab her favorite speckled tin camping mug.

Ellen cut out dough shapes with a jar lid, turning them on her floured table, lining them all up on a cookie sheet, but Greta interrupted by resting her bushy head on Ellen's shoulder; she was not quite awake.

"Good morning, darling." Ellen nestled into Greta's brown hair pillow.

Eyeing the biscuits, Greta took a pinch of the cheese I'd just grated and sprinkled frosting over each.

"I get the big one," she stated as if already decided. Avoiding my protest, Greta turned to contemplate the large hourglass Chemex balanced in its bubbling bain-marie of hot water. Grabbing its narrow wooden neck, she filled her cup, a spill of milk from the rooster creamer, then out the back screen door with a slam. I saw Ellen wince, knowing that Gerald upstairs would have been alerted. The day had begun.

Greta went to commune with her four-legged equine animus, Cricket, and would be out in the backyard, sitting slumped over on horseback while they wandered around the yard as one, nibbling weeds, sipping coffee.

Kristin tiptoed downstairs in her floral nighty. The first words from her mouth were "Where's Greta?" The two girls were inseparable.

Ellen stopped whatever she was doing, even as she turned up the oven for a timed bake. The biscuits remained blobs on their tray as she took off her apron to collect Kristin up in her arms, cradling the sleepy little girl.

"Greta's outside, of course." She glanced to the backyard. "She lives on that horse."

I had to say it: "A horse is a horse, of course, of course." Ellen's eyes glimmered, recognizing my referencing to the cornball TV show *Mr. Ed*. But Kristin just thought her older brother was weird.

Ellen attempted to brush some of the knots from Kristin's mane, and I took the initiative, sliding the tray of biscuits into the oven. Hair brushing was also a part of the morning ritual (Ellen so patient with her yowling daughter). But I was not patient. I was hungry!

While Ellen worked at the frayed ends of an impossible tangle, I poured a bit of coffee into Kristin's pet cup. A china demitasse with a tiny ceramic mouse hiding at the bottom, peeking out only after all the coffee was gone. After her first sip, Kristin cheated and tilted the cup to see if her whiskered friend was still there, looking up, waiting for her.

Ten minutes later, biscuits were done, and Kristin yanked herself free, taking hers on a napkin to the kitchen window where she stood silently munching, watching the shape of horse and rider in the backyard slowly meander back and forth. From the kitchen, Cricket looked like she had some strange oblong growth on her back. It was Greta, slumped over with her coffee cup balanced between the brown mare's ears.

Biscuit finished, Kristin fled outside with a care package, Greta's large rock biscuit wrapped in a paper towel. I saw her hand it over (trading for an empty mug). Taking a seat on the broken scroll-back chair, she waited as her older sister made one more round of the yard. Buttons hopped up into her lap to be petted by tiny hands, but not for long because soon it would be Kristin's turn to ride. Greta gave Kristin a boost up onto Cricket's bare back, directing her every move, holding the reins, leading horse and sister around, never letting go.

Gerald was always the last to arrive in the kitchen, emerging from the stairwell around eight o'clock like a craggy, peg-legged, one-eyed pirate growling at the arcing light of morning, the sun an affront to his senses. Like Faust confronting his inevitable deal with the devil, there was desperation in his baleful stare.

"Ach du Lieber!" He held his hand up in front of eye slits. "The sun is so bright! Is the world on fire?" Mornings were difficult for Gerald.

Life was but a stage, and Gerald lived every moment as if he were making a grand entrance. Lately, though, I'd observed him folding in on himself. He'd turned from a bombastic, loving teddy bear into haunted scalawag. Every action seemed preceded by a disconsolate moan. A cat on a hot tin roof, afraid of his own shadow, cringing at the ringing telephone, heaving a sigh of resignation as the UPS delivery guy knocked.

"What have I signed my life away for this time?" The ugly surprise was not the end of the world but a special delivery from the Musical Heritage Society.

"Vivaldi! Vivaldi!" Gerald held up the new, nondescript, white album in triumph. Music older than dirt, a collection of baroque concertos, and for Gerald, pure crack cocaine.

"Música! Música!" he proclaimed, pushing the record into my hand. "Put it on. Put it on and listen to genius."

Tinkling harpsichord and sweeping violins danced over the amber-tinted fantasy of a sixteenth-century garden or marbled chamber. Our little kitchen suddenly a rococo palace and Gerald (adjusting the air with his wafting dishrag) a slightly rumpled Venetian courtier. A short moment of revelry, and then he was back to complaining about something.

"The speakers sound tinny! Did you do something with those dials?" Of course I was the logical culprit as I was listening to Elton John after work last night. He slapped the rag down and went into the adjacent family room to toggle the receiver. I heard him muttering made-up curses.

"Dagnabbitfrickinfrakin!" He was the caricature of a mad baron, not far from the truth. The correct volume for classical music piped into the dining room and kitchen (according to Gerald) is a fixed, sacrosanct one or two clicks from the twelve o'clock position. Anything below was ridiculous, illogical; above, it was an abomination.

"If you must play your noise, you'd better make sure the dial is back in place before dinnertime."

It was a given: any deviation from Gerald's prescribed center spelled trouble. He was adamant and reinforced his ultimate authority over every detail of the restaurant. Change something (like a notch on the stereo), and you were courting trouble. He worried about how tinny the tinny harpsichords sounded, what was left in the refrigerator, and how many days he could stretch that horrible Hungarian fish soup. He worried about what that tourist last night (picking at painstakingly prepared lemon chicken) was thinking. "What did he say? Why didn't he lick the plate?" The innermost thoughts and table manners of strangers were always in question.

He worried about the deepening dent in his butcher block, about the grease that could never be scrubbed entirely away from underneath the stove hood, the sputtering pilot light on the back burner, and what the health inspector would say if he made a surprise visit.

The joints of his fingers, toes, elbows, and wrists were in such pain. How would he make tonight's dinner unforgettable? How would he debone all that salmon if his fingers and wrists were on fire?

"It's like being stabbed with a knife!"

How did he please everyone and remain sane? What would the bank do the day after tomorrow if he didn't make the late payment, and how fast could he reinvent the wheel? He mumbled about how Ellen's cat, Buttons, stared at him with hatred.

"That cat will claw my throat out while I sleep. I've seen the devil in her eyes. What have I ever done to her?"

I'd seen him hiss at poor Buttons and stamp his foot purposely to scare her.

An ambulance siren wailed somewhere, and he looked up with expectation. "Hoohoo! My ride is here! They might close us down. Haul me off to the poorhouse, or the loony bin." Men in white coats could come storming in at any moment with a special jacket just for Gerald. He did seem a bit crazy.

He was always very concerned that the carrots were sliced au julienne enough. "The thinner, the better!"

He was concerned that inclement weather would kill business and even ruin the clean front porch by blowing dirt onto the just-swept steps. He was worried about dirt. That was why we kept the kitchen clean and made sure it stayed that way. It helped Gerald feel better; it calmed him down.

Strong coffee in the morning was crucial.

I'd gone over the kitchen and picked up a dish, wiped away biscuit crumbs, knives back on the rack, phone messages listened to, notes posted, and reservations marked in the book. I'd plated a perfect biscuit in the valley of his butcher block; the kitchen was spotless. Vivaldi's viola de gamba flowed like warm butter from the small speaker tucked in a corner.

Gerald returned from the bathroom with his face washed, hair smoothed back, both sides of his mustache pointing in the right direction, eyebrows arching as he surveyed the kitchen. But he was still not awake yet. Even with both eyes open, he looked right through me. However, he did see the coffee cup in my outstretched hand, and he grasped it with both paws. A long, slow sip, head tilting back, and a mighty exhale.

"Ahhhhhhh! The elixir of life!"

I felt like a doctor or drug dealer, handing the morning fix over to my father, who would be only half a man without it. It was only then (too late) that I saw the glinting architecture of a new spider's web in the crook of a window, a bug dangling. Gerald saw it too.

"Nature be damned! Those damn spiders can't leave well enough alone!"

A quick swipe and the spider was gone, and I scolded myself for missing it. I was preoccupied with coffee. I was glad the girls were already outside (avoiding Gerald), waking up on their own terms, riding slowly around on horseback. Gerald used to be funny and suave and sweet; now he just barked.

"Where's your mother?" He shot with his eyes.

"She went to the store. She's getting stuff on the list." I pointed to the blackboard — milk, eggs, flour, dry yeast, matches, light bulbs.

"That's something you could have done. Ellen has many more important things to do than shop for matches!" he barked.

"She wanted to go."

Ellen slipped out the door while Gerald was still in the bathroom. He took his coffee, biscuit, and clipboard from the kitchen into the warmed-up dining room, the French doors banging back and forth in his wake. A brief puff of wood smoke, a trail of coffee and burnt cheese lingered while Gerald and the morning got to know each other.

I heard the little fire out front crackle and pop in time with the Vivaldi minuet. No other word from Gerald as he settled in to read the morning paper. An abalone diver was missing. There was an accident on Highway One when a redwood log fell off a truck. Weather was predicted to be temperate with morning fog.

Gerald had his list on that clipboard. Ideas for tonight's dinner, necessary foodstuffs kept in the refrigerator or cupboards, and some that were not (many of which I'd probably be sent out for later). A cobbled-together menu with enthusiastic circles around beef, salmon, and black bean soup and an angry question mark next to dessert. Connecting each circle, Gerald's pencil-scratched webbing translated into a tiny script, squashed down into the bottom right of the page. These few words would guide our day.

Ellen returned with her groceries, and as I put them away, she slowly erased the blackboard of its outdated list, her damp cloth turning letters into clouds. I caught a small sigh as she poured herself another cup of tea, taking a cold biscuit and her own little clipboard to sit with Gerald out in the dining room. They were talking about what it would take to make their menu, delegating tasks, and because they sat for so long, maybe they were also planning out the rest of the week. I hoped so, since then a measure of stress would not again hound them down the stairwell tomorrow morning, spreading like a virus around the kitchen. Sure enough, I was given my shopping list and told to be back before one o'clock, the sooner the better.

"Our lives depend on it!" Gerald gestured, sweeping wide, then pointed to the door. "Do not tarry! Drive like the wind...but don't kill anyone."

He handed me his list, a wad of cash, and a couple of signed checks. "Make sure you get receipts and no pit stops, no dawdling! You have soup to make!"

Everything was high stakes. I looked up at the blackboard, which had now been altered to reflect today's to-do list, written hastily over this morning's smoky remains.

Saturday Menu:

Beuf Roulade, Salmon Almandine, Black Bean Soup, Salad, Chocolate Genoise, Lemon Merengue

On my list, Gerald had drawn flourished, large, baroque letters:

Lamb, Ham Hock, Salmon, Butter Lettuce, Sprouts, Carrots, Yellow Onion, Green Beans, Celery, Parsley, Lemons, Bittersweet Chocolate, Dijon Mustard.

The lamb for tomorrow maybe, but everything else was critical for tonight's dinner.

Pressure was on. Even just standing there reading the list was procrastination. I could be driving, shoving lettuce in a bag, spinning right around, and flying back. Life flashed before me in the seconds it took to read and mentally map out my trajectory up and then back down the coast. How fast could I throw this soup together and then get the dining room set for dinner, and what new drama would be waiting for me when I returned? Probably a hundred other tasks Gerald had thought up. I had to hurry before he thought up anything else! If only I had six arms and could be in all places at once. If only I could be somewhere else.

Thank goodness black bean soup was relatively straightforward. I liked mashing all those beans through the sieve. I got a strange satisfaction, mashing things. Becoming more familiar with what it took to create food here in the café, I learned there were many steps, each one just as important as the one preceding it. A myriad of details all contingent on the next, and there never seemed to be enough time.

As we were always finishing by the skin of our teeth, I was surprised things went as well as they did. Given what I knew, seeing how chaotic it always seemed to be, I knew one odd thing could throw the whole train off track. I had to get that salmon home quick.

Everyone played a part, and I knew that I was doing my bit, but I could always do more. I could be more enthusiastic about helping Ellen and Gerald, but it was just not that interesting, and I could never do what they did. I was not and could never be as good as they were with food. I couldn't coax the flavors from meat the way Gerald could, plot an entire meal for fifty people every night, create from scratch a set of perfect pear tarts, a family of browned rum canelé, or the building blocks of fresh bread every day like Ellen. I didn't want to do that. I hated it, in fact, and I could see that they were both beginning to hate it as well.

I was a much better drawer than a cook. I'd rather draw a picture of a soup pot than make the soup that went in it, but I could pull this recipe together. I knew this one by heart: pot of water, black beans, onion, ham hock, herbs, and a finishing spoon of sour cream. I could taste the tang of beans on my tongue. Blended up (with salt and pepper to taste), this soup gave me the impression that I'd traveled to a foreign country, and I'd made it by hand.

Confidence bolstered my nerve. I was helping to create a positive experience. Soup would be made, and everyone could breathe a little bit easier. Maybe I'd even get to eat some later.

Gerald went to the freezer to pull out beef for defrosting, Ellen was elbow deep in bread dough. I reached for the car keys in the basket by the telephone and was heading for the door, but then I remembered, I'd better soak those beans first. Gerald noticed me with my coat on, filling up the big soup pot.

"There you go, using your noggin." An arched eyebrow, a knowing smile, Gerald thinking what a good apprentice I was, what a great chef I'd make. He was wrong.

I didn't know what exactly it was I wanted to do with my life, but it was not what Gerald had in mind. He was going to be bitterly disappointed when I didn't follow in his footsteps.

I pushed the speed limit up to the butcher's in Cleone. Gerald had called ahead, so lamb was wrapped and waiting. It was almost a relay race as I held out my hand to receive (offering a check in the other), rushing in while also turning to go.

Lucky me! A parking spot right in front of the little market. Vegetables, lemons, mustard, and chocolate in a bag and lickety-split, I was down to Noyo harbor where Popeye's grandpappy had two massive whole salmon also wrapped and ready, heavy, fishy, and wet.

Zooming back down the coast, passing tourists unpracticed at driving while taking pictures at the same time, I shifted and signaled, sped up and down the small hills, around curves, past trailers, and sea-bleached wooden barns, cows and sheep, fields of green grass all sliding by in a watercolor blur. Glittering ocean flashed between rhododendrons and mossy cliffs. Road signs and directions were meaningless as I swerved up the hill to the herb farm, my last stop. I could see Gerald back home pacing, his breath ragged, eyes rolling.

"Where is that boy?"

Sprouts and fresh parsley in the bag, and I hit the retro rockets; I'd landed. Turning off the motor too soon before shifting back into first, the VW bus rattled and jerked. Startled, as I came barreling up, a raven hurled epitaphs down at me from the telephone wire.

"You're late! You're late!"

I barged into the kitchen, the screen door banging, arms full of bags, raven barking, telephone ringing, kettle whistling, Gerald yelling, Greta yelling back. I was home.

"Why do I always have to remind you of your duties?" Gerald accused Greta.

"I know exactly what to do and how to do it!" she countered.

He grabbed the grocery bags roughly from my hands. I'd been fast today, but it was never fast enough. I thought the future promised us flying cars.

"Well, then, get to it! We've been right here—where have you been all day?"

Ellen looked from one to the other, acknowledging the old argument; it was like a recording. Everyone knew where Greta had been. Riding Cricket around town or down to the beach, up a trail and back, then mucking out her stall, brushing hide and mane, spending every waking moment outside.

"Go clean yourself up. You stink to high heaven!"

The phone was still ringing. I turned to answer, but Ellen reached the phone first, putting her floured prints all over.

"Good afternoon, Café Beaujolais! Hello? Yes, hello. Café Beaujolais. Hello? Sir, sir, I'm sorry, but I'm afraid I can't understand you, oh yes, hello. Yes, we have room for four. At seven? Yes, I believe we can do that. Your name? Your name, sir. Oh, you're flying in from San Diego. Yes, yes, I understand. May I get a phone number…well? We'd appreciate a call if you're going to be late. We're looking forward to the evening, thank you, oh! He hung up." She held the phone away from her face as if it had stuck its tongue out. "I didn't get his number."

Gerald wrinkled his forehead, eyebrows drawn together, mustache twitching, lips pinched into a tight frown that sometimes lasted all night.

It was not like it hadn't happened before. People made reservations and then left the wrong number, or they didn't even show up. They arrived late, bringing along more guests than they'd booked (or we had room for) and demanding a dish that we hadn't prepared or sending something back to be cooked again. This drove Gerald crazy. Or sometimes they'd leave without paying, usually just forgetting but still leaving poor Jim to have to scamper outside and chase them down the block.

It had become painfully apparent that we could only control what we did there in the kitchen, with little or no reach upon the rest of the world. The expectation that people would act more or less like civilized adults upon entering the café (our home) was a fantasy. The unspoken contract was to treat someone like you'd want to be treated yourself, and if that failed, the customer was always right.

Whenever something off program reached back to the kitchen, everything stopped for a second with a ricochet of searching eyes. Absorbing information, reeling from anxiety, searching for an answer. A moment's imbalance, but common sense always won.

The crying child ruining dinner for the rest of the room. How long to wait before crossing a name off (and giving the table away to someone impatiently standing in the hallway who drove up from the Bay Area), only to have the late party show up and be angry their table had been given away? Not getting the full picture but having to decide, moving heaven and earth. There were sometimes ugly surprises. Life was messy, perfection elusive.

Ellen was usually the sober, guiding voice that calmed everybody down, and she spoke gently now.

"I'm sure he'll show up. He sounded…emphatic." Ellen's graceful sweep away from the phone back to her bowl of bread dough was all that was needed. Gerald relaxed, the weight of the world shifted, and he turned to unwrap salmon.

Two whole fish as long as my arm lay across his butcher block, their glazed eyes looking at nothing. Taking his sharp fillet knife, he leaned down and expertly sliced their bellies from head to tail, opening the fish to reveal a shock of pink laced with tiny white bones. I knew he'd be bent over for at least an hour as there were lots and lots of bones, each one having to be handpicked out, but it didn't take that long for his back to stiffen up.

"Mein Gott im Himmel!" He stretched the German out while hinging his back in a spasm of pain. Gerald had many phrases from several fancy European languages that he'd employ in just the right moment. All those years of singing opera, Gerald was always the actor, the star of his own personal drama.

We kept offering to raise the butcher block on bricks, so he didn't have to stoop over and suffer, but he always poo-pooed the idea, preferring, I guess, to groan, stretch and then continue to complain about it. I thought he may like to make noise as he worked, distracting his busy mind and maybe letting the rest of us know that he was still there. Ellen and I would look at each other. How could we ever forget?

One o'clock and the sun beamed into the kitchen from all sides, illuminating the blue table in the center of the room as if it were molten glass. I covered the blinding gleam with my cutting board and the various tools I needed, tasting beans, skimming off floaters as they steeped in a simmering bath. They were exactly as they should be, with the tiniest bit of crunch left. By dinnertime, they'll be soft and perfect. In went the ham hock, more water, chopped onion, celery (leaves and all), two carrots, whole garlic, bay leaf, a dash of cayenne, and fresh pinch of thyme from the bunch hanging above Ellen's pantry table.

Two o'clock. Turn the heat up slightly. I had until four to get all my other chores done. Ellen had her bread baked. The loaves were stacked under the table and covered with napkins. Now she was concentrating on the chocolate genoise and lemon meringue. The tang of fresh lemons hovered above deeper meat, herb, and toasted bread smells. Beef roulade in the oven, Gerald returned to work on the salmon. There was a mound of collected bones and a few pieces of fish that couldn't be used, ending up as stock. Maybe Buttons would even get a treat. Gerald would hiss and then feed her as if to say, "I'm sorry."

Greta was on her own out in the dining room ironing and folding freshly laundered napkins, lining up perfect stacks in the glass cupboard.

There were pots and pans to wash. Utensils and various metal and driftwood tools, pans, bowls, dishes, and glasses, everything just as important as the other, needed for service later this evening or in the morning. Tackling the glasses first, I filled the three sinks out back with near-boiling water. Wash, rinse, and then sterilize. Gloves on, wineglasses in and out. None had broken or cracked (a personal triumph), and they looked like refracting crystal jewelry steaming dry on the rack. Dishes and tools and finally pots, the chore girl scrubby getting a workout, my hands withered and webbed in hot water.

Greta vacuumed the dining room, competing with Wagner (and Gerald) on the stereo. A commonplace commotion, Valkyrie warriors belting out operatic battle cries just above a motorized din. I was reminded of when we'd stripped the floorboards in those first days. I thought of Jesús. Returning the glasses to their cupboard, I waited for the inevitable.

At any other time, Gerald would be lambasting Greta for disturbing the reverie of this musical interlude. Still, because it was crunch time (also because she was doing her job), he remained mum; he just turned the music up. Apocalyptic thunder rained down on our little kitchen, and the newly cleaned glasses tinkled on their shelf.

"Gerald! For god's sake, turn that down!" Ellen was holding her ears, a smudge of meringue on her cheek. Like a scolded boy, Gerald lowered the volume and then shut off the music completely. Greta's oblivious vacuuming finished; the gulf of silence felt like a body blow. Gerald was taking a time-out, it seemed, disappearing along with the music.

I found him out on the back porch stretching his back between sips from a bottle of Pinot Noir, feeding Buttons her savored salmon bits. The sun was behind the water tower now, casting a looming shadow over the garden.

"My fingers are burning." He held up his two hands as if they were on fire. My own hands were still hot from dishwater, and I took his right hand between mine and let the heat seep into his swollen, bony fingers. His eyes closed, and he floated away, momentarily losing balance, and I had to grab him by the arm. Buttons, startled, darted away, but I held on to Gerald, who left his body for a moment.

What to do next? Chop firewood or clean the bathroom? The light was shifting, so it was the pile of just-dumped wood out back. Cedar, pine, oak, and a few leftover chunks of redwood, left where the hippie dude emptied his truck behind the shed. There was rough comfort in setting up a chunk of wood, choosing the center mark, wielding the rusty ax, and splitting the log in two. A nice pile loaded up and then delivered to the stove inside. I took out my frustrations on stupid lumps of wood, about my uncertain future, about my many scary secrets, the mistakes, and imperfect behavior. A clean chop, and they were all split, whittled down to size.

I still had the toilets to scrub and then soup to finish. Time was precious.

Shifting into automatic, I shoveled out the ash from the morning and set up a new log construction with today's crumpled paper, the matchbook set and ready for a five o'clock lighting.

When I returned from cleaning the bathroom, Ellen was in the dining room handwriting tonight's menu page. Her set of pens and ink bottles lined up, hand poised for a graceful attack. Her delicate, calligraphic script, always a work of art.

Hors d'oeuvres:

Spiced Mushrooms

Chicken Liver Pâté

$2.00

Table d'hôte:

Soup du Jour (Black Bean)

Bread & Sweet Butter

Entrée du Jour (Boeuf Roulade/Salmon Almandine)

Fresh Vegetable

Brown Rice Pilaf

Tossed Green Salad

Coffee/Tea

$10.50

Dessert:

Chocolate Genoise/Lemon Meringue $1.50

I slipped the menus into their sleeves then took the larger copy out to the street. It was so quiet under the darkening sky. Nothing moved, and I hovered for just a moment in the space between now and the business about to rain down on our kitchen as we approached five thirty: the witching hour.

The sizzle and scent of herbed bacon permeated the kitchen, but as I passed by Ellen's pantry table, warm chocolate perfume rose in competition. Her genoise sat cooling on wire racks as she whipped fresh cream to be piped on later in decorative florets.

It was three o'clock—time for me to finish the soup. A short window before service, before Ellen, Gerald, Greta, and Jim become automatons, robots of efficiency who would require every inch of space, both psychic and physical. I needed to be done and out of their way. When my prep was finished, I could disappear and retreat to the garage, to my safe space. Smoke a joint, dance around to my new Todd Rundgren album. I would have at least an hour before I start hosting.

The beans were perfectly cooked, soft but not mushy. Now came the fun part. Ladling soup into a sieve and mashing the contents into another great metal pot with Ellen's well-worn driftwood spoon. The soft veggies, onion, garlic, and beans pulverized into steaming, soil-colored paste. A quick sip asked for a pinch of sea salt—another taste, perfect. Pot on the back burner, flame on simmer, a final dollop of sour cream would be added as it was served into a tureen or single bowl.

Gerald needed a quick, emergency dicing of carrots for something. I didn't even ask; I just got it done. As I chopped, I reached down under the blue table with an odd carrot stick. Little sister Kristin was hiding there, snuggled up with her articulated stuffed bear, Tina. She camped under the table some nights, out of the way, wanting to be close to us as we all scrambled about, still a part of the action.

Jim arrived at four thirty with a voluptuous bouquet collected from neighbors' yards along the walk to work from his studio across town. How he got away with it without reprisal was impressive. His rationale was that nobody would miss a few flowers since there were so many everywhere. Nobody paid any attention. Gerald noticed, though.

"Did you snag those flowers from the other side of town or just down the block?" I swore I'd seen those dahlias right next door.

Jim was an artist, so he took his time arranging the burst of color in a vase out in Fleurette's foyer. Hopefully, a customer wouldn't recognize their prize bloom greeting them for dinner.

Before I could make my escape, I took the list of scribbled reservations from the kitchen and transcribed them into the big black bible out front. I did a double check, making personal notes about a remembered person, a recalled conversation, if there were kids (we didn't have high chairs). Someone who was a good customer, a recognized name, a birthday, a requested entrée or wine choice, a question mark next to a possible conflict, blocking out the allotted two hours per set, or leaving blank tables that could still take diners.

Here was that rude person who called this morning; I put his party at the table by the piano entrance. Then my heart bounced. Peter Sellers! Party of two at seven o'clock. I wonder who he'd bring tonight? It was always a different woman. He liked table eight (in the corner). That meant I had to move someone. Mr. Sellers got a VIP, was circled, alongside a caricature of the Pink Panther.

I could already hear Gerald muttering about how disgusting the overcooked meat and vegetables were. Mr. Sellers always ordered the same thing, and he liked everything reduced to an overcooked pulp.

"The English have no taste buds." Gerald just had to say something, but it was with far less bite than his criticizing me for not informing him about Mr. Sellers earlier.

"You could have warned me. I would have started boiling his vegetables an hour ago." It was a sideswipe of a joke. Even though he was of course pleased that a movie star frequented our restaurant, deviation from Gerald's perfect menu was an insult.

I wondered who took the reservation and didn't tell him. It wasn't me. Maybe Ellen, not mentioning it because she didn't want to antagonize? Or Jim earlier in the week, collecting the magnificent bouquet tonight because he knew who'd be sitting in his section? Or it could have been Greta, who simply didn't give a damn.

It was a tempest in a teapot, so I was not listening to any more bickering. All my chores were finished, and I could walk away out to the garage. Plenty of time to get stoned and dress up for my role as host. I got to greet Mr. Sellers and his date, then transferred back into the kitchen for the rest of the evening. The joint was exactly where I left it, and a quick couple of puffs got me in the mood.

It was sweet fun riffling through the racks of costumes, making spontaneous choices based on how I saw the evening going. It was Saturday night and Peter Sellers was coming, so the ducktailed tux over a silver lamé T-shirt, black slacks, and my good pair of red Converse sneakers were perfect. Rocker chic married to functionality.

One more sing-along with Todd, who mourned a love gone sour.

"I'll come around to see you once in a while…"

I wondered, was the object of his affection in prison or the state pen?

Ambling from the garage, along the rose-strewn path and up the back steps, I wondered what kind of apocalypse I'd be entering. Then again, it could be like church. My parents could be napping, the pots all lined up silently steaming on their own, towers of white dinner plates stacked on the blue table, waiting.

Everything was put on hold until I unlocked the front door at five thirty. I wondered who would be out front. Sometimes people were early, and I'd watch them wander back and forth, picking blackberries from the wild tangle across the street before I let them in.

Not quite a church, not yet a zoo, Gerald was still cutting away at salmon fillets; it looked like the last one. Pink steaks were displayed like triangular slabs of candy.

"That's it!" He dropped the knife and slowly unbent from the butcher block. "A perfect ten from this monster fish." Hands wiped, he reached for the medicinal red wine. Then he saw me.

"You are not hosting looking like that! Go wipe that lipstick off immediately! This is not the Moulin Rouge!"

Ellen looked up from her spot piping mocha buttercream frosting onto genoise.

"The lipstick is a bit much, Eric."

I figured they'd say something like that and begrudgingly wiped off the blood-red lipstick. I'd liked the symmetry of how my lips matched my sneakers. They hadn't said anything else, so I was good to go (and I'd just reapply when I was out in the foyer).

Greta saw me, and I read her lips.

"Are you?" she mouthed.

I nodded slowly and formed the silent words "Oh yeah!"

"Maintain" came her follow-up. Another part of the evening ritual, a dare and challenge wrapped together. Greta always looked for me and then acknowledged my altered state with a wink of conspiratorial sisterhood.

I knew she was high as well, probably gone out to the shed for a quick toke or swig of the expensive wine she'd filched. How she could focus on waiting tables while buzzed was one of her special talents. I'd freak out, break things, spill on people, or say something scandalous, bringing Gerald down on me hard. I always attempted to play it straight.

I'd be Mr. Mellow out front. The practiced script of meet and greet, rehearsed delivery, and curated outfit projecting a professional in charge. Even still, sometimes I just had to wing it as far as bouncing people around, and there was a perverse thrill in the panic. Maintain. Every weekend was a new situation, a new chance to get it right.

The new Vivaldi album would be in constant rotation tonight. I'd also slipped in Gerald's other new favorite: Pachelbel's Canon in D. The classical aural smorgasbord would guide diners in their savored experience (while also informing Gerald that I did indeed listen to and appreciate his music).

Rob, the tall young man who'd been hired as weekend dishwasher, arrived. I'd seen the new pile of pots and pans waiting for him already out back. Where did they come from? He saw me applying more lipstick.

"You're never out of character, are you?" he said with a knowing smile. Rob had become a new, unexpected friend, and we'd sometimes spend hours drawing together or playing dress-up. He was an anomaly among straight men in that he liked to do all the things I did, while certainly not being gay in any way. He was a writer, a poet, and one of the smartest people I knew. It gave me some confidence, triggering an old wound, knowing that if Rob liked me, I couldn't be that stupid.

Greta lit the candles, the fire was going, Jim lined wine bottles up along the counter and then gave me a nod: he was ready. The antique mantle clock started ding-donging five thirty, and sure enough, I could see some people gathering out in the street. It was showtime.

Before I opened the door, I must alert the kitchen. *Here we go!* I had to ask, "Are you ready?"

Noting the looks of heightened anticipation, my parents' eyes slightly wider, their stations neatened up, new towels tucked in their clean aprons. The kitchen was warm and scented with herbs, meat, chocolate, a whiff of lemon, the tang of wine. Gerald had a new bottle of Beaujolais ready by his butcher block. Ellen sipped her tea. Break a leg!

CHAPTER 28

KENOPSIA OF ANEMOIA

Sunday was deliciously slow. The café was closed as we recovered from the debacle of the night before and sheltered in place. On Sunday, the café became, once again, just home.

As usual, I was the first one awake, and there was the coffee setup waiting for me; all I had to do was turn on the stove. Watching the kettle, listening to a rising whine of hot water and echoes of last night's drama.

Last night had begun poorly when the lady who grew the sprouts found a staple in her salad. There was hand-wringing, comps, and apologies, but then it was determined that the staple came from the very bag of sprouts she'd brought us.

The obnoxious doctor from San Diego had arrived late, already drunk, and loud, barging right past me in the foyer. I had to redirect him back to the table I'd set up by the piano. He wanted to sit down next to Peter Sellers and Elke Sommer.

Meanwhile, Jim turned into a silly clown when Peter Sellers and his bombshell wife sat at table eight. It was amusing to watch him transform from a sophisticated, wizened gentleman into a curtsying manservant.

"He's so, tiny!" Greta was nonplussed.

Shouting over everybody, telling stupid jokes, Dr. Disruptive started banging on the piano, ignoring poor Jim's encouragement to please, be quiet. Why did I seat him near the piano?

"Am I disturbing you?" He banged even harder. Customers complained, some left, Jim was helpless, Sellers and Sommer observed aloof from the corner, Greta watched as if it were a sideshow. Another Saturday night at the Beauj.

My shuffling bare feet and the sticking cupboard drawer were explosive violations in the morning quiet. Accidentally nudging a chair; sounds of a streetcar screeching. Disturbing the pristine, newly cleaned kitchen reassembled from last night, I searched like a burglar for a clean coffee cup.

Pots and pans on the stove, plates, spoons, cups, dishcloths left where they fell, the discarded remnants of last night had been left scattered about like a crime scene, yet somehow, this morning, everything was magically put back together. Sometimes I couldn't find what I'd used just the night before, so whomever put everything back together didn't live here.

Our friend Juliette had sneaked in the side door as I locked the front, she and my parents chatting, staying up late, finishing off a bottle of wine. Maybe she was the one who rearranged our universe?

As the filter dripped, I nibbled a cookie from the box of English shortbread, remembering Gerald's horrified look as I told him about the trouble out front. He could hear his precious upright piano being abused. No mention of the red lipstick I wore.

He'd spun in place but was helpless (in the middle of a delicate salmon procedure). He'd have marched out there to give that guy the riot act, but Peter Sellers's entrée was near plating. So, Ellen took off her apron, smoothed her hair back, and went out to face the jerk.

"Sir, you need to please be quiet. You're ruining the evening for everyone." When she came back into the kitchen, she was flushed, shaking, furious.

The banging had stopped, a brief lull, and then, suddenly, the double doors burst open and Dr. Asshole stormed in.

Ahhhh, the savored, silent calm of morning. Sitting on my stool by the back door window, I watched the new sun angle in, glinting off hanging metal spoons. Coffee was hot, a faraway crow coughed, someone was chopping wood. I sat and contemplated the rusty orange of a new nasturtium creeping over the porch railing.

Ellen was still in bed letting the morning begin without her (almost unheard of), but after last night, she certainly deserved her rest. I was glad she lingered. Her absence predicted that today could ramble and stretch out slowly, randomly, with no agenda. A healing balm of slowness, today was all ours.

"Who the hell do you think you are?" I could still hear Dr. Shithead standing there in the kitchen last night, his slurred voice blaring. I saw Jim cowering, Greta holding back laughter, Ellen with a full pastry bag of buttercream quivering in her hands. Everything stopped.

When Ellen's pastry bag went up defensively and aimed, my better angel stepped in, gently coaxing her hand down, facing the belligerent Dr. Douchebag.

"She's the owner of this restaurant, and you need to GET OUT!" I shouted in his face.

He didn't know what to say to a bushy-haired teenage circus performer with red lips and an elephant-size chip on his shoulder. He backed up, sputtering. His group left; the dining room applauded.

Front door slamming; the drunken people screaming and yelling out on the street. I watched them huddle together, holding each other up, lurching away until they were bouncing dots on the horizon. Harmony had finally been restored, Pachelbel making an encore performance. Peter Sellers sent compliments to the chef.

Sitting on my morning stool, acknowledging this new day, the echoes of last night began to fade away. An old Ford truck rumbled down the street, taking long minutes from the top of the slope to turn by the A-frame real estate office. In that infinity, I reexamined my instinctual response (protecting Ellen), but there was more.

Contradiction yanked at me. Even though I'd stood up for Ellen, it felt like I may have also done something terribly wrong, something I might regret, something that could blow up in my face.

I'd never dared to fight back before, but this time something had snapped. Standing up to a monster in a world full of monsters, I was primed and ready for a fight after a lifetime of being tormented by bullies, my lipstick a red flag of rebellion. *Don't fuck with me or my family!*

This guy would never come back to our little restaurant, he'd probably tell all his friends not to come, he'd write Gerald a nasty letter, he'd write the newspaper. I could end up in trouble. I'd always been told that the customer was always right. No, in this case, the customer was not right. The customer was a dirtbag.

With the sun beginning to warm up the kitchen (and my caffeine buzz kicking in), I wanted to help usher in a brand-new day. I should make pancakes! Ellen always made me pancakes when I was feeling down, and I had a short stack ready when she finally descended the stairwell, subdued, wearing her comforting blue sweater. A shower and then maybe a walk was all she looked forward to this morning. She might even do some reading or draw out in the garden. What a luxury to fill a morning's serene space with nothing more than your presence.

I made the girls a small menagerie of animal pancakes (which species was up for debate). Greta ate half of a "horse" and then mated the end with a "pretty girl" pancake, her centaur nibbling raspberries next to a river of maple syrup. When Gerald appeared, he collected his hot plate of perfect silver dollars and a medicinal cup of coffee, but instead of retreating out to the front room and fireplace, he sat next to the butcher block, joining us in recounting our restless dreams and last night's adventures.

"You became a man last night," he said to me. "I'm proud of you, boy."

Not at all what I had expected from Gerald. Stumbling forward into adulthood was uncomfortable and weird. Flying in the face of protocol, taking a big chance, wearing lipstick, and shouting at the drunken jerk. I made it all up as I went along.

Ellen thanked me for coming to her rescue and for subverting a buttercream disaster.

Everyone enjoyed their pancakes, thankful for the coffee and for Eric growing a pair. There was no mention of lipstick or Peter Sellers, of possible fallout or the loss of money. Dr. Dickhead faded away like a broken fever.

The girls finished and went outside to the stable; Ellen helped me clean up while Gerald perused his paper, still in the kitchen, not moving from the blue table, the center of our world.

"This is what it feels like"—he gestured grandly—"this is what they mean about right livelihood."

He was looking at me again as if to say that *you, Eric, need to understand that this is your right livelihood.* Why did he have to go and ruin a perfectly good breakfast?

"Eric, what say we go to a movie matinee?" He was reading the small ad for the Coast Cinema in Fort Bragg. "Our favorite director has a new film!"

I didn't know who'd directed *The Great Race, Those Magnificent Men in Their Flying Machines*, or *It's a Mad, Mad, Mad, Mad World*, but if it had a pie fight or a crazy chase scene, I was all in.

"Remember those art house cinemas in San Francisco? Remember *The Seven Samurai? La Belle et la Bête?* Remember *The Bicycle Thief? Chushingura! The Seventh Seal? 8 and 1/2? La Dolce Vita!*" He listed his favorite films and raised the coffee cup high to salute fond memories of those tiny, dark theaters with just Ellen, Gerald, and me huddled close, a big bag of popcorn between us. Before the sisters, before moving here to Mendocino, when the world was still young and in black-and-white. I'd learned about pathos and irony by reading foreign faces and subtitles.

"Federico Fellini has a film about ancient Rome!" Gerald's eyes widened as if someone was giving him a million dollars. I pictured burning temples, orgies, big hair, and dark sunglasses.

Driving to the theater up the coast, past fields and mini-malls, architecture turning prefab drab, road signs advertising Wood Delivered, across the Noyo bridge, by the generic restaurants all serving fish and chips or chowder, past the lumber yard of piled-up dead trees, into the suburban blight of Fort Bragg. A grid of sad bungalows and lifeless streets cornered with once-grand Victorians, now vandalized as pizza huts and sports bars.

The shit-brown movie theater was a squat, pockmarked box surrounded by low scrub clinging to gravel. The only color was a clean, bright poster for *Fellini Satyricon.* Two beautiful young men in Roman tunics, their bare legs hugging a white horse.

I liked the audacious subtitle: "Rome before Christ, after Fellini." A sly come-on miraculously defacing the bland facade of the theater. How Fellini sneaked into Fort Bragg, of all places, was a minor revolution.

Gerald and I were the only two people in the theater; no one knew (or cared) about this uprising. This was our exclusive screening, and the coup was that Gerald and I also shared something else in common. But I didn't discover that until much later.

Late Sunday morning, people were still in church praying for forgiveness, while Gerald and I slumped in our seats eagerly anticipating whatever debauchery Fellini might throw at us, and I couldn't believe my luck! From the very first shot, the handsome, sweaty, blond hero (wearing a miniskirt) yelled for his male lover into the dank, stylized set of a Roman bath, and it just got better from there.

It was like a nonlinear R-rated Shakespearean soap opera; now I knew why the woman behind the ticket counter looked Gerald and me up and down. *The rest of the world is in church, and you two are here for the orgy.*

My box of Milk Duds forgotten, melting on my lap, hiding painfully tented jeans. Sneaking a peek at Gerald sitting next to me, I saw he was leaning forward, alert, beret cocked, popcorn kernel by kernel delivered automatically from bag to open mouth. Gerald adored his foreign films. I like naked men.

"I loved all the lurid colors and theatrical, surreal sets."

Driving back home, away from the Quonset hut slum of Fort Bragg and blast site of *Fellini Satyricon*, I unpacked my impressions of what we'd just experienced, still tingling and spent. It was only the cinematography and production values that I could verbalize.

"It felt like I was right there but, at the same time, still dreaming." An impossible time trip back to a place that seemed somehow familiar.

"That's Fellini's gift," Gerald explained. "Neo-realism. Staged events that look as if they're naturally playing out, like real life. A fantasy based on reality, the randomness of events bleeding into each other."

I got it. Glamorized ancient Roman life, the casual violence, crude yet strangely modern attitudes, the indifference toward homosexuality, of owning a slave. It was all normal and had appeared so real. It was real! I saw myself as the thief, the self-important actor, the one-eyed gladiator, the elegant nobleman, the coquettish maid, the towering, masculine Minotaur. I was the sex slave.

I was also a ferocious clown emptying Ellen's pastry bag of chocolate buttercream into the arrogant stranger's face. A lovely fantasy that I could so easily visualize and that had almost happened. Why hadn't I just grabbed that pastry bag and done the deed myself?

Eat chocolate, asshole!

I felt the weight of a projected reality settle and then whisk away as we crossed the graceful Russian Gulch bridge, a view of sparkling water and then onrushing trees. That hadn't happened, but it could have, and it certainly was satisfying to think about.

"The music! Oh, that Nino Rota is a master at evoking nostalgia for a time and place."

Of course Gerald focused in on the discordant sound score using early instruments, a sweet, melodic theme percolating throughout. He was driving but not really looking at the road, staring through the mist of time, humming the sad, alien melody half-remembered.

Gerald was right—this movie had given me a sense of woozy nostalgia for a purely fictional experience and then placed a brand-new perspective on my everyday dramas. Life was what we made it.

As we pulled up in front of our little house, I finally said it.

"Those men. They were so beautiful."

"Yes" was all Gerald said. "Yes, they were indeed."

CHAPTER 29

ACCIDENTALLY
ON PURPOSE

I was living out in the garage, which I'd come to learn was where the hearse carriages were kept. Practical, since the cemetery was right across the street. Shortest ride ever.

With no insulation, it was an icebox out there. I always thought about coffins and dead bodies as I slithered into my mummy bag at night. A dead mayor or prostitute lying in the cold corners waiting for a funeral, for relatives or paperwork.

Lying still, zipped up and enveloped in goose down with the hood cinched around my head, I was listening in the pitch dark to every suspect creak or groan, recognizing the personality of this old place. Dry wood breathing or restless ghosts?

At seventeen, I decided to move out here for more privacy. On my own but still attached, the kitchen and food and family still within reach but easily shut out. There was electricity but no running water, no sink or toilet, so I had to scamper outside at night sometimes over cold stones and dirt to use the bathroom. It was at night that I questioned my decision. There was always something lurking in the shadows.

But it was my very own space and so worth it. Not just a room but a separate, unique environment that I could mold into whatever I wanted. Not subject to criticism or parental direction; nobody wanted anything to do with this dank, empty garage. Home to spiders, mice, dust, ghosts, and a frizzy-haired adolescent freak.

My sleeping space was just up the wooden steps, near the door. A pallet frame, standard army-issue mattress, dingy pillow, and Mountaineer mummy bag provide spartan comfort. A used roll-top desk, companion elbow lamp, and long, rough plank shelves once full of rusty tools were now crammed with dog-eared books. I spend a lot of time huddled under the lamp studying comic books or newspapers, Ray Bradbury, Robert A. Heinlein, or Frank Herbert. Sealed up tight in the bag with a balanced plate of secreted almond crescent kipfels near my mouth.

An open closet area held my everyday clothes, seeded with collected costumes. I seemed to have one of everything. The vintage brocade jacket occasionally worn with favorite flared cords. The heavy, moth-eaten black wool cape (thrown on some gloomy days), demanding that I march directly down to the Headlands and stand at cliff's edge. The wind swirling, ocean crashing, cape flapping like a great bat.

A ragged newsboy's cap, a box of bow ties, a pair of red leather platform shoes I clomped around in when feeling brave, overtly sassy, or resentful. The purple feather boa (worn only once to a party) still tempted me every time I reached for a turtleneck.

Next to the fringed vest and patchwork, pom-pom poncho, the musty tuxedo got pulled out of its garment bag when I played host for the café. Camouflage fatigues, sailor's bell-bottoms, and Italian clown pantaloons hardly came off the hangers (but I knew that they were there). A favorite was the crushed top hat I found in a box, worn any chance I got. It tamed the mushroom head of hair and gave me a sense of skewed authority. Sometimes I fell asleep in that hat, mashing it even farther (the spring long ago having given up). I'd wake up looking like the cockeyed master of ceremonies or a pirate accountant.

The chair near the plank bed was piled with magazines and my tossed uniform: T-shirt and jeans. Worn until stiff, they retained the angular creases of my legs and arms, the knobs of pointy knees. I could step right in and face the world.

The rest of the garage was an artist's studio. Shoving old threshing equipment and automobile parts aside, sweeping away dust, cobwebs, and gunk, I cranked up Elton John, Stevie Wonder, or David Bowie and flailed about. I had plenty of space to work out routines and practice signature moves. I could throw my arms out, lunge, spin, and flip my head around without knocking anything over. The person I saw reflected in the full-length mirror was a dervish, an elf, an acrobat, a mime, an Elizabethan courtier, the fourth Musketeer, or sometimes, he was just a clumsy hunchback.

There was enough room to model several different staged areas. Different lighting and maneuvered scrims, heavy curtains pooling on the ground, draped, or pulled back by a tasseled sash revealed other, more intimate spaces. Like assembled panoramic Easter eggs, private environments could only be accessed by following the maze.

I'd mounted several theatrical explorations out here. A grand retelling of Winnie the Pooh. A chorus girl version of a Busby Berkeley musical where the bit players staged a coup and fired the big-time producer, creating their own elaborate, impossible extravaganza, and an original melodrama based on Carrie Nation, the pre-Prohibition temperance movement figure infamous for wreaking havoc in saloons with a Bible and hatchet.

Writing long-winded monologues on the evils of liquor and fear of God, I'd begun to understand her frustration and the never-ending job of cleaning house.

Rehearsing into the night with my friend Molly (who was always in character, wearing her pinched eyeglasses and starched, black crinoline dress, waving around the antique hatchet we'd found), she inhabited the role. Bellowing sermons, smashing old bottles and lumps of wood from the backyard, she could have won a Tony Award.

A large drafting table I set up under the big south-facing window was always covered with sketches for imagined children's books, fantasy novels, elaborate murals, or impossible Rube Goldberg contraptions that brushed my teeth by way of the chicken coop.

Various nails poking out of beams were convenient pegs for considered, sketched ideas. The walls a scrapbook gallery for dancing figures, battling superheroes, vintage film stars, and cartoon studies of hunky men wearing tights. Hidden behind all the other drawings, I'd amassed my own fantasy porno corps du ballet. I worried that if Gerald ever pulled off a drawing of Renaissance bards or science-fiction creatures, he'd discover my true secret obsession: bulging tights.

Purloined copies of *After Dark*, an entertainment magazine that seemed to feature lots of beautiful, shirtless men in provocative poses were scattered about (the evidence right there for anyone to see). One copy remained under the bed, its pages discolored and stuck together.

My favorite two books were always open, their pages bent, spines broken: *Hollywood and the Great Fan Magazines* and its smarmy sibling: *Hollywood Babylon*. I read and reread the stories of Golden Age Tinseltown debauchery, studying the immaculate faces, perfect bodies, and salacious rumors surrounding these celebrated, now long-dead movie stars. The accounts of unimagined wealth, displays of grit and glamour, shady dealings, and horrible, sometimes sloppy, deaths exposed the mundane normality behind all the breathless hyperbole.

I illustrated a scene starring Greta Garbo in the style of Edvard Munch. The great Garbo wailing into her vanity mirror, on the brink of insanity.

"I want to be alone!"

Another panel revealed a pensive Tyrone Power, sitting legs akimbo, wearing only his tighty-whities.

The garage had become a living museum for my private collection of fantasies. My secret hideaway, like the wardrobe in *The Chronicles of Narnia*. A drafty oasis where I could escape to and regroup before braving the inevitable, all-too-real outside world.

Some weekend days I barely opened the door (peeing in a bottle), nibbling on crackers and cheese, only appearing in the café kitchen for dinnertime, risking being swept up in the nightly performance. Hunger made me do crazy things.

Besides sleeping or reading, dancing, drawing, or sulking, I some-times just sat at the drafting table and gazed out the window observing the changeable sky, the strange clouds, the fuzzy edge of a fog bank looming. Seagulls careened on erratic wind gusts. A raven sat on top of a phone pole doing exactly what I was doing, simply watching.

The wobbly lines of picket fences marked the division between dirt and pavement, weeds, flowers, and wind-bent trees, the tiny cars zoom-ing by on the faraway highway. The little house across the street butted right up against the cemetery. A solitary older woman with a trained parrot lived there.

Sometimes pulling in laundry from the outside clothesline, the wom-an would bring out the bright-green bird who perched patiently on the basket, watching as she folded her sheets. I would watch the raven watching the parrot, who watched the woman (careful not to let billow-ing sheets touch the ground). The parrot was oblivious to the raven, who finally got bored and flew away.

Looking back down at my table: a large, detailed drawing of a dragon curled up, its pile of scales folding over and over. The dragon smiled down at a small boy, who offered up a flower.

One day in a sleepy funk, I reached into the closet and put on what I thought was an all-concealing, extra-large sweatshirt. Something dull and colorless, exactly how I felt that sodden morning. I didn't care what I wore, didn't want to go to school (or face the intimidating, complicat-ed world), and it was only after walking across town and down my new high school hallway that I realized in horror, following scrutinizing, laughing eyes of classmates that I was wearing an old lady dress.

My worst nightmare, being outed and confirmed as a fag/weirdo—and I'd done it to myself! Here I was in a faded-pink shift, one of the costumes forgotten but still hanging around. I turned on my heel and marched swiftly back home, missing the first class.

The rest of that day was a mix of irritation and an odd, new, percolating thrill. Inadvertently, I'd stepped out of my safety zone. Costumes were fun, and they were empowering and appropriate occasionally (wearing in a theatrical performance), but I'd never intentionally worn a dress in public, as myself! This was a transgression that I'd avoided like the plague. It was scary, but it now also suddenly triggered an electric, subversive glee.

Walking back to school in my T-shirt and jeans armor (wrestling with the intriguing contradictions and possibilities of a pink dress), I vowed to try it again, only the next time, it would be on purpose.

CHAPTER 30

PROM DATE

In high school, I became Queen Elizabeth's consort. My new friend Liz had a predilection for wearing stiff, vintage brocade dresses and on occasion, flowing velvet capes.

A curated mass of brunette hair swept up in a brooch, her needle-point gloves clutching an ornate onyx bead bag, sturdy arched heels clip-clopping her royal presence down our high school's echoing hall-way between a widening path of jeans, sweatshirts, and dirty sneakers, she commanded the room.

Her costumed appearance told of time lavished on the preparation of an assumed persona. Of lacing up a whalebone bodice, manicuring the perfect pleats of a taffeta skirt, applying a lightly powdered Elizabethan face and blood-red lips recently kissed by a vampire, and thinking about just how much lace would be practical in the cafeteria lunchroom.

Liz projected a stylish, manifest superiority, holding herself apart from the general rabble of petulant teenage ruffians.

From my spot at the end of the long lunchtime table, I observed Elizabeth's skillful etiquette. Whatever was on her tray seemed a royal repast. Tuna fish sandwich or sloppy joe, they were delicacies managed with a studied pinky finger. Her manners rendering even Jell-O a luxury, the plastic spork a scepter directing attention to the circumference of a fruit cup. I stared as my PB&J dripped.

It was a serendipitous twist of fate that I'd encountered Elizabeth in my current exacerbated state. Flailing away at the dictated eleventh-grade course of study (enrolled in after the Headlands School shuttered), I felt like a broken-down Sir Pellinore unhorsed and limping, tilting for the Questing Beast. With a head for drama and no heart for football, I found high school was a nightmare.

Alone at my end of the cafeteria table, I wallowed in friendless discomfort, my contemplated sandwich a meditation of slow-motion strawberry ooze.

High school's society of competitive neanderthal posturing demanded that I conform, and I balked. It felt like dying. I wasn't a jock, didn't fit into any category that I recognized. Yet somehow, Elizabeth saw my potential.

"Is that a hand-knit sweater?" she asked without looking.

Nothing escaped her notice. The large, rust-colored cable fisherman's sweater I'd borrowed from Ellen was, indeed, painstakingly hand-knit. Ellen was a maniac with yarn and that Elizabeth had noticed (while also saying nothing about the fact that it was a woman's sweater) alerted me to her appreciation of fashion statement, not to mention a sense of discretionary aplomb.

In my attempt to camouflage my gangly frame in any extra-large all-encompassing shroud, Ellen's heavy woolen sweater muted all sharp angles, and I could pick up a sandwich (uncouth elbows propped on the table) by letting voluminous sleeves fall away from the creep of jam. A napkin kept hidden in the extra fold bloomed strategically to assist unlicked fingers.

My red sack sweater and white napkin flag attracting Elizabeth's eye, I must have looked like a modern-day motley fool and in short order was welcomed into her royal sphere. The world became exponentially larger that day.

To be near Elizabeth and enter the space she occupied was an epiphany. As an act of survival and curious wonder, I eagerly attached myself and was subsequently lifted out of a funk. My mind and spirit conspired toward a common cause: the enthusiastic expression of aspirational fantasy.

"It's important to look your best," Liz would say. Fine for a queen whose everyday was better than most.

I had a closet full of costumes that I touched occasionally, but wearing a cloak to high school was asking for trouble. Elizabeth convinced me that it could be done.

I was still smarting from the embarrassment of being caught in public wearing that stupid old lady shift. Even jeans and a T-shirt had felt like not enough camouflage. The red balloon sweater covered my shame.

Suddenly elevated past my self-imposed gutter status, walking down the halls to English class and then safely off the grounds as Elizabeth's escort, I was rendered relatively immune to ridicule, made newly invisible to lurking bullies and the social death traps of high school. Because I was Elizabeth's friend, I was someone of worth.

"Ignore them, and they'll forget all about you," she'd say as I cringed behind her swirling, tasseled shawl. The football hero lumbering past saw only the sweep of cashmere and an armload of books.

To have a steady chum as well-connected as Liz meant everything in high school. The aura of privilege gave me cover, and my confidence grew.

After I applied myself and began to enjoy certain aspects of lessons, the repetition of bite-size challenges, my grades began to improve. I felt a bit less of a loser, more a participant, suddenly finding myself running track and winning blue ribbons.

I'd had a lot of practice running (running away from pounding fists and taunting jibes), and now these long legs were finally good for something. The jerks who'd shoved me up against my locker threatening to "kick my faggot ass" were now clapping me on the back and talking to me as if I were an actual person. I kept running and surviving.

The rugged Northern California coastline Elizabeth and I called home illustrated an individualist's temperament. Epic ocean panorama broken by wind-bent trees, cow-dotted fields, time-honored footpaths leading down to the craggy shores of a secret beach. Bruised Victorian monuments of boxy homes, barns, ragged lines of picket fences dividing earth from sky and sea; spectral wooden water towers (the tallest structures in any town) were bleached scaffolding against unpredictable weather. An unkindness of ravens hovering like animated black tears, wood fire smoke lingering in a sudden chill; this was our home, and it was the landscape of dreams.

Elizabeth's sense of ease both perusing the shelves in our high school library and walking those narrow, rutted roads in a crinkly crinoline gown further solidified her status as royal eccentric. Every step and vista Elizabeth occupied was revealed to be her kingdom. And through Elizabeth's sponsorship, against the canvas of wide-open spaces and newly revealed potential, I created a more accurate version of myself.

"Behavior which would be considered insanity in a tradesman is looked upon as mild eccentricity in a lord." I quoted Peter O'Toole from *The Ruling Class*, a British film that had captured our shared affection for sharp Anglophile humor.

"Here, you'll like this one." She handed me a small book.

The White Peacock was old, mildewed and had the embossed image of fanned feathers on its cover. Elizabeth's whole family loved classic literature, and offering me a book from their personal trove was like being inducted into a sacred society. Visiting Elizabeth at her family's home in Elk was committing to an all-day-and-into-the-evening glimpse at how deposed royalty lived. They read books. Lots and lots of books. The little unincorporated village of Elk (founded by a member of the Donner party) down the coast from Mendocino was a wide space in the road with its own cliff's edge cemetery, a whitewashed post office, general store, and pebbled beach. The place and family, steeped in gothic intrigue, were (to me) as remote as Siberia.

Inside, their little Victorian cottage was an homage to the fabled Bloomsbury group, with colorfully painted walls, gypsy shawls, and heavy curtains scalloped over high-backed rattan and plump rococo chairs. Lounging cats, fountains of pampas grass erupting from a Roseville umbrella stand, smoky daguerreotypes and silhouette portraits of imagined high-born relatives, lovingly displayed onion skin scrolls of the Declaration of Independence and Magna Carta, calligraphic refrigerator lists of fantasy feasts to satisfy a regal entourage, and there were books. Books piled in every corner, books filling every nook and every shelf. First edition books from floor to ceiling; books towering to support the very foundations of the house. When I visited Liz, it felt that I was entering an annex of the mythological Akashic Library. Their home, a gateway of wisdom and knowledge. Out the front door was a rough frontier while inside, the endless stacks of antique books held the wealth of the world.

"The stepping-stones were white in the sun, and the water slid sleepily among them. One or two butterflies, indistinguishable against the blue sky, trifled from flower to flower and led me up the hill, across the field where the hot sunshine stood as in a bowl, and I was entering the caverns of the wood, where the oaks bowed over and saved us a grateful shade." D. H. Lawrence spoke as if he were a next-door neighbor, and I remember thinking, *I'd give my left nut to be able to write like that*. Evoking Lawrence's flowery prose, I transposed his words over everyday conversation. "The cragged ridge of his aching brow spoke a volume of sorrow." I described our miserable social studies teacher. Elizabeth and I had wondered if there might be trouble at home for him.

Either in each other's presence or alone with a thick book propped open, Elizabeth and I examined and then discussed the attitudes, concepts, descriptive passage, opaque wordplay, and actions taken by many a fictional or historical figure. Dense, elaborate, and challenging language structures puzzled out new theories and some delicious, deep, often dark emotional states.

The brooding romance of Jane Eyer, scrappy David Copperfield, whale-fearing Ishmael, innocent well-intentioned but infuriatingly ignorant Candide, wizard's apprentice turned king of England, various haunted governesses, bellicose barons, plotting scullery maids, tortured orphans, lonely sheepherders, adopted Indians, shipwrecked pirates, or my favorite, the preternaturally beautiful, murderous society dandy who also happened to have a decaying portrait in the attic.

Tales of valor and angst peered at through pages of musty and dog-eared books took on extra significance and began to inform my days. Between piles of dishes and prepping vegetables, I experienced a blossoming reverence for something old made new again. I entered my truer self: I became a bookworm.

Shuffling along in Elizabeth's imposing wake as her newly licensed sidekick, this new freedom gave me heretofore unrealized access to deep thought, self-expression, and renewed appreciation for costume. Besides a voracious reader and pilgrim of romantic ideals, I became a hat person.

"You wear the top hat, and I'll break out the crown jewels," Elizabeth dictated a Friday ritual dare. The weekend was imminent, so we could wear whatever we wanted; there would be no reprisals, forgotten the day after.

But hats were only the beginning. Parading around in a blaring tasseled band jacket or ridged Australian khaki Desert Rat uniform, pair of well-worn jodhpurs, buckskinned Florsheim wingtip shoes and knee-high army socks, my wild hair-mop contained in a wine-red version of my father's Basque beret (pushed back to reveal newly pensive brow), I affected the chiseled statue of a beanpole, bushy-haired aristocracy.

Scarves, silk ties, and cufflinks made a showy comeback. My moth-eaten wardrobe of pirate blouse, ducktails, and yellowed butler's gloves were no longer off-limits. I embraced the spitting image of a fop. The only thing missing was the gruesome portrait out in the wine cellar.

At one point during the school year, a visiting poet corralled a willing bunch of us bored egghead students to plumb the depths of our roiling psyches and attempt a creative exposé.

"Write about what moves you, what informs you," suggested the wild-eyed teacher. "If that doesn't work, write as if you were someone else."

He marched back and forth in front of the class, leaning in for emphasis, his pointer finger making a point.

This either-or exercise enabled me to project my inner Virginia Wolfe longing for the attentions of Vita Sackville-West, or Edgar Lee Masters with sorrow knocking at his door, the murky humor of Edward Gorey's strangling ficus plant tickling my wicked funny bone. I wrote:

> "I was afraid of climbing up
> I took the rope and made a sling
> there was no reason
> for a swing or guide or measure
> I could see the world from here
> but across the sea and land and green
> it looked as cloudy as the grave."

Teachers freaked out. Parents were called into the office, and I explained that I was only following the direction of my instructor. I'd put myself so thoroughly in the mindset of a depressed and lonely noble, financially ruined and grieving, abandoned by his true love (I didn't mention the hunky sheepherder part). There was nothing to live for, and yet, the desolate beauty of the cold ocean and rolling fields seen from my lofty attic gave me pause.

It was easy to picture all of that, given where we lived and from what I was reading. But I had no intention of offing myself. As angry as I was at having to wash dishes in order to eat, there were still so many books to read.

I stopped writing poetry and again concentrated on short stories. My forgotten tale of a bedraggled medieval kitchen grunt privy to magical goings-on in the tower. The machinations of a bewigged French merchant looking to exploit his favor with King Louis XIV (Marie Antoinette a client). A conversation between Grendel and his beastly mother as they sat by the fire gnawing on Viking bones. All still (as yet) unpublished.

Rattling away out in my garage hideaway or lurching through kitchen chores (and grateful for the food), I was adrift in a miasma of fantasy and projected character.

My association with Queen Elizabeth became a bridge to the outside world and of what she embodied as possible. If I kept reading and writing, kept starching those shirt collars and communing with the voices of another era, there might still be a future.

By the end of my seventeenth year, I was on the dean's list, had a wall full of blue ribbons, owed late fees on my library card, and had a semipermanent crease where the red beret lived.

Elizabeth and the rest of my class moved on, but the powers that be flunked me for lack of credit (still catching up after the unrecognized free school years). I'd made great strides but hadn't been quite good enough, and in a fit of pique, I dropped out, never finishing high school.

As a final act of rebellion and theater, I accompanied Elizabeth as her prom date. Wearing my butler's tails, ruffled shirt, prerequisite red carnation, sharkskin pants, and wingtips, I was a proper (if slightly rumpled) courtier.

Her royal highness dressed in a heavy, full-length, sky-blue gown beaded neck to toe with crystals. With a pearl necklace, dripping pearl earrings, and more beads woven into her intricately braided hair, Elizabeth floated above the earth as if suspended on a gurney.

Posing for a snapshot in the high school gymnasium under festive crepe paper, a regal and composed Queen Elizabeth and her messy, foppish consort made quite the couple.

CHAPTER 31

SUMMER OF '42

In 1971, when I heard that another movie would start filming in Mendocino, I shrugged. More mad money made as an extra! Another chance to be discovered! Yeah, sure, OK, whatever. More like another long day of standing around then being dismissed as if never having been there at all. The hundred-dollar bribe, cheap compensation for willingly, choosing to be a piece of meat. The whole thing, an elaborate waste of time. Chagrin had tempered my idealism.

The last experience had been such a letdown. I'd been so enthusiastic about playing a zombie. Involvement in the exciting art of filmmaking became, less exciting. There was the sobering realization that it was all so tedious. Once I figured out that no, I wouldn't be scooped up and that yes, it was all so super boring, my overblown fantasy deflated. This time I ignored the newspaper's printed casting call.

I'd gotten over being used as a human prop (just a job), but the unexpected shock of being chided by my very own two friends Sean and Annie had been the bigger disappointment. Still stewing, stung from such an unexpected source, and caught off guard, their criticism triggering all my insecurities. They'd laughed at me for trying so hard, shamed me for being so into it, my total commitment, so not cool. I was now reassessing our friendship and my place in the world.

In their critique I'd also received the sideways message that I was still such a novice at making and keeping friends. It had always been difficult, but now suddenly, it was even slightly dangerous. Simply exercising a bit of self-empowerment, expressing myself, and then being mocked by my supposed friends felt, well, unfriendly.

Without knowing, Sean and Annie's jab had reopened a festering wound. I was living with the knowledge that something was wrong, that I was broken. Underneath all my bravado and bluster, I was an insecure, terrified mess. I already knew that what all the bullies were yelling was indeed correct (that I was a faggot), but it seemed my worst fears had also been realized. Authorities had also recently labeled me as mentally challenged.

To help my basic education (after having dropped out of high school), Ellen and Gerald hired two teacher friends as private tutors. With their accredited help, I could at least get a GED. I could get a diploma and then maybe go to college.

But after a few frustrating months of study with these two tutors, they proclaimed at a formal sit-down that in their educated opinion, I was damaged beyond their ability to repair, that they were done trying to "fix" me, and that I was quite possibly retarded. Now, it's evident to me that ADHD might have been the culprit, but back then, that was on no one's radar.

Ellen, Gerald, the two esteemed teachers, and me sitting around table eight. The adults talking about stupid, developmentally disabled Eric as if he were a failed lab experiment, a blob, with me sitting right there.

"This is outrageous!" Gerald rejected the diagnosis, ending his friendship. Was he offended on my behalf or because his newly simple-minded son reflected so poorly on his parenting skills? If I was "special," then what did that make him?

I also remember thinking about how cruel grown-ups could be. These two teachers passing judgment so casually around cheese and bread and a glass of wine. Another day, another picnic, another execution.

I wasn't just grumpy; I was despondent and angry, and even my friends were now pointing fingers. Their observations punching hard on the red-button issue. I couldn't trust my own body, my choices were flawed, my mind playing tricks. I was a lost cause. I seriously considered suicide for the first time.

"Those stupid movie people," I snarled. It was easier to blame the strangers repopulating our little hamlet.

I was unsure if I could be Sean and Annie's, or anyone's, friend (because to be someone's friend meant opening up, making myself vulnerable) when I knew even the smallest comment stabbed. I thought long and hard about maybe joining a monastery. I imagined living out my life in some cave, making candles or cheese.

I opted to observe the new film project from the sidelines as, once again, streets were blocked off and the old garage across from The Sea Gull transformed into the facade of an old movie theater, a pox of trucks, trailers, and equipment a blight upon the land.

Sean, Annie, and I sat on the corner barbershop's scalloped steps watching in amusement as harried movie people tried to wrangle oblivious locals away from their "set." Their looks of confusion and consternation were snort inducing. Walkie-talkies crackling, arms waving, the truck rumbling by ruining a shot.

I took a long hit, then passed the joint to Sean, thinking back to when Gerald and I had first visited Mendocino. That garage had been a store, and there'd been an old wooden Indian sculpture standing outside.

As I sat there, I also sat apart in a deep funk and noticed that my simmering resentment had somehow, weirdly, given me an edge. Sean and Annie were acting slightly differently toward me. My mood swings had made me cool again.

As I watched the movie people scurry about, a pervasive dread loomed in the periphery. I felt that it could all be over at any minute, that destruction and chaos loitered just underneath the placid, idyllic landscape I observed every day. In 1971, near-constant nuclear testing was blowing holes in the world; airlines seemed to be crashing with frightening regularity; there were antiwar riots everywhere; people were getting shot on college campuses. Every other day a headline in our local newspaper announced someone's son getting killed in Viet Nam. Soon, I knew, it would be my turn. At eighteen, I would have to register for the draft.

I visualized the earth cracking open to release volcanos, fire, devastation, Armageddon, an earthquake severing Mendocino from the mainland, radiation from a bomb, a meltdown poisoning everything. These busybody movie people swept up in a sudden tidal wave, everything falling apart.

"And...here's Paul Bunyan," I deadpanned. Another unobservant lumberjack lumbered through camera sight lines. The script girl threw her papers down, arms raised, people yelling at each other—the body language of exasperated sheepherders.

Directly across from the garage/fake movie theater, The Sea Gull restaurant had become an ad hoc staging ground and watering hole for the cast and crew. We watched their entertaining, frustrated machinations while sitting there on the barbershop steps next door. Sean, Annie, and I built stories, predicted outcomes, tempting fate by remaining here, just out of camera range yet well within the Hollywood invaders' view. I expected at any moment for someone to come over and shoo us away, or to maybe beg a toke.

At night, the Beaujolais was everyone's hangout. Movie people had money to burn, and they wanted the best. Gerald was delighted that every night's second seating had been bought out. He put up with demands and extra late hours, as the cash flow was a shot in the arm.

At this point, I had a set daily routine with some late-afternoon breaks when I could sneak out to the shed for a quick smoke then return to the bustling kitchen, altered and ready to focus. I made soup and prepped veggies, working like a machine, doing what needed to be done, powering through chores.

Getting stoned elevated my experience of mundane tasks and made the job tolerable, even enjoyable. Despite my epic sulk, I found that I could hone in on details and work like the devil while slightly high. I wasn't a mathematician, I didn't give a flying fuck about science or sports, but I was efficient at kitchen work. I lived in a restaurant, so my skills were in demand, and with one or two puffs, I could direct focus and do the job.

The challenge of completing something, of doing several things at once, and knowing that I contributed was sweet, nourishing satisfaction. I showed myself that I was able to work, I was pretty good, I wasn't stupid, and getting stoned lightened my mood significantly. I didn't dwell so heavily on doom scenarios but was free to put my energy, instead, toward results. It wasn't just work anymore; this was living.

Sometimes I even whistled that stupid song from Disney's Snow White animation, as a self-aware soundtrack and motivator from the backyard to the kitchen. It was felt good to enjoy my job.

Movie company people took up residence in the front rooms of the Beaujolais, and the nightly ritual became an informal company party of sorts. They lounged, we served behind the scenes, and then occasionally, someone would come into the kitchen, break the fourth wall, and engage with us.

One night, the star of the movie herself, Jennifer O'Neill, in a pair of cutoffs, out of makeup, and wanting to escape the boisterous dining room, joined my sisters upstairs and taught them how to crochet. I couldn't help myself—I wanted to witness a movie star hanging out on the edge of Greta's bed demonstrating a hook and pearl, so I barged in with the excuse of looking for a book—and yes, I was probably stoned.

CHAPTER 32

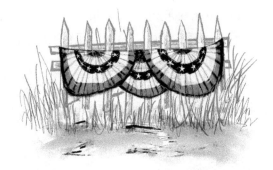

FAME AND FORTUNE

The 1972 Fourth of July parade down Main Street was a cookie-cutter ragtag assemblage of small-town Americana, except for one, weird thing.

Besides all the trucks with goats or dogs or even cows in the back, assorted red-white-and-blue bunting draped over bumpers or dragging from back fenders, besides the convertibles with beauty queens and politicians waving, loggers riding atop a newly felled redwood tree, volunteer firefighters clanging their red truck's bell, children running around with balloons, candy apples, and tiny flags; between the Rotary and Lions Club contingents, among library and historical society matrons, rhododendron gardeners, blaringly off-key high school bands, and various somber churchgoers were scattered the other less patriotic but equally enthusiastic, more artistically inclined residents.

Jim Bertram and his cast of the just-opened play *Harvey* stood waving on the back of a long flat-bed truck. Occasionally, someone dressed as a giant rabbit would hop off to pose with onlookers. A rough collection of hippie folk wove in and out of the line of cars and local dignitaries, scattering flowers, skipping, holding hands, waving jubilantly, as if this were completely normal and a most beautiful day to celebrate life.

A passing breeze would pick up the recognizable pong of pot, mixing with sea salt and wet grass.

Greta, dressed up in her fancy, handmade, red satin gown, rode her horse Cricket sidesaddle, their hair and tail brushed to an amber sheen. A car with a loud banner rejecting the proposed RV park slated to be built just outside of town drove by slowly, honking. Some people whooped and yelled back in encouragement. This issue had the town riled up, a petition circulated, and there was desperation in the air as the powers that be in the county seat of Ukiah were ramming this monstrosity through, dismissive of the town's adamant rejection. It felt like this wound would be just one more of a thousand cuts, another inevitable degradation to the pristine beauty of this place, our sweet home.

Real life could be ugly, and it was encroaching fast. The whales were endangered, the Fed always threatening to drill for oil offshore, local, roughneck loggers clear-cutting whole swathes of old-growth forest. In a couple of months, I'd have to register with the draft. Who knew what happened after that?

The typical small-town parade was spiked with mismatched yet co-existing citizens all marching together in no particular order. A peculiar mishmash of the observed holiday, political battles, local events, and spontaneous expression. In the bright sun, Mendocino's eccentric personality was on full display.

One lady in red-white-and-blue shorts and crop-top combo, glitter makeup, and top hat walked gingerly by on high stilts, blowing bubbles between factions of hippies and rednecks. As Sean, Annie, and I observed the cavalcade from the sidelines, I kept waiting for the stilt walker to step into a pothole, be tripped by a flailing, skipping hippie, or bumped by a beauty queen, tumble down into the back seat of her fancy car, or be squished underneath the giant tires of the logging truck.

Sean, Annie, and I were leaning against the wobbly fence that edged the street and bluffs, the white-cropped ocean roaring just beyond.

"So many trucks, so little time," I opined, yawning—the stilt walker picked her way past, not falling.

"Oh, look, another princess in a tiara." Annie pointed out the third or fourth car with a blond, blue-eyed, and bucktoothed debutant.

"Is it Miss Apple Orchard or Potato Peel?"

"Miss Diagnosed, obviously." I sneered. The poor lady's voluminous pageant gown had been caught on one of the unstable poles holding up an awning, and she'd gotten herself twisted somehow. Huge shoulder pads pressing up against her head, balloon sleeves caught and wrapping around her like a straitjacket, it looked like she was having a seizure.

"Off to the ward," Sean remarked, dryly. He gulped his Styrofoam cup of bourbon. We'd come from an impromptu party in one of the nearby apartments, using any excuse to get loaded.

"Oh, that's so sad," said Annie. "I hope she doesn't suffocate." Petticoats blowing up around her, one little hand poking out, the poor woman waved furtively, like an abused Barbie doll being swallowed by an amoeba. We watched the truck lurch past, no one paying any attention, the driver utterly oblivious to the ongoing wardrobe malfunction.

"Hey, here's our ride." Sean waved at the wildly decorated Cadillac sedan rumbling around the corner. I'd seen it before, parked in front of the grocery store, across from the post office. Thoroughly encrusted in buttons, beads, shells, and ornaments. The front hood emblazoned with a phalanx of plastic ducks swimming in perfect formation, the roof bristling with various figurines, swans, lizards, the side panels marching insoles, leading to an eruption of flamingos, horses, and dinosaurs on the back hood. Pink Floyd oozed from the speakers, and the long-haired driver waved back, gesturing for us to join him.

"Dude!" Sean knew the guy and clambered up front. Annie and I got in back, taking our turn to wave out the windows. People on either side of the street watching us in the car, staring, not knowing how to react. This crazy art car didn't need any slogan or sponsor, as it was its own entity—a riot of incongruous found materials proclaiming its presence in a cacophonous subversive, colorful yell.

I watched onlookers' faces as we drove slowly behind the now untangled epileptic princess, their mouths agape. Sean, Annie, and I had suddenly become a part of the performance, our own faces obscured in the crush of pop culture iconography.

Larry dropped me off by The Sea Gull as I had some evening chores to get to. I walked the few blocks back home, feeling as if I'd participated in something more than just a community parade, more than just a hitched drive down the street. When I arrived in the kitchen, Gerald was glowing, singing. He was smiling; Ellen was smiling. What was going on? They didn't smile anymore.

"Eric, we've made it! We're famous!" He gestured to the stack of mail on the blue table. There was a long envelope with an unfolded batch of stapled paper the color of baked clay. It was *Jack Shelton's Private Guide to Restaurants*, the newsletter Gerald subscribed too, read voraciously, hoarded, and collected. The opening article was about us, about Café Beaujolais.

The first thing I read also made me smile.

"The coffee I nursed was absolute perfection."

The restaurant reviewer had come incognito last month. He'd sat right there at table eight and watched Ellen piping buttercream onto genoise, observed Kristin wiping dessert plates, noticed Gerald's goatee, listened to Mahler, ate the bread I was also so crazy about. The way he described his dinner, it was as if he were still there. He loved my cream of spinach soup, Gerald's stuffed veal, the translucent gravy. The perfectly crisp, julienne of string beans, the rice pilaf, even the salad.

He went on and on about Ellen's favorite stilton cheese, her chocolate broyage, and then again, the coffee, ending with how he'd like to take this perfect dinner around to other big-city restaurants and show them how it was done.

I stopped reading and looked into the dining room where Mr. Shelton had been. I tried to picture his face but couldn't; he'd been so sneaky, probably using a pseudonym. Had he come with other people? How many times, and…what happened now?

It was a spectacular, glowing review that corroborated everything we were doing. He'd noticed the details, the quality ingredients prepared with care and imagination. Jack Shelton had given Café Beaujolais a mighty boost.

"It's like a benediction!" Gerald proclaimed. "HE has spoken!" Gerald looked around our little kitchen, beaming at Ellen and me. We'd done it; we had made this.

"And look, we're listed first. Before famous Gallatin's in Carmel, before Nepenthe in Big Sur."

I felt a mild panic rise inside; the thrill of recognition was replaced with a terrible responsibility. Part of me wanted to hide, but I held my two parents in an embrace, feeling the pride move around and around and swell to fill up the kitchen.

Tuesday we weren't open and had the rest of the day to bask in the recognition. Someone with clout, an influential stranger who ate food for a living, had legitimized our little café. We'd arrived.

That night, we ate leftover cassoulet, some of those perfect haricot verts, and a new loaf of bread. There was rum poppyseed cake for dessert. Wine all around, candles, and a fancy sit-down dinner at table eight. We all dressed up, Greta still wearing her red gown. Erik Satie on the stereo. I lit a fire in the stove, and we pretended to be appreciative customers in our very own newly famous restaurant.

CHAPTER 33

SHUFFLING
TOWARD EPIPHANY

By 1975, Mendocino had become a popular tourist destination and the population soared with visitors meandering up and down Main Street, exploring the Headlands, attending the Art Center's various events, or eating in the several restaurants that had sprouted up and down the coast.

The Beaujolais was always busy, and even though work was constant (daily, swirling issues always threatening to hamper an evening's smooth service), the business had become successful and continued to provide a lifestyle.

Proud of my ambitious and talented parents, I could see that I'd been given such a unique experience, and in my small way saw how I'd helped to make the family enterprise work, but I also knew that I'd never be a restaurateur. I wanted to be an actor.

As I was newly freed from automatic conscription when the draft was abolished, theater had become my go-to escape, and I threw myself into all sorts of shows. Serious, artsy plays; bedroom dramas and farce; musicals. I hated musicals. But I got some satisfaction in my latest role, flipping the script, playing the bully instead of the bullied. The audience hissed when my snarling Noah Claypole locked wimpy Oliver up in a coffin. Strangely, it was when the undertaker's front door got stuck, and I had to bang and shove my way onstage, flustered, that people laughed, and when I tried it again the next night, it worked like a charm. Director's notes dissuaded me from stealing the scene a third time, but I remembered the thrill.

Any small achievement was one more than before. Making people laugh sweetened the commonplace routine of another day. I was making something, surviving beyond Charlotte's rejection years ago, past Ray. Once I'd walked out of Charlotte's house, I never saw either of them again, learning sometime later that Ray had died of a drug overdose.

With each new experience, I felt parts of myself shift. Acting out, rehearsing lines, pretending to be someone different, inching by degrees onto a more public stage; every day I also practiced at being me. Eric as I had been but also who I was becoming. Now I knew without a doubt that I was gay.

Besides all the theater experience and amplified awareness of what a body (my body) could do on stage, I took a variety of dance classes and with practice got stronger, more agile. I had more control and to suddenly have more control felt like a superpower.

I grew a chest, my arms toned up, my posture was stick straight instead of slumping along. The gangly, awkward teenager becoming the spitting image of a hippie lifeguard.

I sometimes had to pry the groping hands of lonely, horny women off. Ladies who'd linger at cast parties, inviting me over to their place for a late-night rehearsal. We might be partners on stage, but that was as far as it went. I just wasn't interested.

I did my time at the Beaujolais, moving between the foyer, prep table, and dish pit. Dance classes during the day, multitasking in the kitchen weeknights, and then stage craft on the weekends. Gerald grumbled that I'd made myself unavailable when the restaurant was at its busiest. He was still trying to maneuver me into the role I didn't want. What would he say when I finally told him no, and then shared my big news, that I would be an actor instead of a chef, and that I was a gay actor?

To keep his hounding at bay, I began specializing in certain food dishes for our family meals. Cheese, and then chocolate soufflé became signature contributions.

Beside the cheesy or cocoa goodness, part of the enjoyment was in surprising my parents, intending to distract them from leaning so hard on their envisioned choice of my future profession. Unfortunately, in perfecting the recipes, I instead set myself up for further scrutiny. I only made food when I was hungry, had been told what to do, or could make it work. That difficult soufflé had become a thing, meant Eric was learning, which could only mean that he was also enjoying himself. What they didn't know was that I also avoided the inevitable. I knew that sooner or later; I'd have to spill the beans.

As I carefully introduced frothy whites to cheese and yolk, I'd also mix in the well-rehearsed explanation of what I'd so recently discovered, of who I saw myself as.

Even though it was fun to bust the myth of soufflés being troublesome, getting better at a thing only put more pressure on me to perform...and to tell the truth.

"I made this with love," I'd say, imagining myself presenting a perfectly cooked asiago and cheddar pouf, and then dropping the bomb. "Enough for extra helpings, and crunchy bits for everyone; plus, I have some exciting news!"

Instead, I did my job in the kitchen and would then extricate myself, avoiding the one thing that was foremost in my mind, retreating into my own constructed world of theater, dance, and private longing. There was safety in routine.

Then one day, Michael McCowan exploded on the steps of the Helen Schoeni theater.

"What sign are you?" he demanded in a deep Southern drawl, his purplish eyes burning into me.

He'd just moved to town, and by comparison to anyone else I'd ever met, he was an exotic, fabulous, shimmering peacock.

Radioactive energy raked my skin, capturing me in a tractor beam. His long, wavy, blue-black hair crisped with electricity, diamonds glinting from his ears, full lips in a generous, gleaming grin. He was on fire.

His bright-orange striped silk blouse and yellow Boy Scout kerchief, multi-pocketed khaki-green pants, knee-high socks, pastel strap-on mules, and jangling bracelets of ivory, colored glass, and Bakelite projected a strange new aura, searing right past my jeans and T-shirt armor. A costume and yet worn as naturally as any uniform. I thought I'd seen everything, considered every fashion choice; Michael presented a Westernized, pop culture version of a Hindu deity. Krishna by way of Mississippi. It was November, the sunlight was still weak, but I felt I needed sunglasses.

Paused there on the cement step (reeling from sudden exposure), I felt something stir in me and then fall heavily into place. This was supposed to be. Elemental chess pieces moved into position as Michael and I locked each other in a gaze that lasted a bit longer than was comfortable.

I knew in that moment I was ready. He was the one. Somewhat experienced yet still impressionable, I was impressed (if a bit startled). Flattered, I saw myself on the precipice of the next great adventure, and it had nothing to do with preparing food, acting in a play, or memorizing steps.

Michael focused his lightning bolts, but instead of shrinking, I received his blast of energy, newly recharged. I'd been seen, and from this moment on, I knew I would be more, whether I liked it or not.

Interestingly, I'd just had an astrological chart written up and learned that all my planets were clustered on the left side, indicating that I was a self-starter.

"I'm a Virgo with Leo moon," I answered matter-of-factly, as if that explained everything.

"Mercurial, discerning, critical...and sensual," Michael responded, as if knowing all about me. "I'm a Gemini with Aries ascendant, and I'm here to conquer the world."

Michael had decided on a whim to audition here at the Schoeni for the local Christmas variety show, and with this attitude, he was certainly guaranteed a part.

Even though I was always a bit nervous beginning a new theatrical project, I looked forward to some fun with my new chosen family of like-minded theater folk. I knew everyone; a couple of years ago I'd gone to school in this theater building. The school had closed, but this space was still my other home.

"We're gonna have so much fun," Michael assured me, flashing that hungry smile as he marched us in for the audition.

I remember nothing else about the show except being swept off my feet in the silly tap routine I rehearsed and then performed with Michael and his best pal Ellie—and of then being kicked out of the house.

I learned that Michael and Ellie had moved from Boulder, Colorado, trading mountains for the ocean and a new start. Both self-directed city artists a few years older than me, they'd already lived raucous, full lives, and despite their choice of tiny Mendocino, they both acted as if this was the greatest place they'd ever seen and that this was their town. As I watched, the familiar horizon expanded to accommodate them.

It wasn't long before Michael proved he'd been serious about world domination. Mendocino (he told me) was simply a comfortable launch-pad for his expansive vision. He planned on starting an import/export business, selling his original silk designs to multinational dry goods companies, of dressing dignitaries, movie stars, and popes. Celebrities called him at all hours for emergency wardrobe accessorizing tips. I chopped carrots and washed dishes for a living.

He drove a massive Coupe DeVille the color of a dirty, bruised plum. Faded, dented, seen better days but fitting his outsize personality as if he'd only further extended himself with power steering and deep leather seats. From the back seat lounge of Michael's gigantic car, I was elevated further up and out of the ordinary, the local scenes once again becoming a surreal, toy movie set, and I saw myself moving beyond my limited pathway, life growing larger.

Michael's friend Ellie looked (to me) rather like a tall Morticia Addams recently come from a beat poet's reading. Long, dark hair pouring down her back, world-weary, deeply set dark eyes, her voice perfected in a Patricia Neal finishing school. She loomed. I could hear the sharp intellect clicking away in her words, and though her outward expression was tinged with droll melancholy, there was a puckish glee in how she'd land a bon mot. She was the perfect foil to Michael's brazen bull in a china shop, and I admired her instantly, laughing at their shenanigans, learning from her friendly sparring with Michael. Theirs was a playful yet adult interaction that pushed me, encouraged me to further inhabit my own newly adult nineteen-year-old body. I'd made up my mind.

Now, adopted into their clan, hot and heavy with Michael, and with a fun, all-consuming project, I fed my ever-growing confidence. I could do this. I could come out to my parents.

Michael knew how to tap some (I did not), and he relished his new role as dance master, appraising our every step-shuffle-ball-change like Diaghilev hounding his Ballets Russes. It was Christmas, and all the performance vignettes were of a holiday theme. Our choice of Bing Crosby singing "Winter Wonderland" was ripe for a send-up, and as three tap-dancing snowmen, we could honor the vintage sentiment while also bending convention.

This is also where I got my first taste of how Michael behaved with a bit of power. He'd been pushy from the start, but then given the reins (or rather, assuming the role of director), he badgered Ellie and me to meet his high expectations.

I shared his desire for perfection, but after hours of slamming our feet on the cement floor of his garage, of his demanding and yelling, both Ellie and I reminded Michael that we were not made of wood, that there were no strings to jerk, that he was not a puppeteer, nor a god.

It was here also that a troubling thought passed through me. The immensely talented yet fiery and equally gentle nature of Michael reminded me of someone else I knew. Someone I admired greatly yet still had problems with. Someone who would act like an angry dictator one moment, a warm and friendly mentor the next. Someone who's artistic, irrational temper revealed inner turmoil, repressed anger, a deep hurt, a frightened child. Someone I was sometimes even afraid of. I saw my own father.

Then it hit me. For a hot second I worried that I might actually be as sick as all the myths about homosexuals warned and that, yes, ultimately, here was yet more evidence that I was probably stupid. Potentially developmentally disabled, gay, and with a full-blown Freudian daddy complex. When I finally told Gerald and Ellen about Michael and me, they might point this out and frown on our new relationship, or worse.

I thought in a panic: *Am I sleeping with, having sex with another version of my own father, and am I lying to myself in thinking that Gerald, that both parents, would both be OK with me announcing my gayness? Should I reconsider? Should I break up with Michael?*

But then I calmed down and separated myself from this ridiculous idea. This was a warped cartoon and not real. Now, it was even funny. I was making such a big deal out of nothing. I'd only been encouraged by both parents to express myself in any way I felt was genuine.

Even with the odd similarity, the bossy, obsessive personality quirk that Michael and my father Gerald shared, it was also what made them individual, even attractive. They were amazing, dedicated artists. Both charismatic, both having great humor and depth, both dealing with personal issues that came out in weird ways, and who didn't? I loved my dad, but no, I didn't want to have sex with him. Eww!

Time for a new paradigm. I reminded myself that I'd become successful in my current interests and that I was having fun. Even though Michael was temperamental and childish sometimes, he'd become a wonderful friend and lover. Michael made me laugh, he challenged me, he'd said he loved me, and I believed him. This was working. Soon, very soon, I'd tell my parents that Michael and I were much more than friends, that he was my boyfriend. I'd tell them that I was gay. I was gay and happy. It was all going to be OK.

"Why can't you understand?" Michael almost whined, he was so frustrated. "It's a simple repeat pattern. What's wrong with you?"

I was struggling with all these new tap steps, and he didn't realize he'd prodded an old wound, but I forgave him. I knew what I needed; I needed some space.

The new activation of body parts required some time to rehearse on my own, a bit of complicated rewiring (having never tapped before), and some old habits to finally break. It simply took some time. Working through self-inflicted roadblocks on my own helped imbed the pattern, and soon I began dancing.

"It's a goddamned fucking Christmas miracle!" Michael proclaimed after seeing me perform the routine. He couldn't argue with results. I'd cracked the code.

Michael, Ellie, and I devised simple DIY snowmen costumes from pillows, white sheets, and rope, and practicing again just before dress-rehearsal, I realized that I'd need to tie those ropes much tighter, as all the pillows stuffed under the sheets kept bunching up. The show was a modest success, and we all had a great time. Familiar stage fright turned into energizing showmanship, propelling me across the stage, making people laugh, galvanizing my friendship with Michael and Ellie. We were a troupe, the terrible trio.

Opening night gave us all a taste of reality, Saturday's evening performance saw the audience swell, and then Sunday was standing room only. Word got out that the tap-dancing snowmen were hilarious. On that final across the stage exit, I shuffled so hard those pillows (even with ropes cinched tighter) fell through their confines and ended up around my ankles. The crowd went wild.

Soon afterward, one weekday afternoon when I arrived home sweaty and winded after a dance class, finally prepared to announce myself as a gay man with an amazing boyfriend, I found the kitchen a warehouse of chaotic functionality. Demands were leveled, orders barked, everything had to be perfect. Gerald's equilibrium had been knocked off kilter.

"Check everything again, do it right, don't dawdle!"

What was going on?

"Alice Waters is coming for dinner! I want everything ready!" He was almost hyperventilating.

Alice Waters, the chef/owner of Berkeley's Chez Panisse was coming here to eat!

It was always Café Beaujolais and Chez Panisse, the two most popular restaurants in Northern California. Not a competition but nevertheless a dramatic reveal in how much customers loved eating at our little spot. It was high praise indeed, as we seemed to share a customer base. Gerald was excited and scared shitless.

Even though I knew I wouldn't replace Gerald as chef, I was so proud of both my parents and the incredible food they made. After such a long and difficult struggle trying to make a go of this café, their Herculean efforts were bringing the world to us, to Mendocino. Now, the great chef Alice Waters was coming. It meant everything to them, almost as if Julia Child herself had decided to beam in from outer space. I whisked through my tasks and asked for more, setting aside my big announcement. I wanted to support Ellen and Gerald. This would truly be a moment to remember.

They went all out. Oysters en brochette, delicate beef consommé, juicy NY steak with port wine and shallot reduction. Ellen made several cheesecakes to be served with a mote of fresh raspberry sauce. Everything was elegant, beautifully prepared, and we were all ready when Jim alerted us that she had arrived with her guests.

Service went without incident, every plate going out quickly, returning empty, sauce wiped clean with ends of Ellen's perfect bread. One after the other, every customer arrived, ate, enjoyed their dinner, and then exited, with compliments to the chef.

And still we waited, anticipation ratcheting up. What would Alice Waters say or do? I was busting to tell my parents my big news but waited.

At some point toward the end of the night, the double French doors swung open, and she entered the kitchen. I could see Jim's face on the other side of the glass, watching. She stood there and looked around, taking everything in, and then, she left, without ever acknowledging Gerald or Ellen, without saying anything. Nothing. It felt something like a dismissal, or even a strange backhanded compliment. As if her precursory glance might have said: *You did all that in this simple space?*

Instead of being crushed with disappointment, to my great surprise, Gerald and Ellen heaved a huge sigh of relief and then began to laugh. They'd made such a big deal out of the great chef coming to visit, putting such pressure on themselves. So invested in Alice Water's approval, they'd both been at the top of their games, and thanks to Alice the night had gone perfectly. Yet the evening had ended in such an anticlimactic way. Or had it? I still had my news.

Suddenly, it wasn't important whether a bigwig had liked the café or not. Her mere presence, that she'd even come to eat and not said anything, was the reward in and of itself. Ellen and Gerald had been seen. That was when the curtain opened, and I revealed myself.

CHAPTER 34

NERO FIDDLED

One short year later, everything had fallen apart, and even though I wasn't directly responsible, I'd played a role because of my willful ignorance. I certainly felt guilty; I was a deserter, I'd abdicated my heritage, I wasn't going to be a restaurateur. This had always been Gerald's plan. I was twenty, and I'd moved out and had other dreams.

Gerald had tried in vain over the years to groom me as his apprentice, but it hadn't worked. I'd disappointed him by not diving in and taking control. Fatally intimidated by the science and business aspects of running a restaurant, I could never achieve what my parents had pulled off. Gerald didn't help his cause any, referring to the restaurant business as a special needs child.

"The constant screaming!"

Oh yeah, this was precisely what I wanted to do with the rest of my life.

Instead, here I was dressed up like the Artful Dodger in my ragged tux and tails pacing out in the street, watching customers flee the little French café that used to be my home. Shifting hurriedly into their coats, wandering away in confusion, people seemed to recognize me.

"Why didn't you do something?" their blaming eyes said.

Tonight was closing night. After tonight, it was all over, and I could never call the Beaujolais home again. Even the latest review, a positive write-up in hallowed *Gourmet* magazine, appreciative of the several menus tasted over time, hadn't been enough to sway the tide. Published too late for any genuine effect, even though it was nice to see Café Beaujolais receive recognition from a national magazine. In 1976, Ellen and Gerald sold the Beaujolais, and tonight was the Pitsenbargers' swan song. It was the end of an era.

A sold-out prix fix dinner, and even though I'd moved out a while ago (living with Michael), I wanted to be a part of this evening's final hurrah, so just like old times, I played host. A theatrical gesture and my private ritual of closure.

Michael and Ellie were also drafted to wait on tables. They'd never done anything like this before, but Jim had quit, disgusted by Gerald's ridiculous tirades, and Greta refused; she'd also left and was living with her boyfriend. Kristin and Ellen were gone. It was just Gerald and last-minute hire Marilyn slogging it out to the finish.

Michael and Ellie were fully aware of my fallout with Gerald, my parents' divorce, and all the reasons for the café's demise. They knew that Gerald had become a raving alcoholic.

This didn't seem to bother either of them in the slightest. It even made their involvement somewhat more interesting. More than simply making some easy money, they had the morbid curiosity of putting themselves potentially in harm's way. Like secret agents going undercover, or a backflip dare off a cliff to see who landed in the water...or on the rocks. This was kind of a joke to them. They were joining the circus for five minutes.

Even though it irked me to see them so cavalier, I couldn't blame them, since I also felt somewhat of an imposter, sneaking back for one more go at playing a restaurant brat. Returning to the crime scene, knowing that my two friends were also getting a taste of what I'd lived with gave me a smug pleasure. Schadenfreude highlighting the paradox:

I'd escaped but was still conflicted.

This was the end of something so monumental. But at this point, it had become pure absurdist theater, messy and dark. I was glad for the company. I knew that Michael and Ellie would have a good time playing waiters on a stage, which also happened to be the ruins of my home, a local landmark.

This was my last performance as gatekeeper. The host, an arbiter of gracious living, hanging coats up and pulling chairs out for ladies, providing the first impression for strangers, handing over the expectant, monied VIPs to Michael and Ellie, and whatever came next: a meal, a speech, or perhaps an ugly scene. I hadn't even talked to Gerald. I didn't need to; I knew he was drunk. Still, I hoped that it all went down smoothly and without incident. Fantasies die hard.

Out here in the street, I noticed how comforting the grit felt under my feet, how it sounded crunching sweetly as I walked back and forth.

This was familiar terrain, the street. I always seemed to end up out here when it was too hot inside, and here I was yet again, the friendly earth keeping my body grounded while back inside, the Beaujolais finally imploded. I heard Gerald yelling, yodeling like Tarzan. He was chasing everyone out. People scurried away in every direction; we would never see them again. It was like a toilet flushing.

"What family doesn't have its ups and downs?" I remember Ellen once merrily quoting from that movie *The Lion in Winter.*

She'd sounded cheerful, but it was all an act. She was trying to be funny, trying to protect us kids and disarm the kitchen's shock after yet another blowup from Gerald.

I imagined Ellen as Katherine Hepburn, crawling up those stone castle steps (a queen brought low by her family's dysfunction). Life imitating art. But this was not a movie. My father, the king, had turned into a monster, and Ellen was an injured soul.

Cursing the chicken on his butcher block, the sputtering flame at the back of the stove, a dust mote floating across his vision, Gerald violently lashed out (sometimes with a knife still in hand). He started to throw things, smashing bowls against walls. Someone was going to get hurt.

"Woohoo!" he hooted, seeing us recoil. "Made ya look, didn't I?"

The kitchen had become a sad, fragile place.

Though they still worked together, Ellen and Gerald were wholly different people, not the same two who'd excitedly begun this adventure eight years before. They weren't my loving parents any longer. They were zombies barely speaking to each other from opposite sides of the kitchen—jabs and cutting remarks from Gerald, one-word answers and despairing looks from Ellen.

She could barely stand to work with him, refusing to sleep in the same bed. She moved into a hall closet, constructing a padded, carpeted cocoon. Her precious books on Buddhist meditation and esoteric teachings bricked the narrow walls, the chosen words of encouragement her closest friends.

A closed door meant do not disturb, and it broke my heart. Ellen shut the world out.

Gerald drank alone, mumbling and growling to himself, clanking around the kitchen, singing bits of opera, and then making squealing, honking sounds like tuning in to a ham radio station.

Ellen spent more and more time in her closet, sinking into depression, not keeping up with the restaurant's workload, so Gerald was forced to hire someone else.

Marilyn was a large, tough lady who could have been a prison matron. She put her head down and got the work done, not taking any shit from Gerald, who treated her with begrudging respect.

Looking back (out here next to the blackberry bushes), I could point to Gerald's drinking as the beginning of the end. Or maybe it wasn't—maybe it was just one more thing. There'd been so many times when it could have all gone up in a puff of smoke.

Poor Gerald. We'd all become acutely aware that he shouldered the restaurant's financial troubles on his own, and it caused him no end of worry.

"We are not in the black!" he'd declare, his eyes panicking. He'd seen the apocalypse, and if Gerald was worried, then we should be too. What my parents had built could all come crumbling down.

Yet he refused to allow anyone's assistance, claiming that it was his responsibility and his alone, as he was the man of the house. This attitude got him into trouble. Gerald had been like Zeus. He was a god, all-powerful, all-knowing. He could make a potato taste like a million bucks, but he couldn't keep the accounts flush. His court of supplicants, his family, encouraged him to hire an accountant or at least delegate tasks, but he refused and instead dug himself deeper.

In addition to the long, unforgiving hours of labor, Gerald's crippling arthritis and gout had damaged his hands, wrists, and ankle. He was in terrible pain. Recurring bronchitis would almost kill him, but he still worked, and then there was the constant drinking—his favorite beverage, wine for pleasure and then more wine for the pain. Wine of any shade, blend, or appellation was guzzled day and night, against doctor's orders, despite Ellen's plea for common sense.

And there was something more. Beyond physical complaints and mounting daily troubles, Gerald wrestled with something very old, very deep. It had something to do with his personal history. We'd heard stories of how demanding his Midwestern childhood had been. Growing up on a farm during the Depression was almost unimaginable.

Sometimes Gerald would remind us that he'd had to walk for miles, swim across a river, and push through blinding snowstorms to get to school! His bravado slipped somewhere between comedy and tragedy, but underneath the tall tales, something else gnawed at him. He refused to talk about it. We only wanted to know what bothered him. We wanted to help.

"That was then! This is now!" He'd shut us down. The old sadness never gone but kept hidden, and now with fewer filters, it raged, and was spilling out. Preferring his misery to any clear-headed solution, Gerald acted like an injured, trapped animal. He didn't need any help. He just needed more wine, and by the time we acknowledged that it was an emergency, we'd already lost him.

It had seemed so simple to me. You get sick; you get help. But Gerald laughed at any encouragement of a vacation, putting off any doctor visit or therapy, and then our final, desperate intervention tipped the scales to meltdown. He turned on us. We were traitors! We had sabotaged him and the restaurant. Ultimately the solution became, how do we take care of ourselves?

There went another couple running. How many times had I done just the same? Burst out of the side door and taken off to the far other side of town, down to the Headlands, or to the carved-up bench above Portuguese beach? As overwhelming as it was at home, even though there was no fix for what was happening, I could still appreciate what I saw as my future. I was not my father.

The rift between Ellen and Gerald widened after she dared to make an outside friend. A like-minded, New Age philosopher, Tai Chi teacher, and astrologer. Stuff that didn't interest Gerald in the slightest but that threatened his shaky hold as authority figure. Will was a gentle, soft-spoken man who reminded me of the way Gerald used to be. Ellen spent her free time taking classes from Will and always returned home refreshed and enthusiastic. Of course, Gerald became jealous.

"A little afternoon delight at the studio?" he mocked her. I don't think she and Will were having any kind of liaison, but they might as well have been. Gerald believed they were and projected his worst fabricated nightmares. Ellen was simply trying to have a life.

After he hit her, she moved out. That was it; there was no going back. The shock wave was a stark, ugly checkmark that ended something. Then he hit Greta. But she surprised him by giving as well as she got, serving him with a wallop. That woke him up for a moment. She and Kristin both left, still young girls but fiercely independent. They each had boyfriends and found work elsewhere. A divorce followed in short order. Gerald was on his own.

My spot out here at the end of quiet Ukiah Street was almost like another room traversing several intersecting planes of space and time, encompassing my life's messy laboratory. I'd lived out here as much as in the actual house. Out here, the toxic issues of the moment could somehow dissipate. Out here, I could see myself.

Last year was when Gerald had thrown me out.

"Begone! You are not my son!" he bellowed. Grabbed by the back of the neck, he hustled me from the kitchen. Gerald pointed to the great beyond with his powerful god finger. "Do not darken my doorway! I never want to see you again!" The earth tilted; I was falling.

How quickly my triumphant announcement, the euphoria of freedom, had turned into such an ugly melodramatic turning point. My affair with Michael and the overwhelming relief of finally accepting the truth, the breathless decision to declare myself.

I'd steeled my courage and was also greatly relieved. My big news! This would be difficult, but I needed to tell Ellen and Gerald. My confidence buoyed in knowing that all my life, despite the confusion and longing, at least I knew that my parents would support me. They'd only ever encouraged me to seek beauty, to do anything and to be whatever I wanted to be.

"I'm gay," I'd finally announced.

It turned out they supported anything but that.

In an instant, Gerald turned from my funny, bombastic role model of a father into a Wagnerian supervillain.

Cast out onto the street, in shock, I watched as the garage doors were slammed open and all my stuff came flying out. From cherished son, potential apprentice, to persona non grata. Suddenly, I didn't know my own father.

The next day, he denied everything, poo-pooing my exasperated recriminations and the sisters' corroborated story, their unstinting support.

"Oh, I never did that! There you go, exaggerating again!" He shut down any further talk, any counsel or reasoning.

"Do not speak!" He held up his hand. "The subject is verboten!"

"Just give him some time" was all Ellen said.

Gerald refused to listen or offer any further information, retreating further into his private sulk, ignoring me altogether. I became almost a nonentity, and I left soon after, moving in with Michael.

At the very end, Gerald blamed us, his own family, for ruining everything. It was we who had abandoned him. It was our fault that the restaurant was closing. Café Beaujolais, the dream, the glorious food, and the charming, if clumsy, learning curve—our wonderful family had exploded it all. It was over.

Quiet now. People had disappeared, and the street was empty—a meditative, familiar silence comforts. Standing still had its benefits. I could see shadows moving inside. Was that Michael? Maybe I should go in there and see what was going on?

Earlier, I'd followed protocol by calling to confirm everyone, marking names, indicating the one or two openings, taking numbers in setting up for the night. I couldn't help but flip back to the beginning of the big, thumbed-through reservation book and look at one of my first entries: Peter Sellers and guest. I'd drawn the Pink Panther sneaking off the page.

Giving a final preservice scan of the dining room, I saw Michael was sitting at table eight with Ellie, drinking wine.

"When in Rome." He toasted the air. Gerald had given them wine, or maybe they'd poured out what was left from a forgotten bottle.

Why not? It was a party, it was the last night, none of it mattered anymore. I heard Gerald in the kitchen singing some garbled tune. I didn't want to go in there.

He was wasted, whooping, whimpering, and snarling, going through the motions, a knot of contained chaos. I could see Marilyn through the swinging doors; she seemed her usual (as much as I knew what her usual was, in such a short time) harried and grumpy self.

I asked Michael if he needed anything, showing him the reservation book and the first parties to arrive, but he waved me away as if I were distracting him.

"This will be a piece of cake." He shrugged, his colorful silk blouse hissing over broad shoulders. Michael always came off as eminently confident, capable of taking on any challenge. I wondered if tonight might just put a chink in his bravado.

Ellie was her always unflappable, imperious persona. Wearing a black turtleneck, her long, jet-black hair clasped behind her back, observing my world through those large, dark eyes—who knew what she thought?

Gerald was singing in the kitchen as if it were just another Saturday evening, or as if serenading cows back home in Le Claire, Iowa.

I went back out to the foyer to await the first customers, glancing at Fleurette against the wall. She looked wan and ghostly, gripping her basket of flowers protectively. I wished I could have saved her. I'd made my choice, and it was to survive beyond the broken dreams of my parents.

Once dinner was in full swing and I'd welcomed the last guests, I made a final lingering wander about the dining room. The cute little tables, scroll-back chairs, the dusty rose fleur-de-lis wallpaper, crackling fire, mantle clock, prints of wildflowers and smiling, cheerful country maids, even that oblong eye in the wood floorboard that always stuck out. Things seemed to be normal enough, the facade intact, people enjoying the dinner of tender duck breast in black current sauce and loaves of bread, baked earlier by a young woman named Margaret, who'd answered an ad. I could see that they weren't Ellen's loaves, but nobody cared.

There was something off, though. Used plates were stacked and shoved aside; empty glasses lined the sideboard. There was a disheveled quality, the room unattended, the two new waiters nowhere to be seen. Once the food had been served, Michael and Ellie didn't care anymore. They were doing it for the money.

I looked down at a couple sitting at table eight, the table where I'd spent so much time puzzling over life's possibilities, illustrating menus, eating my own special dinner. Their water glasses could have used a refresh; a napkin lay on the floor. Bolstering myself, I was about to enter the kitchen through the swinging doors when suddenly Gerald came bursting out. I almost didn't recognize him. He was wearing an army fatigue flack suit with half his face painted blood red, the other shiny black.

Performing a drunken, whooping dance like a tall, gangly ape, his arms swinging, eyes bulging, he lunged at people, growling, snarling, picking food off their plates and gobbling like a ravenous animal.

A woman screamed, forks dropped, wineglasses smashed. From that point, I remember my fruitless attempt to stop him, putting myself in his way, between him and shocked customers already halfway out of their chairs. He roughly pushed me aside.

"You!" he snarled, showing his teeth. Then he leered down at some poor woman. "Enjoying your meal?"

I pulled at his sleeve, pushing him away but ready to dodge swinging fists. Plates and glasses and food were flying, crashing. I saw Michael appear in the background. Gerald kept wrenching free from my grip, continuing his insane prancing through the dining room, banging on the upright piano, howling like a wolf.

He collapsed for a moment against the wall then gathered himself, returning to the wreckage of dinner, slamming his hands down on a table. Everything was clattering, spilling. He was crying out as if he'd been stabbed. People pushed past me, and I followed them out.

Now, here I was in my designated spot out on the street. I took a short, shocked tour of the cemetery next door as Michael and Ellie cleaned up the mess left in the dining room. A bigger job than they'd bargained for.

"That duck was so good." As we drove home, Michael described eating what was left off someone's abandoned plate. "I'd just delivered the plate when Gerald came bustin' out. All that food just sitting there; those people left it."

Scandalized customers had provided Michael and Ellie with a staff meal. I hadn't eaten. I'd lost my appetite.

303

CHAPTER 35

BFFS

Gerald and I would move from Mendocino to San Francisco and then back again, over and over, at various points in each of our lives, for years. Each time back in San Francisco was for re-creation, to have an adventure, to make a dent. This time (we'd tell each other), it would be different; this time, it would be better. Our city would sharpen the edges, polish rough spots, and give us a boost. That was the idea anyway.

San Francisco was the place where Gerald had himself recognized his own beginning. In the early 1950s, Gerald left the Air Force and moved to San Francisco, molding himself as a bohemian artist. Introduced to Ellen at a party, quickly married, and then soon after, I was born.

It was also the place we'd forged our father-son relationship. When I was a child, we did everything together. I sat on Gerald's lap while playing the upright piano, snuggled between my parents at art-house cinemas, the opera, and poetry readings. I was introduced to life, to their San Francisco, and the many gifts this glorious city offered. Even when we moved across the bay to Berkeley, it was in the city where we knew all lines met. San Francisco was the center point.

Gerald and I would take field trips back across the Bay Bridge to the city every other Saturday. A dedicated pilgrimage to the grand San Francisco Opera, the incredible de Young Museum, the giddy insanity of Playland, or the enigmatic penny arcade under the Cliff House. With the city's vibrant, still preserved history coexisting right alongside chic modernity, I felt my psyche's tendrils take root.

San Francisco had given both my parents a revitalized confidence. So even in Mendocino, even as a reimagined restaurant family, our sensibilities and core beliefs still held a connection to our old home, San Francisco. Café Beaujolais was filled with curated furniture pieces from SoMa antique warehouses, a turn-of-the-century aesthetic married to a New Age focus. San Francisco was where we looked for clues. Plus, it was where the tourists who visited our tiny coastal bubble in summer predominantly came from. We depended on a more sophisticated city palate and wallet. For a new business struggling in a postage-stamp-size village, San Francisco was still providing.

Everything was connected. The challenging drive was a cathartic part of the experience. Back then, setting out from San Francisco was a commitment of about four hours until you reached the remote little outcropping of land on the North Coast. Gerald and Ellen worked their butts off to make the journey worthwhile.

Gerald had commuted from Berkeley every weekend while he apprenticed at Norman's, racing up Highway One to our little Victorian fixer-upper, then driving helter-skelter back down to the Bay Area, to do it all again the following weekend. One Friday afternoon, he hooked up a utility trailer loaded down with the twelve-burner stove he'd purchased and driven the entire route at five miles an hour.

"The stove drove that car!" he collapsed, shaking from exhaustion in our arms. "Mr. Toad's Wild Ride!"

On my first nervous solo attempt in 1971, the city was my kickstart into adulthood. Enrolled at the Academy of Art, I imagined the city would help turn a seventeen-year-old high school dropout into the true professional artist I knew I could be.

I forced myself into classrooms full of strangers and nude models, attempting to wrangle raw talent and full-blown social anxiety, spending most of my monthly allowance on expensive art supplies, ignoring hunger and sometimes the rent.

After school, a saunter up and down Castro Street gave me an education in the gay lifestyle and some personal responsibility. Disco was brand-new; hippies still camped out in Golden Gate Park; Harvey Milk hadn't even opened his camera store.

But my city was growing up all around me, right along with me; a modern skyscraper in the shape of an obelisk rose up downtown. I watched it pointing higher and higher, up and above all the other tall buildings, and felt myself also reaching, knowing that I'd better also hurry up and become something. And exactly who would I be when the Transamerica pyramid finally touched the sky?

As scared as I'd been on my own, it was in the simple act of walking around San Francisco, to look at and be looked at, that gave me courage. I'd returned to the place that had initially given me life. Now here I was, visible as a young adult for the first time, my awkward, emerging identity both terrifying and glorious. I was living in the city, my city!

But finally, starvation and loneliness drove me back home to Mendocino. I could always draw, but I needed to eat.

In the year that followed, I found a new passion and abilities as a dancer. The fundamentals of strict ballet discipline, ballroom's coordination, and sharp jazz dancing gave me an experience that had nothing to do with restaurants. Living in my skin like never before, I found that jazz dance more accurately defined me. The flash, razzle-dazzle, and athleticism completely transforming my body and a sense of purpose, the performance for my very own pleasure, not for Gerald's or anyone else's.

This was what I was meant to do! I saw myself auditioning for Broadway. I would never wash another dish ever again, and it became clear that I needed to go back to the city and get a real education. So, I returned to San Francisco for a second time in 1973, trading pencils and paper for leg warmers, enrolling in Lone Mountain College's newly installed dance program.

A former Jesuit women's school, Lone Mountain had a towering gothic campus that looked down on the city from a copy of Rome's Spanish steps. The imposing facade and turrets, sculptured grounds, and long, dark, wood-paneled hallways were a fantasy of arch grandiosity, where at every turn I felt the ghosts of an era and a pressure to succeed. Applying newly focused abilities, I was exultant, determined. This time I was doing it right. This time San Francisco would be the stage I needed. This was the real thing.

The city became one big open-air studio. Lunging into a pirouette, or grandejeté over a crosswalk, performing for classmates and gawking strangers, I tempted fate. Always practicing, incorporating the varied terrain into how I moved within it, I literally danced around the city.

But I also needed to make money. I'd been too scared the first time around (letting myself flounder in malnutrition and paranoia), and this time I bit the bullet and got a job in a restaurant busing tables. I fed myself and was a step closer to independence.

It did seem ironic to be working in someone else's restaurant while also trying to become a performer (like Gerald had once been). I saw a zigzagging yet parallel path, and even though he wasn't with me, I could still hear Gerald barking in the back of my mind, his voice a goading inner monologue demanding that I work harder, not be lazy, to do exactly as he said "because I said so!" I wanted to please him but also to be well free of him.

I made it as far as an entire semester. After initially splashing out, the novelty of being bold and self-sufficient resulted in abject loneliness, which I still couldn't tolerate. No encouraging teacher, job, or beautiful stranger could satisfy my longing for and lack of security. After time spent in the studio, I always seemed to end up alone, learning that any acquaintance made at school was also competition. I couldn't keep any friendship outside of class, and despite all my efforts to remain strong and focused, I faltered. My earnest routine became a mundane exercise.

From the confines of a cold dorm room, I thought bitterly, at least washing dishes and making soup in the restaurant had produced positive results; at least there I could dream. To live in Mendocino was like being in a dream, and I yearned for the serenity and anonymity of dreaming.

I moved back to Mendocino, worked at the restaurant, and decided to finally come out. I'd known since I was a kid but had avoided the obvious. Falling hard for Michael, I prepared to tell my parents, and what a great feeling it was. Revealing to myself (and to the world), an intrinsic, defining characteristic that I'd transformed from fear and self-loathing into joy and triumph. But Gerald didn't react the same way, kicking me out and, on that day, setting in motion a new trajectory for both of our lives.

In 1976, Gerald had barely survived his divorce from Ellen and the sale of the Beaujolais. Sliding into an existential pothole, he escaped to France, walking the pilgrim trails, spending in wild abandon his entire share of the split money (and then some). Returning to the States, he landed at my front door, broke and sick with pneumonia. Michael and I nursed him back to health, gave him money, and enjoyed a reunion of sorts. Then he began drinking again, and when I called him on it, he stole away on our new scooter and drove it into a ditch.

Retreating once again back to the city, this time practically destitute and in debt, no longer a young man, injured by lousy health and circumstance, he hid from everything and everyone, wallowing in self-induced exile.

Gerald moved into a residence hotel in the seedy Tenderloin district, struggling to find any connection to the place that had once given him such a head start. Working in his fallback position as secretary, he was always one paycheck away from being homeless. Depressed, desperate, and alone, he then contracted yellow fever and almost died in the hospital, the doctors pumping gobs of yellow puss from his lungs.

His spirit was broken under a lifetime of deep emotional wounds and his body wracked with pain, and I expected my father's fabulous and poignant story to end here, in the city that had been his real beginning— an ignominious belly flop of a finale to such an incredible legacy.

But then Gerald recovered and moved back to the country, to rural Northern California, where he assisted his brother in a backwoods nursery (and fields of illegal marijuana), making a small fortune for his efforts.

In 1979, three years after the sale of Café Beaujolais to Margaret Fox (the young lady who'd made bread on that last day), I attempted one last time to stake my claim as a bona fide San Francisco resident. I'd split with Michael and was ready for a new experience, ready to face the recurring nemesis of urban loneliness and to then surmount it. I was stronger now. Ready to see what I could become in a familiar yet challenging place and to construct something of value.

Armored up, eyes wide open, with some funds, a job, and even a car, I leaned hard on every access point while in the back of my mind wondering, why did it always have to be San Francisco?

I began to see past whatever nostalgia I'd built for a place and time and once again (I couldn't help it) compare my own experience with that of Gerald's. San Francisco had also been his city. At twenty-five, my dad had walked these very same streets and perhaps felt the same way.

Retracing steps to remembered haunts, I imagined Gerald as a young man skulking at the end of the bar, looking mysterious in his black turtleneck and Basque beret, smoking clove cigarettes, fingering his mustache, flirting with that burley dockworker. My father had been just like me.

In the intervening years, I'd learned quite a bit more about Gerald, about both my parents.

"When your father and I first met and began living together," Ellen had told me about a year after he'd thrown me out, "he came home one night, all beaten up and bloody."

A darkened alley tryst gone bad.

"That's when we decided to get married."

Ellen was always trying to build bridges and make peace between feuding family members, and she knew that I still harbored a grudge against Gerald. He'd been my friend, and now there was a schism. We barely spoke.

Back in 1952, she'd practically dragged Gerald to the courthouse. "We can't go on like this."

Only after they'd come to know each other better, confessed secretive gay lives were revealed. Gerald tricked on the weekend, while Ellen had been living under the thrall of a bossy woman.

"When Gerald was a young man," Ellen described in her calm, collected voice. "He'd been a soloist in the Air Force national band. But one unfortunate day, he was discovered 'picking up the soap' in the barracks shower."

She waited for this news to sink in.

The way she explained it, Gerald had been summarily, traumatically, dishonorably discharged. Losing his job, his standing, never seeing his longtime lover ever again.

"I believe Gerald tried to reach out and call the man once, but the guy just hung up." Her eyes were misty.

San Francisco beckoned. San Francisco was the place where Gerald could be himself.

The city gave him back his life. San Francisco was where life began.

How could this happen, I'd asked? How? How in the hell did they make a family? But then it made perfect sense. It was for survival.

Times were very different then. It was dangerous, sometimes even deadly, to be openly gay. It just wasn't done, an unspeakable offense, a crime. It was moral corruption and often led to suicide. People lived haunted, double lives. People (my parents) become fugitives from their own families, from themselves.

This revelation opened doors for me and further fueled my own adventures in the city, figuring that it was just meant to be. It was supposed to be this way. Since both of my parents were gay, how could I not be? But I couldn't really explain it, since my two sisters certainly weren't. Maybe it had something to do with me being the firstborn and closer somehow to who my parents had been in their former lives? Just after their pact, I'd come into the world—a perfect gay baby. I'd always known.

"I don't know how you turned out this way!" Gerald had said at one point when confronted for the millionth time. I'd come out, he'd then thrown me out, and as I continued to thrive outside of the home (with Michael), his argument lost much of its sting.

I wanted to tell him to just go look in the mirror but couldn't find the courage. I didn't trust him, was even afraid of him, he was so contrary to everything he'd previously been as a loving father.

When Gerald had been my age, he'd had to sneak around San Francisco, the specter of shame following his every move; fear and self-hatred motivating many decisions. He'd married Ellen, and they become each other's saviors, providing cover for each other. Adopting the now antiquated slang of being "beards."

I supposed I was grateful after all (since their coupling had given me life), but their difficult decision was not mine. Times had changed. I'd seen it. I'd been a part of it. Participating in a jubilant Pride march, taking to the streets when gay hero Harvey Milk was assassinated, living as an openly, happily gay man. I'd partnered with Michael for several years. It was who I was. This was me.

And by some fickle chance, I would skate through what was to become the AIDS crisis. Unscathed at the tail end of the '70s, I floated out the other side of the '80s, fully experienced but still somehow innocent—a miracle.

Still, I questioned the choice of San Francisco, even whether the city had anything to do with my personal path. A gay "mecca" was still just a city. "Wherever you go, there you are": Having moved to the city once again, I thought I was supposed to be home but instead found myself at the crossroads looking at my very own dilemma. I knew that there was no there there and that the grass was undoubtedly not greener. I kept on trying, though. San Francisco represented so many firsts.

So, in 1979, I attempted once more to insinuate myself as a genuine resident, renting a room between the kitchen and bathroom, where the pink-haired lady of the house would tromp through at any time. That had been a dumb mistake.

Pretending to be satisfied with the way things were, I became a cynical city dweller just going through the motions, feeling the addictive charge of making it by the skin of my teeth, no glamour in simple survival. This was going nowhere, and something had to change.

Gerald would write me letters from his backwoods hideaway, the glib matter-of-fact telling of his life as a pot farmer illustrated in his expressive penmanship. It scared the crap out of me.

Dear Eric, Another beautiful day in this far away forested Eden! But I'm tired. I barely slept a wink. Spending the night out in the field, both feet laced to trip lines running throughout (to warn of local sabotage and bad neighbors who might steal. You never know who's your friend when it's this close to harvest). The shotgun lying in the grass next to my itchy fingers. Every hoot owl, every mouse, and cricket a warning. The rustling of ripe buds, the sickeningly sweet smell on my tongue, the terror that maybe I'll shoot my brother by mistake! Oh, why did I ever say yes to this posting? I'm not a warrior! I'd rather be indoors, up in the loft with the cat and spiders. I have fresh salmon and raspberries and red wine, so I will survive. After all, we in the country must make do! I hope you're dancing. X Gerald.

Dear Eric, I made a rushed delivery to a strange apartment in San Fran yesterday (never saw a soul), and all the time sweating as if a water spigot had been turned on! Driving in such crazy traffic and making wrong turns (away from cop cars) made my stress level even wetter. I'm sorry not to visit, but I wanted to be done with this. Bags of money under the seat, I feel like a bank robber who needs a shower. I stink from all day on the road and too much coffee. This is the third journey I've made, and it never gets easier, though I have discovered some short cuts. Oh, to be home with the sparrows and deer! The endless peace and quiet of this forest ocean. This is where Ishi wandered out of the bushes to surprise Professor Kroeber, y'know. We are in the hinterland for sure. I hope you're well. **X Gerald.**

Dear Eric, I'd just come down from the field, watering, weeding, checking the fences and taking a lunch break with old bread and cheese (my favorite, but out of wine) when a roar descended! Two huge black helicopters landed just where I'd been, not moments before! Men in flack suits began a controlled burn of our tenderly cared for crop. All gone. Burnt to the ground. Now I have all the time in the world to sit by the creek and dangle my bunioned feet, reminiscing about yesterday. La vie est une aventure! Write to me. **X Gerald.**

I was worried not just because of the high-stakes drama involved and because my father was more or less a criminal living out there in the Wild West, doing things and consorting with an underworld that I wanted absolutely nothing to do with—more than that, he was enjoying this! The blithe, nonchalant attitude was disarming the seriousness of his actions. La-de-da! Just another day in the life of Gerald.

When I was a child, he was my best friend who turned into a bad-tempered taskmaster and bully; he became an addled, crazy alcoholic and destroyer of our family and business; he was the man who rejected me in the most personal way. And he had become someone I honestly knew nothing about. Someone I was reminded, once again, I wanted nothing to do with.

In all the years, I'd never received any apology or even acknowledgment of his terrible behavior. The events had simply never occurred. I'd made it all up.

"There you go, exaggerating again," he always said. It was my fault, his throwing me and all my belongings out like trash.

Obstinate denial had become a hallmark of Gerald's personality. Simply ignoring all the elephants stampeding across our shared history somehow absolved him of any wrongdoing—a narcissistic frightened child's coping mechanism. I hated him, loved him, and pitied him.

I knew his story. Born from a lifetime of repression and fear, subverting his true nature, hiding, living a lie, surviving one disaster after another, rebelling against a cruel society. It had warped his outlook. He was repeating the same self-destructive patterns, without making peace, without cleaning up, without acknowledgment or therapy or responsibility.

Gerald was an outlaw from himself. If I genuinely wanted to become the person my father could never be, I would have to break from him once and for all. After years of skating around his outrageous behavior, I cut him off. We were done. I never answered any of his letters.

But I was concerned for my two younger sisters who still idolized him, beguiled by his reckless naivety. He appealed to their gypsy spirits, living with abandon and little regard for what (inevitably) could come next. Our father could go to prison. He could die alone in a cell or be killed by cops or some shadowy cartel. In my mind, at this point, Gerald was nursing a death wish. He was already a ghost.

Then one morning at the beginning of 1980, in an all too familiar funk (after enduring a parade of people marching through my rented campsite), I set aside my heavy grudge and decided to call him. A spontaneous gesture and timid hope that maybe, just maybe, I might be surprised. I missed my dad.

"Eric! I'm so glad you've called! I've been thinking so mightily about you." He didn't seem drunk, but I didn't trust his good humor. It was usually a smokescreen for some sloppy behavior.

He was sober and healthy, he was happy, and...he was living with a man.

Gerald had been in Humboldt for a few years and then, newly flush with money, decided to up and move to a different city. Not back to San Francisco but an entirely new spot in an altogether different state. A place called Seattle.

"I love this new life and this new city! It's so green. Air as sweet as cake, such nice people." I hadn't heard him this enthusiastic in a very long time.

"Good food everywhere and so much to do. Music, theater, and dance. Seattle is a cultural smorgasbord. I see something every night all within walking distance. It reminds me of San Francisco in the 1950s when I'd first discovered it." Gerald wasn't high on wine but an aesthetic and artistic euphoria. He sounded like the father I knew so long ago.

After my shock, I confessed the ennui I'd been trudging through.

"Get away from that place," he urged. "Come live with Ken and me until you can get your own spot. There's an apartment opening in the same building; I'll put a word in. Please come. You can dance again, make art, meet new people. You will love it. I would love it."

As I drove my beat-up Corolla away from what used to be the one and only city, toward Seattle and Gerald, I thought, *This is a pretty big risk*.

Up the coast, past the place that had been our hometown, sleepy little Mendocino was still resting there on the sea's edge, and I felt it reach out.

Poppies will make you sleep. Poppies.

I drove right past without even stopping.

Seattle was everything Gerald had advertised. Barely contained gardens overgrowing fenced yards. Lush trees reaching up into arbors, over intersections, buildings crowded by greenery. At once both shaggy and elegant, quiet streets lined with quaint Craftsman and deco brick apartment buildings named after grand old ladies or dignified institutions. A rambling, industrial, public marketplace burrowed underground in a labyrinth of obscure novelty shops, while upstairs vendors threw fish back and forth as if performing in a carnival. Seattle felt like the place I'd grown up in (that other city), only removed sideways about fifty years. It felt like home.

I arrived in April, just before Easter, and got a job promoting a local chocolatier, riding a wobbly bike around in a giant bunny costume. Becoming familiar with the neighborhoods, I got some serious exercise (burning off excess calories from eating chocolate), and I made people laugh. Disrupting downtown office decorum and creating a bit of silly havoc was my kind of job!

Gerald's new boyfriend, Ken, was instantly familiar. Slim and fond of purple, he wore long, beaded necklaces and a little decorated felt cap. He was a philosopher, scholar, a sprite with a winking smile, and Gerald was crazy about him.

They'd decorated the small apartment like an Art Nouveau fantasy. Sumi ink scrolls hung down the walls; wide silken scarves draped over the bed. There was Toulouse-Lautrec, Matisse, Degas, Hundertwasser. All of Gerald's favorite artists reflecting the visual landscape of his imagination. There was a piano, the smells of food, incense, and flowering jasmine. Collected vintage plates under potted ferns, gold filigree painted along the door frame to create a unique threshold shrine. It was as if the world I'd grown up in had been transported and re-created; hung against the wide walk-in closet door was Fleurette. Even a bit ragged along the edges, ink scraped off in places, she still looked as sweet and free (though now, a bit tired) as when she'd graced the Beaujolais. As I felt the gulf of time undulating, I found myself wondering, what happened to the blue table?

Gerald and Ken had their names inscribed in tiles at the waterfront marketplace to commemorate their bond with each other and with Seattle. This was their city, and Gerald was delighted to share it with me.

We walked everywhere. Up and down hills, through neighborhoods of close, comfortable bungalows, down into the old part of town where high, turn-of-the-century arched windows, thick stone facades, and bumpy cobblestone streets met glittering asymmetrical towers of glass and steel. It was all new yet comfortably familiar.

We ate sashimi in the International District, took in a film at the Grand Illusion Cinema, admired the city's Japanese garden in the glowing green arboretum, a classical concert at Cornish College of the Arts. Just like old times, Gerald and Eric painting the town.

A week after arriving, I was back in my tights and leg warmers, stretching on the floor with a room full of strangers at Dance Center Seattle. This would be my first modern dance class.

In walked a tall, feral feline of a man wearing zebra-striped leggings.

All arms and legs, barefoot, picking his way carefully across the floor (almost prowling), he casually glanced at the group as we sprawled before him. This was our teacher. Everyone quickly stood up, and I could feel a sense of awe ripple between them as if a king had entered and he were assessing his subjects. Blindingly handsome, shoulder-length blond hair cut in a shagged mane, he had the appearance of Farrah Fawcett or a young Dutch master.

Stopping directly in front of me, his flint-blue eyes looked me up and down, blatantly judging me worthy or not. I met his stare with a defiant look of my own. I'd signed up and paid my eight dollars for class just like everyone else, though now I was questioning if I might've been too confident.

As quickly as I'd felt the heat of his appraisal, he turned gracefully, dismissive, taking a center spot on the floor, and began the class.

Later, I had to admit that I was indeed out of my depth. This class had been too advanced. Struggling with the rapid-fire, twisting, reaching combination our teacher threw at us, I quickly became a stumbling, bumbling mess. Steps were flying past my ability to pick up, none of the movement in my vocabulary. I wasn't the only one who had difficulty keeping up, but it still burned. I thought I was ready for this.

The whole weight of my Lone Mountain fiasco reared up and pulled me under. The jeering, nasty nagging, my angry, injured ego stabbing. If I wasn't dancing, if I couldn't keep up, if I couldn't learn and fast, then who would I be?

I told Gerald about this after class in a corner coffee shop, and he reached over and put his larger hand on mine.

"Keep trying! What's one class? You've only just begun." He squeezed and looked at me with his sly, knowing eye. As discouraged as I was, it was nice to be encouraged, to be motivated by Gerald once again.

"Eric, I want to tell you"—he hesitated, beginning to tear up—"I am so sorry for, well, for everything."

Suddenly he was crying, tears rolling down his face dripping onto the half-eaten croissant. "You know, you have given me strength. Your example showed me the way."

What was happening?

"My whole life has been spent running away from fear, of trying to find myself around every corner, and of never looking in the very spot where I was."

I stared at him. He'd been saving this.

"It's always been vivre l'instant présent! Live for the moment! To look back is to suffer, and there is only the now. There is so much regret, but here we are, a new beginning. We have this chance, and there is so much to be thankful for."

I was a stone in a river, feelings rushing by in a frothy mix.

"I assume you know why I was so upset about you coming out? You were so young, and I wanted to protect you."

I held on to my cold coffee cup.

"I didn't want what had happened to me to happen to you. I know I overreacted. The context was different, but it was, you see, also the same. Being gay was a curse."

Being jealous, drunk, and vindictive hadn't helped, I thought. But here Gerald was, baring his soul to me like never before. I'd never heard such empathy, clarity, such a sincere apology, such a genuine, brotherly gesture from him, or from anyone.

So many times I'd reached out to him, and he'd never been available. Gerald had lost himself and chosen to ignore everything because, I guessed, it hurt too much. I'd always wished for some sort of closure, and now here it was, at long last.

I saw something else. In writing Gerald off, I'd also unwittingly boxed myself into a selfish position of my own. My very own precious pain. I saw it lying there, wriggling on the table between us—the Great Coveted Injury that hobbled how I related to my father and the world.

"Eric," he continued, "it's your example that helped me to come out. Finally! You've lived such an honest, risk-taking, adventurous, full life. And I see why you were so happy to reveal your true nature. It's a revelation."

Where was I? Who was I talking to? The river of feelings came tumbling out.

"But, Gerald, don't you know? You're the one! It's you who taught me how to be me!"

My tears pouring. "I quite literally could not have been me without you. You're the one who taught me how to recognize, and to embrace, freedom. You permitted me, gave me every opportunity to explore and to be brave, and I did! I didn't become a chef, but I still followed in your footsteps."

People in the café were starting to glance at the two grown men in the corner openly crying, holding each other.

And Gerald was right; the only thing to do now was to go back and take that class again. Push past clumsiness and maybe learn something. Resilience had also become one of my collected skills.

But first, wanting to let go and just dance, I dragged my father, my new gay best friend, out to a club. I needed to reconnect to the beats and my muse; I needed to not think so hard about where I placed weight on which count, of what the count was, of where my feet were. I needed to move!

Halfway through my beer, sitting at a small table along the edge of the dark club, Blondie began singing "Heart of Glass." That was it. I couldn't wait any longer. It was now or never. If I kept waiting for the right song, the perfect moment, past shyness, past judgment, fear of failure, I'd never do anything. It was a very old argument.

Be brave! Get out there! Show the world (and yourself) what you can do. Be free, my inner voice, my father's voice, encouraged, and I felt the old traps fall away.

Nudging through bodies and ready to join the music, I saw him. On the opposite side of the small dance floor, my teacher (the leonine blond D'Artagnan) also stepping out.

There was a spark of recognition that passed between us as we met in the middle of the dance floor. Wade came close and said, "You're glowing under the light, just like in the studio today."

ACKNOWLEDGMENTS

This book is a love letter to both of my exceptional and inevitably human parents, Gerald and Ellen Pitsenbarger. I owe everything to them, my first and most important friends in this world. Their greatest gift: teaching me how to express myself. I'm so proud of what these two were able to accomplish, creating such a fabulous thing in Café Beaujolais. Their efforts helped to transform people's expectations of good food and provided me with the experience of a lifetime. Despite the trouble, the disfunction and drama, it's by their example that I was able to build a career in the service industry and, as such, to become a better human.

My two sisters, Greta and Kristin, are like the earth to me. Walking with them through the long process of writing this book; reflecting on the many good (and not so good) times, all the details, and corroborating events; and enjoying our exclusive, mutual support group have been fundamental. Greta and Kristin represent the model of grit, grace, and resiliency, and I cherish my experience participating in both their lives. Also, they've saved my butt more than a few times, and I'm so grateful.

The team at Duende Press: developmental editor Rebecca Pillsbury, copy editor Kristin Thiel, publicist Bryan Tomasovich, and designer Antonio García Martín all gave their personal, and professional, deft attention to my passion project.

There is a cadre of readers who gifted me with their focused and encouraging attention:

Lodi McClellan's insightful real-time commentary, editing choices, and blast of affirmation provided the next steps forward.

Stacya Silverman's shared experience writing her own dramatic memoir, her canny observations, and her suggestions helped to solidify and endorse my voice.

Alice Laskin, new to my story (other than what she'd heard about in our working relationship), helped confirm my account's messages. An educator and the child of an author, she offered a savvy and perennially enthusiastic encouragment that has buoyed my vision.

Georgia Ragsdale is a mentor and friend. A practiced performer, comic, and gifted memoirist, Georgia has an ear for timing that has lifted me as an actor, writer, and clown.

In particular, Eleanor Cooney (not only portrayed in this story but also a published author herself) is one of my prime examples of what a committed writer is. Eleanor will always be the source I refer to as I recount my first attempts. Her first, encouraging pearl of wisdom? "Keep writing."

I feel like this whole story has led to what I now have with Wade Madsen—we are two like-minded individuals who appreciate the same things while supporting and instigating each other's endeavors. Wade has always been my best friend, teacher, and critic, and it's through him I found catalytic permission and a sparkling example. Wade is a force, and I'm inspired to be my best, often silliest self. As I worked out this long-gestating project, Wade has heard every story as it's been written and offered his thoughtful support. Thank you, Wade, for your trust in me. I love you.

A bevy of GoFundMe contributors, who all donated at various times along the road to self-publishing, provided more than financial support—they gave enthusiastic reassurance that my story could become a book.

And finally, to the village of Mendocino, itself a character in this story; synonymous with my personal fable and with Café Beaujolais, more than a physical place or destination, Mendocino is a frame of mind and sacred ground that provided me with the space to grow and discover my truest self. I would not be me without Mendocino.

Thank you, all.

ABOUT ERIC

Eric Neil Pitsenbarger is a visual artist, writer, and occasional performer. Designer of book covers, blogger for performance venues, ghost writer of other artists, and an award-winning food server, this is his first book. He lives in Seattle with his husband, Wade.

Photo by Tom Schworer

"The author's early home life is nothing like what we find in most coming-out/coming-of-age stories. If you expect 'normal, you'll be disappointed."

Eleanor Cooney

"A revealing account behind Mendocino's most well-known restaurant. Eric presents a rich kaleidoscope reflecting a complex family story intermingled with the improbable creation of a restaurant dream. From early years through adulthood, his perspective reflects sensitivity, insight, and wisdom that are at times poignant, caring, hilarious, and ultimately satisfying."

Margaret Fox

"*Beaujolais in My Blood* is a rollicking you-are-there account of a boyhood spent deep in 1970s Bay Area Bohemia. All the classic components - unconventional parenting, wild childhood freedoms, beat poetry - are here and colorfully represented, but it's the surprising deviations and unearthed secrets that you remember most."

David Schmader

CPSIA information can be obtained
at www.ICGtesting.com
Printed in the USA
JSHW051930170223
37851JS00003B/37